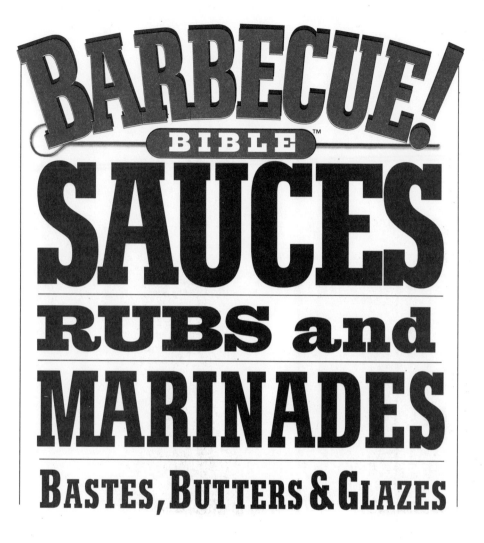

BARBECUE!

BIBLE™

SAUCES

RUBS and

MARINADES

BASTES, BUTTERS & GLAZES

BARBECUE! BIBLE™

SAUCES

RUBS and

MARINADES

Bastes, Butters & Glazes

by STEVEN RAICHLEN

Illustrations by Ron Tanovitz

WORKMAN PUBLISHING, NEW YORK

Library of Congress Cataloging-in-Publication Data

Raichlen, Steven.

    Barbecue Bible! sauces, rubs, and marinades, bastes, butters & glazes /

    by Steven Raichlen; illustrations by Ron Tanovitz

       p. cm.

    ISBN 0-7611-1979-5 (paper)—ISBN 0-7611-2013-0 (hc)

     1. Barbecue cookery. 2. Barbecue sauce. I. Title.

TX840.B3 R355 2000

641.5'784—dc21   00-026060

Cover design by Paul Hanson

Book design by Lisa Hollander

Cover photographs by Greg Schneider

Book illustrations by Ron Tanovitz

Workman books are available at special discounts when purchased in bulk for premiums and sales promotions as well as for fund-raising or educational use. Special editions or book excerpts can be created to specification. For details contact the Special Sales Director at the address below.

Workman Publishing Company, Inc.

708 Broadway

New York, NY 10003-9555

www.workman.com

First printing May 2000

10 9 8 7 6 5 4

To Barbara
Who lights my fire

ACKNOWLEDGMENTS

The most pleasurable part of writing a book is thanking the people who helped make it possible. This one is built on the wisdom of thousands of pit masters and grill jockeys around the world.

In particular, I would like to thank:
My wife: Barbara
My agent: Angela Miller
My stepson and recipe tester: Jake Klein
Recipe tester: Elida Proenza
Editorial assistant: Heather Short
Photographer: Greg Schneider
Web master: Benjamin Wilchfort

My friends at Workman Publishing:
Editor extraordinaire: Suzanne Rafer
Pubisher: Bruce Harris
Copy editor: Susan Derescky
Editorial assistant: Kylie Foxx

Designers: Paul Hanson and Lisa Hollander
Sales and licensing folks: Janet Harris, Jenny Mandel, Pat Upton
Publicity: Ellen Morgenstern and Jim Eber
And, of course, the one and only Peter Workman

Barbecue buddies:
Karen Adler of Pig Out Publications, Jim Budros, "Oklahoma" Joe Davidson, Ardie Davis, Dr. Rich Davis, Judith Fertig, Cal Fussman (Perfect Man), Ron Harwell, Brian Heinecke, Don Hysco, Jake Jacobs, The Kansas City Barbecue Society, Paul Kirk, Ted and Donna McClure, Jack McDavid, Janeyce Michel-Cupito, Donna Myers, Lindsay Shannon, David Sparrow, Skip Steele, Jim "Trim" Tabb, Charlie Trotter, and Carolyn Wells

CONTENTS

BUILDING BETTER
BARBECUE
THE FLAVOR FACTOR

They're the foundation of world-class barbecue, the cornerstones on which unforgettable live-fire flavors are built. I'm talking about the barbecue sauces, rubs, spice pastes, marinades, and mops that transform ordinary grilled meats and seafood into barbecue of the highest distinction. They're the essential seasonings that give grilled fare its character, personality, and very soul.

And they're about to make you, the grill master, look like a million bucks.

One thing's for sure: Never has interest been keener in these not-so-subtle boosters of flavor. Spice sales are skyrocketing (up 62 percent in the last decade); and chili consumption has gone through the roof (188,000 tons at the very end of the millennium versus 105,000 tons in 1980), as Americans hunger for big-flavor foods that pack a wallop to the taste buds. In the realm of bar-

becue sauces alone, there are now more than 750 different commercially bottled varieties to choose from.

Despite the proliferation of barbecue sauces, rubs, marinades, and bastes, a great deal of confusion surrounds them. What's the difference between a dry rub and a wet rub? When do you use a spice mix or a marinade? How long should you marinate your favorite meat or seafood? What's the best way to baste or glaze? When should you apply the barbecue sauce? What do grill masters in other countries serve with grilled fare? How do the pros use rubs, marinades, and sauces to make championship barbecue every time?

This book explores the answers to these and other questions. For rubs, marinades, and sauces can make all the difference between serviceable grilled fare and world-class barbecue. There's no shortage of commercial rubs, marinades, and barbecue sauces, and many will produce tasty barbecue. But if you want to achieve truly extraordinary results and express your culinary creativity to its fullest, at some point you'll want to concoct your own.

Before we begin, a word about

nomenclature. Oceans of ink have been spilled about the true meaning of barbecue. To some, it's a catch-all term for anything cooked on a grill or pit. For others, barbecue refers to a specific type of meat (usually pork or beef) cooked by means of an equally distinctive cooking technique—long, slow smoking with indirect fire. Yet others use the word barbecue to describe a cooking device (the so-called barbecue grill), a dish (pulled pork in North Carolina, for example, or brisket in Texas), or even a cookout.

In Miami, where I live, and on the American East and West Coasts in general, barbecue refers to any sort of food cooked with live fire. The method can be direct or indirect. This is the way I use the term in this book. I acknowledge that this isn't the way certain Texans, Kansans, and North Carolinians see matters, but for the sake of expediency, please humor me.

A STRONG FOUNDATION

Anyone can grill a steak or smoke a brisket. But cooking great barbecue involves an intimate knowledge of fuels and fire control as well as considerable expertise in using rubs, marinades, bastes, glazes, and sauces. In a way, the process is similar to building a house. The contractor has to know how to select a site, dig a foundation, build a frame, do the finishing work, paint, decorate, and landscape, using the proper tools and construction methods.

Building great barbecue as well, requires the right tools (smokers and grills), the proper methods (flame and heat control), a solid foundation (the rubs and marinades), good finish work (the bastes and glazes), attractive paint (the barbecue sauce), and pleasing landscaping (the salsas, relishes, chutneys, mustards, ketchups, and other condiments served as accompaniments). Get these elements right and your barbecue will be very much at home on the plate, on your tongue, and in your belly.

Not every dish requires all of these elements. That would be overkill. But a lot of traditional American barbecue (Kansas City–style ribs, for example) features a soak in a marinade; a dusting with a rub; a generous basting during cooking; a glaze during the final grilling; and a barbecue sauce for serving.

Some years ago, I had the opportunity to watch one of the most decorated teams on the American competition barbecue circuit—Apple City from Murphysboro, Illinois—prepare the ribs that won the grand championship at the Memphis in May World Championship Barbecue

Cooking Contest. I was exhausted just watching the process! Each rack of ribs was painstakingly trimmed with a scalpel, then marinated overnight in a tenderizing bath of lemon juice and apple cider. No baby was ever toweled dry more gently than those ribs or more lovingly dusted with baby powder than the way the boys from Apple City sprinkled the bones with an eighteen-ingredient spice mix affectionately dubbed Magic Dust. (The formula is such a closely held secret, quipped the team captain, Pat Burke, that "no team member knows more than three of the ingredients.")

Once in the smoker, the ribs were sprayed repeatedly with apple cider to keep them moist, reseasoned with rub for extra flavor, and varnished with a barbecue sauce—flavored with apple cider (what else?!)—to give them a handsome sheen. Come time for the judging, the sauce was served on the side to allow the judges to experience the extraordinary flavor of the ribs without distraction.

Americans aren't the only barbecue masters to make such elaborate use of marinades, bastes, and sauces.

When I was in New Delhi, I watched tandoori masters marinate lamb first in a tenderizing marinade of palm vinegar and lemon juice, then a flavorizing paste of yogurt, aromatics, and spices. The meat was basted with butter during grilling and served with mint and onion chutneys by way of barbecue sauce and a cooling yogurt dip called raita.

All this may sound complicated. It *is* complicated, but you needn't feel intimidated. As you read the chapters in this book, you'll learn everything you need to know about rubs and seasonings, marinades and bastes, glazes and finishing sauces, barbecue sauces, relishes, and chutneys. You'll meet some of the greatest living practitioners of the art of live-fire cooking and you'll learn how they use rubs, marinades, and sauces to create winning barbecue every time.

You'll find lots of great recipes—many of them award winners—but even more important, you'll learn how to create your own rubs, marinades, and barbecue sauces. That is the goal of this book: To help you become a more confident, creative cook yourself.

SOME BASIC DEFINITIONS

This book is divided into seven main chapters, one for each of the flavor-enhancing components of great barbecue. Throughout the book you'll find recipes and boxes that tell you how to put them together. Here's a brief overview in order of when the components are used in the cooking process, along with some basic definitions. Note that there can be considerable overlap between categories: All wet rubs are marinades, for example, but not all marinades are wet rubs.

SEASONINGS: These are mixtures of salt and spices used to season foods before and during grilling. Seasonings differ from rubs in that salt is always the primary flavoring and that they are applied just prior to and/or during the cooking.

RUBS: These are mixes of spices, herbs, seasonings, and often sugar that are used to give a base flavor to the meat, rather than season it. Rubs are usually applied to the meat several hours before cooking, so that a marinating effect takes place. Rubs foster the formation of a crust.

DRY RUBS: These contain only dry ingredients. They are sprinkled over the food like a powder.

WET RUBS: Also known as **spice pastes,** these start as dry rubs, but a liquid—often water, oil, or yogurt—is added to create a thick paste. This paste is smeared on the meat, where it works in a way similar to a marinade.

MARINADES: These are liquid seasonings—a mixture of herbs, spices, aromatic vegetables (such as garlic, onions, and peppers), and flavorful liquids (such as olive oil, lemon juice, vinegar, and yogurt). The essence of a marinade is its wetness: The meat acquires its flavor by means of soaking. Marinades benefit meats in ways other than simply adding flavor. The acids in the marinade (wine, lime juice, vinegar) tenderize the meat by breaking down muscle fibers. The oil and other liquids keep the meat moist during cooking. Thus, marinades are particularly well suited to lean, dry meats, such as chicken breasts and game.

CURES: A special type of marinade, cures have a high salt content. The salt "cures" the meat by drawing out moisture. It also imparts a briny flavor all its own.

BASTES: Liquids applied to foods as they cook are called bastes. Basting serves two purposes: It keeps meats moist and fosters the formation of a flavorful crust during grilling. A baste can be as simple as apple cider sprayed on ribs with a mister or as elaborate as the lemon-saffron-butter mixture brushed on shish kebabs by Iranian grill jockeys. Bastes usually contain some sort of fat—olive oil or melted butter, for example—to seal in the juices.

FLAVORED OILS: Often used for basting, flavored oils can also serve as marinades, sauces, and decorative drizzles.

GLAZES: Resembling bastes in that they are brushed on the food as it cooks, glazes, however, are applied toward the end of cooking to create a shiny coating. Most glazes contain sugar, which caramelizes during the cooking process, creating a sweet, flavorful crust.

FINISHING SAUCE: A uniquely American invention, a finishing sauce is brushed on meat at the end of or after cooking to keep it moist and flavorful until serving. Finishing sauces are usually found on the competition barbecue circuit, where they help keep the meat moist until judging.

BARBECUE SAUCE: To many people, barbecue just isn't barbecue without it. In the United States alone, there are more than 750 commercially bottled barbecue sauces and literally dozens of regional styles. Barbecue sauce ranges from the sweet, smoky red sauce of Kansas City to the mouth-puckering vinegar sauces of the Carolinas to the white mayonnaise-based sauce so beloved in northern Alabama. Like Italy's pasta sauces, which are meant to be served with a specific kind of noodle, barbecue sauces evolved to accompany a specific kind of meat. South Carolina's sharp mustard sauce, for example, neutralizes the fat in a barbecued pork butt. The watery thinness of North Carolina vinegar sauce allows it to be readily absorbed by the pulled (shredded) pork so popular in this region. This book includes a full chapter of American barbecue sauces and another full chapter of the barbecue sauces popular elsewhere in the world.

SLATHER SAUCE: This catch-all category includes a large number of condiments that are slathered or smeared on grilled fare and barbecue before serving. Ketchup and mustard are slather sauces; so are aïoli (Provençale garlic mayonnaise) and romesco (Spanish roasted vegetable and nut sauce). Slather sauces are generally thicker than conventional barbecue sauce. (The exception here is ketchup.) Many contain eggs, oil, or cream, such as tartar sauce, béarnaise sauce, or horseradish sauce.

DIPPING SAUCE: A condiment you dip cooked barbecue into. Thai peanut sauce is one of the quintessential dipping sauces; so is Cambodian dipping sauce. While you find dipping sauces in many parts of the world, Southeast Asia is their epicenter. This makes sense, because for Asians, barbecue means tiny kebabs and paper-thin slices of meat, which are just perfect for dipping in tiny bowls of flavorful sauce.

CONDIMENTS: Salsas, relishes, pickles, sambals, chutneys, and other intensely flavorful accompaniments are traditionally served with barbecue. As a rule, condiments are too thick to qualify as sauces. They're served a spoonful at a time with simply grilled meats and seafood. Their explosive flavors round out the barbecue experience, particularly in Mexico, India, and Asia.

SALSA: This vibrant Mexican table sauce is the preferred companion to barbecue south of the border. Mexican salsas come in a dazzling variety—from the simple *salsa frescas* of northern Mexico to the robust roasted-chili-and-vegetable salsas of Oaxaca and the Yucatán. Mexican salsa inspired many of the new American fruit salsas, popularized by cutting-edge chefs at trendy restaurants and served with simple grilled poultry and seafood.

RELISH: Mixtures of chopped vegetables or fruits, relishes are usually chunky and often pickled or seasoned with vinegar and sugar. The sharpness of vinegar or lime juice in a relish heightens the smoke flavor of grilled fare.

CHUTNEY: "A strong, hot condiment compounded of ripe fruit, acids, or sour herbs, and flavored with chilies and spices" is how the august *Oxford English Dictionary* defines chutney. That pretty much sums it up, except to say that chutneys were born in India, where they are still traditionally served with curries, stews, and rice dishes. It took the young Turks of the New

American cuisine to pair this venerable condiment with contemporary grilled fare and barbecue. Spoon a chutney over a grilled salmon steak or chicken breast and you'll see a meal—even an everyday weeknight meal—in an entirely new perspective.

ABOUT THE RECIPES IN THIS BOOK

The recipes in this book come from a wide range of sources. Many are traditional, having been perfected over decades, sometimes centuries. It would be impossible to identify their creator. Others I collected during my three-year tour of the world's barbecue trail. I suppose you can say I created some of these recipes, although in barbecue, as in mathematics, we stand on the shoulders of giants. Others were developed by family members and friends. My stepson, Jake Klein, a gifted chef and accomplished pit boss, threw himself into this project with an enthusiasm matched only by his love of bold flavors. Jake ran my test kitchen and he contributed dozens of great ideas to the book.

Other recipes come from celebrated pit bosses, grill jockeys, and chefs from all over the country. Over the past few years, I've attended a lot of barbecue festivals, including Memphis in May, The Kansas City Royal, and The Jack Daniel's Invitational. In the process, I've made a lot of friends on the competition barbecue circuit.

Many have graciously shared the recipes for their prizewinning rubs and sauces

As I've traveled around the country, promoting the art of live-fire cooking, I've gotten many of my classically trained chef friends interested in barbecue. I asked such giants of contemporary cuisine as Charlie Trotter and Thomas Keller to create barbecue sauce recipes for this book. I think you'll be amazed by some of the "gourmet" barbecue sauces offered for the first time here from some of the nation's top chefs.

But whenever and from whomever I get a recipe, I always run it through my test kitchen. I try to stay faithful to the original, but never at the expense of taste.

In the following pages you'll find the results of my collecting—more than 200 recipes for rubs, spice pastes, marinades, barbecue sauces, ketchups, mustards, salsas, chutneys, relishes—in short, every seasoning and condiment you could possibly need for making and enjoying great barbecue. Use them singly or in combinations, with the foods I suggest or however it strikes your fancy.

I've tried to include something for everyone: basic sauces and seasonings for the neophyte; professional preparations for the expert; classic rubs and barbecue sauces for the traditionalist; cutting-edge flavor combinations for the adventurer; downhome, common-sense seasonings for the basic barbecue guy; and downright exotic ethnic preparations for the culinary globe-trotter. I've also included recipes for complete dishes, using the sauces, seasonings, and condiments in this book.

There are two ways to use this book: read it from the beginning or browse through it randomly, marking recipes or taking notes in the margins. Follow some recipes to the letter and use others as springboards for your imagination. If you don't have a particular ingredient on hand, experiment with another. (Remember: There's no such thing as a mistake in the kitchen, just a new recipe waiting to be discovered!) Add these recipes to your repertory as they are or customize and make them your own. Sometimes, the best dishes are those you make when you cook by the seat of your pants.

And please keep me apprised of your efforts. Ask me questions; share your ideas and results by visiting me on my web site:

www.barbecuebible.com.

You can leave a message for me on the Ask the Grilling Guru page. It may take me a few days to get back to you, but I will answer every question.

Above all, have fun! Remember, barbecue isn't brain surgery.

—*Steven Raichlen*

A REFRESHER COURSE

EVERYTHING YOU NEED TO KNOW ABOUT BARBECUING AND GRILLING

A good sauce or rub or marinade can go a long way toward helping you make superlative barbecue, but in the end, there's no substitute for mastering the basic principles of fire management and heat control—and understanding the difference between barbecuing and grilling.

I assume that if you've bought this book, you already know something about lighting and using your grill. Below is a crash course for neophytes, a refresher course for seasoned grillers, and an opportunity to make sure we're all on the same page when it comes to basic vocabulary.

Live-fire cooking features one of two basic techniques: grilling and barbecuing. Grilling is practiced by grill jockeys all over the planet and is by far the world's most popular method. Barbecuing is primarily a North American phenomenon, but it's also found in Mexico and the Caribbean. In this chapter it refers to a specific cooking technique that's slow, indirect, and heavy on wood smoke. Elsewhere in this book, the term barbecue is used in the generic sense of live-fire cooking.

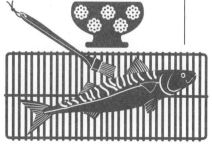

GRILLING: Cooking pieces of meat directly over the fire. The fuel can be charcoal, gas, or wood embers. Because you're working directly over the fire, the heat is relatively high (400°F to 700°F) and the food cooks (and burns) quickly. For this reason, grilling is generally reserved for relatively small or thin pieces of tender meats, such as steaks, burgers, sausages, chicken breasts, fish steaks or fillets, as well as shish kebabs, vegetables, breads, and tofu. Grilling is a quick process, requiring 2 to 10 minutes per side to cook the food, depending on its thickness. The high heat and quick cooking sears the surface of the food, giving grilled food a delectable crust and flame-seared flavor.

BARBECUING: An indirect method of cooking. The food is cooked in a closed chamber next to, not over, the fire. The classic device for barbecuing is a pit, traditionally a trench in the ground, today a metal box or barrel with a fire box at one end and a cooking chamber at the other. Barbecuing is traditionally done at a much lower temperature than grilling—200°F to 300°F—and because the food is located away from the fire, you can cook larger, tougher pieces of meat to tenderness without burning them. The traditional meats for barbecue are briskets, ribs, and pork shoulders. The fuel can be charcoal, gas, or wood embers, but whatever you use, there's always the presence of wood smoke. Indeed, this smoke is the defining flavor—and very essence of barbecue.

INDIRECT GRILLING: A hybrid method that combines some of the heat, speed, and searing of grilling with the leisurely smoking of barbecue. Indirect grilling involves cooking food next to, not over, the fire, but directly in the fire box and at a higher temperature than you would for true barbecue. Indirect grilling is great for cooking whole chicken, turkeys, rib roasts, and other large pieces of meat that would burn if you tried to direct grill them. The higher heat (350°F) allows you to cook a chicken or ribs in, say, 1½ hours, rather than the half day you'd need for conventional barbecue. You can add wood chips or chunks to the fire to generate smoke, much as you would do in a barbecue pit. But you don't need a pit or even a smoker, because indirect grilling is designed to be done in a commonplace kettle or gas grill.

ROTISSERIE COOKING: A special form of indirect grilling. A bird or roast is cooked on a rotating spit next to, but not over, the fire. To set up a grill for rotisserie cooking, arrange the

coals in two parallel rows, one in front of the spit and one behind it. The food rotates in the center. On a gas grill, you'd light the front and rear burners, doing the cooking over the center, unlit burner. On some grills, you'd use only a single row of coals, generally behind the spit.

Grilling, barbecuing, indirect grilling, and rotisserie cooking, then, are the four methods you'll find in this cookbook. Master them and you'll rule the world.

HOW TO LIGHT A GRILL

Before you can actually grill, you need to know how to light a grill safely—a procedure that has daunted more than one would-be grill master. Fortunately, the process has gotten considerably easier, thanks to new technologies and grilling equipment.

CHARCOAL GRILLS

My favorite (and the environmentally correct) way to light a charcoal grill is to use a chimney starter, an open metal cylinder with a wooden handle and a grate in the middle to hold the coals. You can buy a chimney starter at a grill shop or well-stocked hardware store—purchase the largest one you can find. Chimney starters have considerable advantages over traditional ignition methods: The coals light evenly all at once and you don't need any lighter fluid, which can

give your food a petroleum taste.

Place one or two crumpled sheets of newspaper in the bottom section of the chimney starter and your charcoal in the top. (Or instead of newspaper, use one or two paraffin starters —available at grill stores.) Place the chimney on the bottom grate of the grill, light the paper, and stand back. First, you'll see a thick coil of black smoke, then flames; the coals will glow red in 15 to 20 minutes. Holding the starter by the handle, dump the coals into the grill and rake them into the desired configuration, following the instructions below.

I'm a big fan of natural charwood, also known as lump charcoal, craggy black pieces of pure kilned wood that lack the chemical binders and coal dust found in commercial briquets. Charwood is sold at grill shops and natural foods stores or you can order it by mail order (see page 281).

For my money, though, the best fuel of all is hardwood. You can buy it in easy-to-use chunks (2 to 3 inches in diameter) at grill shops and hardware stores. Any hardwood is a candidate for grilling, including hickory, oak, pecan, apple, and mesquite. Place the hardwood chunks in the chimney starter and light as you would charcoal. The embers will glow red in 10 to 12 minutes. Get ready for some of the best grilling you've ever tasted.

GAS GRILLS

To light a gas grill, follow the manufacturer's instructions. Most gas grills have electric ignition devices these days. You simply turn on the gas and push a button. Always leave the lid open when you light a gas grill. If you don't, you run the risk of a gas buildup under the lid, which could literally explode like a bomb. Make sure all the desired burners are lit by holding your hand over them before you close the lid.

HEAT CONTROL ON A CHARCOAL GRILL: Using a three-zone fire

Although gas grills outsell charcoal grills two to one in the United States, charcoal has its partisans. If you love the act of building and tend-

ing a fire, you probably prefer cooking on charcoal. Charcoal burns hotter and drier than gas and many people argue that it gives you better flavor. The chief drawback of charcoal is heat control: There's no thermostat to turn to raise or lower the heat.

But there's an easy way to control the heat on a charcoal grill: Build a three-zone fire. To do this, rake half of the lit coals into a double layer over a section (roughly a third) of the bottom of your grill. Rake the remaining coals into a single layer in another section (another third). Leave the third zone (it should be a little smaller than the other two) free of coals. You now have three heat zones—high, medium, and low—one for searing, one for cooking, and one for warming. If the food starts to burn over the hot zone, simply move it to the medium zone or warm zone. You'll never burn your food again.

HEAT CONTROL ON A GAS GRILL

Nothing could be easier than heat control on a gas grill. You simply adjust the burner knobs to the desired temperature. I'll often set one side of the grill on high and the other on medium to free me from having to adjust the burners. To control the heat, I simply move the food back and forth.

ALL FIRED UP

O kay, you've got your rubs, marinades, and barbecue sauce. The only other thing you need to know is how to manage your fire. Here's a refresher on grilling and barbecuing.

DIRECT GRILLING ON A CHARCOAL OR GAS GRILL

Simply place the food to be grilled directly over the fire. When using a three-zone fire, start the food over the hottest zone and move it to a cooler zone once it's seared to finish cooking. Should the food start to burn or give you flare-ups, simply move it over the unlit zone of the fire. When I work over charcoal, I move the food often, jock-

eying it from hot spots to cooler spots. This is what makes grilling a sport, not a science, and it's why grilling is so much fun. When cooking only one or two steaks or chicken breasts, you don't need to fuss with a three-zone fire. One hot zone and a little unlit space is all you'll need.

INDIRECT GRILLING ON A CHARCOAL GRILL

To indirect grill on a charcoal grill, light the coals in a chimney starter, then rake the embers into two piles at opposite sides of the grill. If your grill has side baskets, place the coals in them. Place an aluminum foil drip pan in the center, under the grate. Place the food to be indirect grilled on top of the grate in the center, over the drip pan, away from the fire, and cover the grill. Adjust the vent holes to obtain a temperature of 325°F to 350°F. You'll need to add ten fresh coals per side every hour and leave the grill uncovered for a few minutes to allow them to ignite. If smoke is desired, toss ½ cup soaked wood chips on each pile of coals every hour. (See Smoking on a Grill, page 6.)

INDIRECT GRILLING ON A GAS GRILL

To indirect grill on a two-burner gas grill, light one side to high. Cook the food on the other side, away from the fire. On a three-burner gas grill, light the far right and left (or front and rear) burners, and set the food in the center away from the fire. On a four-burner gas grill, light the outside burners and cook the food in the center.

BARBECUING ON A GRILL

To barbecue on a grill simply indirect grill at a lower temperature. How low? A competition pit boss will tell you 225°F. To save time, you can go as high as 325°F. You'll need to work at the higher end of the range on a charcoal grill, as it's harder to keep the coals lit at the lower temperatures. On a gas grill, simply adjust the burners to the desired temperature. When barbecuing, you always use smoke.

SMOKING ON A GRILL

Wood smoke is the very essence of true barbecue and it certainly adds complexity and robustness to ordinary grilling. In the old days, you had to start with logs, but now you can buy a dazzling variety of woods in chip and chunk form. Use them to give your live-fire cooking that old-fashioned smoke flavor. Your food will never taste the same again.

Any hardwood can be used for smoking. The classic wood of the American Midwest is hickory. New Englanders favor maple and apple; Southerners, pecan; Pacific Northwesterners, alder; Texans and Hawaiians,

mesquite. (Hawaiians call the latter *kiave*.) Oak is the wood preferred by South Americans, Europeans, and by most contemporary American chefs.

In terms of flavor profiles, the fruit woods (apple, cherry, peach) are the lightest, followed by alder, maple, and oak. (Oak is great for lamb.) The nut woods (hickory and pecan) have a more pronounced smoke flavor that goes great with pork, while mesquite is the strongest—best suited to robust meat, like beef.

The first step is to soak the wood chips or chunks in water, or beer, cider, or other flavored liquid for 1 hour. Drain the wood and you're ready to smoke.

To smoke on a charcoal grill, simply toss the chips on the coals—under the food if direct grilling or in the side baskets if indirect grilling. For indirect grilling, figure on 1 cup wood chips every hour.

Smoking on a gas grill can be easy or challenging, depending on the model. Many grills, like the Viking, Lynx, and DCS, have special slide-out smoker drawers with independent burners. Simply place the chips in the drawer, light the burner, and wait for the smoke to appear. The advantage of this system is that you don't need to move the grate to load the chips in the smoker box and you can smoke even when running your grill at a low temperture. If your

GAUGING THE HEAT
OF YOUR GRILL

In the recipes, I ask you to preheat your grill to various temperatures—high or medium-high for direct grilling; 225°F to 350°F for barbecuing or indirect grilling. Which is easy, if your grill happens to be one of the dozens of models that come with built-in thermometers. But how do you judge the temperature if your grill lacks a heat gauge? It's really very simple.

When direct grilling, place your hand about 6 inches over the coals or gas burners. When the grill is hot, you'll be able to hold your hand over the fire for 2 to 3 seconds (count one Mississippi, two Mississippi, three Mississippi) before the heat forces you to pull it away. On a medium-hot grill, you'll be able to hold your hand over the fire for 4 to 5 seconds.

When indirect grilling on a charcoal grill, align one of the vent holes in the grill lid so that it's over the food, not the fire. Place a thermometer in the hole and leave it there for 5 minutes. You should get a pretty good reading of the temperature inside the grill.

Gas grills don't normally have vent holes in the lid. Fortunately, most gas grills come with thermometers. If yours lacks one, the only thing you can do is drill a hole in the lid and insert a thermometer.

A final option is to buy a grill thermometer or instant-read meat thermometer from a mail-order company like the Grill Lovers Catalog, P.O. Box 1300, Columbus, Georgia 31902-13000; tel: (800) 241-8981.

gas grill lacks these features, place your chips in the smoker box (a perforated metal box provided by some manufacturers or available separately at a grill shop or hardware store). Or loosely wrap the chips in heavy-duty aluminum foil and make a few holes in the top with the tip of a knife. Position the smoker box or foil packet over or as close to one of the gas burners as you can get it. Preheat the grill to high and run it at high until you see copious amounts of smoke. Then lower the heat to the desired temperature and barbecue or grill as desired. Note: When smoking on a gas grill with a nondedicated smoker box and burner,

burn all the chips at once.

Well, that covers the ABC's of barbecuing and grilling. On to the equipment.

TOOLS OF THE TRADE

The right tool for the right job, insists our contractor friend, Richard Knight. You don't need to invest in a lot of specialized gear to make great barbecue. (Although a lot of guys do. After all, we boys love toys.) But having the right equipment can go a long way in making barbecue easier and more fun. Here's what you need to become a master baster and sauce maker.

IN THE KITCHEN

BLENDER: In our rush to modernize our kitchens, many of us have shelved the mixing device of our youth—the blender—in favor of the more high-tech food processor. The latter is terrific, but there are some tasks that are just better performed in the blender, among them combining herbs and oil to make vinaigrettes and flavored oils for basting. Buy a sturdy blender with a tight-fitting lid and use it for blending liquid concoctions or making smooth purées. When using a blender, add the wet ingredients like the oil or tomatoes first, then the solids. A blender blade works better on liquids.

CAST-IRON SKILLET: Perfect for toasting spices and roasting vegetables. The thick metal spreads the heat evenly. And you don't have to worry about scorching a nonstick surface. Cast-iron skillets serve another valuable purpose: They're great for cracking peppercorns and coriander seeds.

Loosely wrap the seeds in cloth and crush them under the bottom of the pan.

CHEESECLOTH: Useful for tying loose spices in a small bag to add to marinades and sauces. For a high-tech version, wrap the spices in a piece of aluminum foil and perforate the package with a fork.

CONTAINERS FOR MARINATING: These include bowls, baking dishes, roasting pans, disposable aluminum foil pans, and even heavy-duty zip-top bags. Be sure to use nonreactive bowls and pans—that is, vessels made of glass, ceramic, plastic, or stainless steel. Do not use aluminum or cast-iron pans; these metals sometimes react with acidic ingredients, like vinegar or lemon juice. When using zip-top bags, place in a bowl or baking dish to catch any leaks.

CUTTING BOARDS: Wood or plastic? Good question. Just when I was all set to recommend plastic, which you can run through the dishwasher, *The New York Times* runs an article asserting that you get less bacterial contamination with wood. (The exact chemistry of this phenomenon is unclear, but it has been scientifically proven.) Actually, it's a good idea to own several cutting boards; that way, you can dice onion or garlic on one and cut up chicken on another. Choose a cutting board large enough to do a clean job;

at least 12 by 15 inches. Whichever kind of cutting board you use, place it on a damp dishcloth or paper towel to keep it from sliding on the counter.

FOOD PROCESSOR: When it comes to reducing herbs and vegetables to flavorful seasoning pastes, nothing can beat a food processor. Buy a model with a wide bowl and strong motor. When using a food processor, add the solid ingredients like the onions, tomatoes, and celery first, then the liquids. A processor blade works better on solids.

INJECTORS: Marinades are great for applying flavor to the surface of a food. But what if you want to put the flavor deep into the heart of the meat? There's a simple tool that looks like an oversize hypodermic needle—the injector—and grill jockeys use it to make some of the most succulent barbecue in the world. To use a meat injector, you place the marinade or basting liquid in the cylinder and insert the needle into the center of a turkey breast, pork shoulder, or roast beef. A push of the plunger injects the flavoring deep into the meat. Many companies manufacture injectors. One good brand is Chef William's Cajun Injector (see Mail-Order Sources, page 281).

JARS: What good is a homemade barbecue sauce without a jar in which to store it? If you're home canning a large batch of sauce, the best choice in my book is the Ball jar, recognizable by its flat lid and ringlike collar. The sturdy glass jar comes with calibrations on the side, so you know exactly how much sauce you have. The flexible lid pops up if the jar is improperly sealed—great if you're preserving the sauce for later use. Ball jars are available at most supermarkets and hardware stores. However, none of the recipes in this book need to be sterilized and canned. Each one comes with the length of time it will stay fresh if properly refrigerated. Although I like to use canning jars for storing sauces, rubs, and condiments, they will also keep well

in the thoroughly washed and dried regular jars.

KNIVES: Buy good knives and take care of them. Taking care of them means washing and drying by hand (never leave a knife in the sink) and keeping the blades honed with a sharpening steel. The knife I've been using a lot these days is a razor-sharp, cleaverlike knife manufactured by a Japanese company called MAC. For a catalog, contact MAC Knife, Inc., 9630 Kiefer Boulevard, Suite D, Sacramento, California 95827; tel: (888) 622-5643; fax: (916) 854-9974.

MEASURING CUPS AND SPOONS: Accurate measuring may seem like the antithesis of the creative spirit. A pinch of this; a splash of that—aren't these the measurements used by pit bosses to create some of their most inspired sauces? True, many great condiments have been whipped up on the spur of the moment, but if you

want to be able to reproduce your results and make a second batch of that exquisite sauce, you need to measure accurately and chronicle your efforts on paper. Get yourself a set of measuring spoons and measuring cups (including some glass cups with spouts for liquids), if you don't have them, and force yourself to use them and record any new or changed measurements.

MIXING BOWLS: A set of nested metal mixing bowls is essential kitchen equipment for any aspiring sauce meister. Choose a bowl that's large enough to allow for vigorous mixing without spilling ingredients all over the work surface. This ought to seem self-evident, but you wouldn't believe how often I've watched a big guy grab a tiny bowl and proceed to scatter the ingredients all over the kitchen.

MORTAR AND PESTLE: Visit a Cuban or Indonesian or Italian kitchen and you'll find a utensil that's almost as old as cooking itself: a mortar and pestle. Nothing beats this ancient, low-tech device for pounding garlic and spices into aromatic pastes used for seasoning barbecue.

Why does a mortar and pestle work better than, say, a blender or food processor? Well, consider for a moment the chemistry of an onion or garlic. The flavor of these ingredients is intensified when the sulfur compounds in them are brought into contact with air. What results is a mild form of sulfuric acid, the compound that makes you cry when you chop onion. The smaller the pieces of garlic and onion, the greater exposure to air and the more forceful the flavor. Pounding foods in a mortar with a pestle pulverizes the pieces and maximizes the flavor. When you buy a mortar and pestle, look for a deep bowl (at least 6 inches deep) with at least a 4-cup capacity. Small mortars and pestles may look nice, but the ingredients will soon be scattered all over the work surface. The best place to buy a serious mortar and pestle is at an ethnic market. Buy them from the people who use them.

SAUCEPANS: You can't make barbecue sauce without them. When choosing the right pan for the job, I look at three things: size, material, and construction. The pan should be large enough to allow you to simmer and stir your sauce

without it spilling over. This means at least a 3-inch clearance between the surface of the sauce and the rim of the saucepan. But choose a pan that's too big and the sauce will form such a thin layer on the bottom, it will either burn or evaporate too quickly.

The pan should be made of a nonreactive material, especially when working with acidic ingredients. Copper, stainless steel, enamel, and anodized aluminum are good candidates. Avoid plain aluminum and cast iron: These materials tend to react adversely with lemon juice, vinegar, tomatoes, and other acidic flavorings. The construction of the pan is important, too. You want a pan with a thick base and walls, so that the heat spreads evenly. Thin pans tend to have hot spots, which will scorch or even burn your sauce. Finally, the pan should have a firmly attached (riveted) handle, preferably of a nonconductive material, so you don't burn your fingers. This should seem obvious, but I've seen more than one grill meister spill a prize sauce because of a wobbly or hot handle.

SCALES: Invaluable for accurate measuring—especially for odd-shaped ingredients, like dried tomatoes or chilies. Buy a kitchen scale at a cookware shop.

SPICE MILL: As any Indian housewife knows, the secret to great flavor is to start with whole spices. Toast them in a skillet, then grind them in a spice mill. Most of the major appliance companies sell spice mill/coffee grinders. Once you've designated a coffee grinder for spices, don't use it for coffee (or vice versa).

VEGETABLE PEELER: Invaluable for peeling cucumbers, carrots, and celery as well as removing thin strips of lemon and orange zest.

WOODEN SPOONS AND WHISKS: The basic tools for mixing. Buy wooden spoons with long handles—they'll keep your fingers cool when stirring a pot of bubbling sauce—and use them for stirring thick mixtures. When it comes to getting the job of mixing done thoroughly, nothing can beat a whisk. Buy several sizes of whisks, preferably with thick handles, which are easier to hold than thin ones. Use whisks for mixing both rubs and sauces. And don't forget the ultimate tool for mixing rubs: your fingers. When you mix a rub by hand, you can break up lumps of brown sugar or salt or crumble spices between your fingers.

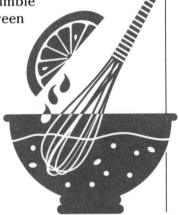

AT THE GRILL

BASTING BRUSH: Having gone to the trouble of making a great baste or barbecue sauce, buy a good brush (or several) for applying it. The ideal brush will have natural bristles and a long handle, so you can use it without burning your arm.

GRILL MITTS: Buy a few of the long-sleeved variety to protect the skin on your arms.

MISTER: Hang around the professional barbecue circuit long enough and you'll see guys spraying their meats with what looks like a plant mister. What they're doing is spraying apple cider or lemon juice on the meat to baste and sweeten it. You can buy a plastic mister at a hardware store for a couple of dollars. Use it for any water-based basting mixture, from apple cider to Worcestershire sauce. To spray a flavorful coat of extra-virgin olive oil on grilled meats, you'll need a mister with a heavy-duty pump. The best-known brand is Misto, available in housewares and cookware shops.

MOP: "Are you crazy?" screamed my wife, as she watched me preparing to use a kitchen mop to apply a barbecue baste to a smoker full of ribs. History neglects to tell us who first had the idea to "mop" a sauce on smoked meats, but he (or she) was one ingenious pit boss. If you have a large quantity of ribs or chickens to baste, a long-handled kitchen mop is the perfect utensil. Of course, you want to use a clean mop—make that a brand-new mop that has never seen action on a floor. You also want to be sure it's 100 percent cotton and you should wash and rinse it well before using. This is a big tool for a big job, so it would be overkill at most family cookouts. Cookware shops sell pint-size mops that are perfect for back-yard grilling and are guaranteed to amaze your guests.

TONGS: The handiest tool in your toolbox. Choose sturdy, long-handled, spring-loaded tongs, available in restaurant supply houses and cook-ware shops.

A WORD ON FOOD SAFETY

My research on barbecue has taken me literally all over the world. I've eaten satés at street markets in Thailand, chicken *tikka* at tandoori joints in India, and *anticuchos* from itinerant food sellers in Peru. Much of this fare came from street vendors, who work in what seems to most North Americans like horren-dous sanitary conditions. But during three years on the world's barbecue trail, I rarely got sick—a tribute to the sterilizing powers of fire as well as to an intuitive understanding of basic notions of food safety on the part of the world's grill jockeys.

The most important risk to avoid is cross-contamination. Here are a few basic rules to keep your barbecue safe.

RUBS: Wear surgical-style rubber gloves (found in most pharmacies) when rubbing meats—especially chicken—with spice mixes. This keeps any surface bacteria off your fingers. Throw the gloves away after each use. Barbecue great John Willingham has a nifty trick: When he plans to handle several different types of meat, he puts on an equal number of gloves, one on top of the other. He peels one glove off after each use, thereby avoid-ing cross-contamination.

MARINADES: Marinades are great fla-vor enhancers, but they can also carry contaminants. Follow these simple common-sense tips and your food will be safe every time.

■ When marinating meats or seafood for a brief amount of time, you can do so at room temperature. For more than 30 minutes (15 minutes on a hot day), keep the pan in the refrigerator. Tightly cover the marinade with plas-tic wrap to keep any food odors from spreading.

■ Most marinades are meant to be used a single time, then discarded. If you want to reuse a marinade, boil it for several minutes first, then let it cool to room temperature. Put it and the food into a clean container. Store, covered, in the refrigerator.

■ Some marinades are flavorful enough to be used for basting. There are two ways to do this safely:

Set aside a quarter of the marinade before you add the meat or seafood. Use this portion for basting.

Boil the used marinade for several minutes before using it for basting.

BASTING AND GLAZING: Basting should be done toward the end of cooking—or at least, after the surface of the food has been seared. If you brush a baste or glaze on uncooked or undercooked food, you run the risk of contaminating the basting brush and any remaining baste.

BARBECUE SAUCES: When serving barbecue sauces, squirt them from squeeze bottles or spoon them over the meat. When serving dipping sauces, place a single serving of sauce in a tiny bowl or saucer, providing one for each eater. Never dip cooked meat into a communal bowl of sauce.

CUTTING BOARDS: Never cut cooked meat on the same board on which you cut raw food. Always use different cutting boards for raw meats and any other ingredients you may be using, like vegetables or tofu. Scrub dirty cutting boards with soap and hot water.

PLATTERS AND PLATES: It's so tempting. You bring your steaks to the grill on a platter. You've forgotten to fetch another for serving. So when no one's looking, you grab a paper towel and wipe the offending platter. At least that's what I do, or did until my wife caught me. I now always bring two platters to the grill: one for raw meat and one for the cooked. Never the twain shall meet.

Following these simple tips will keep your barbecue safe and your guests happy.

SEASONINGS

AND

RUBS

I've always been fascinated by the simple alchemy by which good assertive seasonings are melded into a harmonious whole. Clearly, I'm not alone. Wherever you find people grilling, you'll find spices, and wherever you find spices, you find signature rubs and spice mixes that give barbecue its personality.

This chapter focuses on the rubs, spice mixes, and seasonings used by grill masters the world over. In America, pit bosses use rubs with greater imagination and with a freer hand than anywhere else on the planet. This chapter has something for everyone: a quick, easy, all-purpose Basic Barbecue Rub (page 23); a Kansas City Sweet and Smoky Rub (page 24); and a fiery Lone Star steak seasoning (page 27).

From beyond America's borders, experience an electrifying kebab spice from Spain (page 45); a fragrant rosemary rub from Tuscany (page 44); and even an offbeat seasoning from Bali (page 20).

Whether you're trying to increase the flavor of your barbecue or simply reduce the overall fat, chances are there's a rub or spice mixture in this chapter that can help you. You'll never have to use a commercial blend again.

SEASONED SALTS AND PEPPERS

BASIC SEASONED SALT

Sprinkle this mixture on steaks, chops, chicken, fish—on just about anything you cook on the grill.

Virtually every recipe cooked on the grill calls for salt and pepper. In a perfect world, you'd dose the salt and grind the pepper fresh every time. This is not a perfect world, however, and having a batch of premixed seasoned salt on hand can save a lot of time and trouble. There's no shortage of commercial seasoned salts, but most of them are loaded with MSG and sugar. The following formula may seem simple, but it reacts in complex ways on your taste buds. The coarse crystals of salt and cracked black peppercorns give you little bursts of flavor. The black, white, and cayenne peppers provide three different sorts of heat. Black pepper is the most aromatic; white pepper has a stinging, front-of-the-mouth heat; while cayenne is pure fire that's chiefly experienced deep in your gullet. Put them together and you get a seasoning mix that makes just about everything on the grill taste better. Note that some people like a touch of sweetness in their seasoned salt, others don't, so I've made the sugar optional.

1 cup coarse salt
  (kosher or sea)
¼ cup cracked black pepper
2 tablespoons ground white
  pepper

1 tablespoon cayenne pepper
1 tablespoon sugar
  (optional)

Combine all the ingredients in a bowl and stir or whisk to mix. Transfer to a jar, cover, and store away from heat and light. The salt will keep for several months.
Makes 1¼ cups

SMOKED SALT

One of the best ways to give foods that smoky grilled flavor is to season them with smoked salt. You can buy smoked salt, but it's easy to make your own from scratch and it tastes a lot more natural. Moreover, you can customize the smoke flavor, from the elegance of oak to the delicacy of apple to the robustness of hickory, and so on. Here are four methods for smoking salt, both indoors and outdoors. Smoked salt keeps well in a sealed jar. If it starts to cake after a few months, flake it with a fork.

SPECIAL EQUIPMENT

2 tablespoons hardwood
    sawdust (if smoking
    indoors)

2 cups wood chips, soaked
    in cold water for 1 hour,
    then drained (if smoking
    outdoors)

2 cups coarse salt
    (kosher or sea)

Stovetop Smoker Method: Place the sawdust in the bottom of the smoker. Spread the salt in a thin layer in an aluminum foil pie pan and place it in the top of the smoker. Place the smoker over high heat. When you start to see wisps of smoke, reduce the heat to medium, tightly cover the smoker, and smoke the salt for 20 minutes. Cool the salt to room temperature, then transfer it to a jar, cover, and store away from heat and light.

Wok Method: Line the bottom of the wok with aluminum foil (a 6-inch square will do) and place the sawdust on top. Set a round wire cake rack in the wok. Spread the salt in a thin layer in an aluminum foil pie pan and place on the wire rack. Place the wok over high heat. When you start to see wisps of smoke, reduce the heat to medium, tightly cover the wok, and smoke the salt for 20 minutes. Cool the salt to room temperature, then transfer it to a jar, cover, and store away from heat and light.

SMITTEN BY SALT

It's an edible stone—and a biological necessity—and barbecue would be unimaginably dull without it. I'm talking about the one food we eat daily that's neither plant nor animal, the world's most popular seasoning: salt.

Salt is the single most important seasoning you'll ever use for grilling and barbecuing. To most of us, salt means the tiny white grains sold in cylindrical cardboard containers. But salt comes in a bewildering array of colors, textures, and even tastes.

Indians love black salt (*kala namak*), a blackish-brown or blackish-pink salt with a smoky, almost sulfurous flavor. Talk about reinforcing the smoke flavor of barbecue! When I was in Hawaii, I chanced upon a red salt that was colored with edible clay—the traditional seasoning for the pit-roasted pig at a luau.

Salt comes from two primary sources: mineral deposits in the earth and evaporated sea water. Mineral deposits furnish rock salt; the ocean, sea salt. Freshly mined rock salt is the coarse, gray-white stuff we sprinkle on driveways to prevent them from freezing. To make common table salt, the mineral is dissolved in water, purified, evaporated, and dried. It's precisely this purification process that makes commonplace table salt my *last* choice for grilling. Table salt is salty (actually, it burns the tongue), but it has none of the rich secondary flavors of sea salt.

Kosher salt is another story. Slow, gentle boiling of rock salt produces large, flaky, pyramid-shaped crystals that are slow to dissolve on food. Because kosher salt doesn't melt right away, you get pointillistic bursts of flavor when you bite into a grilled steak or fish fillet. Kosher salt is the everyday salt in my kitchen: I always have an open bowl on hand for sprinkling. Besides, cooking is about sensuality and the coarse texture of kosher salt feels great between your fingers when you take a pinch.

Sea salt is made by evaporating sea water. Traditionally, the water was channeled into shallow seaside basins, where it was left to evaporate in the sun. Unlike rock salt, sea salt is loaded with flavorful minerals from the sea, including iodine and calcium and magnesium chloride. These minerals give sea salt a richer, tangier flavor than mineral salt.

The ultimate salt goes by the whimsical French name of *fleur de sel* (salt flower). Made by the traditional solar evaporation method, this deluxe sea salt has a lovely briny flavor. It's salty, of course, but it doesn't burn your tongue. It's slightly moist, as you'd expect sea salt to be, and it even looks as if it's loaded with nutrients and flavor components, being grayish, not dazzling white.

Things sure do come full circle: My great-grandmother probably would have called this off-colored seasoning "poor person's salt" and would have been appalled by its price. Look for *fleur de sel* in gourmet shops.

Charcoal Grill Method: Set up the grill for indirect grilling following the directions on page 5. Toss the wood chips on the coals. Spread the salt in a thin layer in an aluminum foil pie pan and place it on the grate away from the fire. Cover the grill and adjust the vent holes to medium heat (350°F). Smoke the salt for 1 hour. Cool the salt to room temperature, then transfer it to a jar, cover, and store away from heat and light.

Gas Grill Method: Preheat the grill to medium. Place the wood chips in the smoker box and preheat until you see smoke. (See the directions on page 5.) Spread the salt in a thin layer in an aluminum foil pie pan and place it on the grate away from the fire. Cover the grill and smoke the salt for 1 hour. Cool the salt to room temperature, then transfer it to a jar, cover, and store away from heat and light.

Makes 2 cups

SESAME SALT

I love the nutty, roasted flavor of this sesame seasoned salt. I love the flavor almost as much as I love the appearance: snow-white salt crystals, tan roasted sesame seeds, and jet black *kuro goma* (Japanese black sesame seeds). The latter are available at Japanese markets and at most natural foods stores and gourmet shops.

½ cup white sesame seeds
½ cup black sesame seeds
   (or additional white
   sesame seeds)

½ cup coarse salt
   (kosher or sea)
3 tablespoons cracked black
   pepper

Heat a dry skillet over medium heat. Add the white sesame seeds and toast, stirring occasionally, until fragrant and golden brown, 2 to 4 minutes. Transfer the sesame seeds to a bowl and stir in the black sesame seeds, salt, and pepper. Transfer to a jar, cover, and store away from heat and light. The salt will keep for several months.

Makes 1½ cups

TRY THIS!

This salt makes a colorful seasoning for grilled seafood, chicken, and vegetables. Use it on grilled tofu and seitan. It's good on salads, too.

CENTRAL ASIAN SEASONED SALT

TRY THIS!

Generously sprinkle on lamb, beef, chicken, or seafood prior to grilling.

I'm not sure seasoned salt per se exists in Afghanistan, but the spices in this mix are traditional Afghan seasonings for grilling. Use this seasoning to give an exotic Central Asian accent to anything you throw on the grill.

¼ cup coarse salt (kosher or sea)	1 tablespoon dried mint
1 tablespoon cracked black pepper	2 teaspoons ground coriander
1 tablespoon freeze-dried chives	2 teaspoons hot paprika
1 tablespoon dried parsley	2 teaspoons dried garlic flakes
	½ teaspoon ground cinnamon

Combine all the ingredients in a bowl and stir to mix. Transfer to a jar, cover, and store away from heat and light. The salt will keep for several months.

Makes ½ cup

BALINESE SEASONED SALT

TRY THIS!

Sprinkle this salt on grilled chicken, pork, and seafood. It's also great on grilled vegetables.

I first tasted this seasoned salt at the Aman Kila resort in Bali. The striking contrast of flavors—anise and nutmeg for sweetness and coriander and cloves for spice—has made it a favorite in my kitchen. Ground red rice gives the rub a lovely pink color. It also fosters the formation of a savory crust. Red rice is available at Asian markets and natural foods stores. If it's unavailable, use white rice. And, the easiest way to cut a nutmeg is with a serrated knife.

2 tablespoons red rice	½ teaspoon whole cloves
2 tablespoons coriander seeds	½ whole nutmeg
2 teaspoons fennel seeds	½ cup coarse salt (kosher or sea)

Heat a small dry skillet over medium heat. Add the rice, coriander, fennel, cloves, and nutmeg and toast until fragrant, 2 minutes. Do not brown. Cool the spices, then transfer to a spice mill and grind to a fine powder. Add the salt and pulse the grinder to mix. Transfer to a jar, cover, and store away from heat and light. The salt will keep for several months.

Makes ⅔ cup

LEMON PEPPER

TRY THIS!

Sprinkle on as you would normal pepper, but when you want a zesty hit of lemon as well. It also works as an ingredient in rubs, marinades, or sauces.

Many of the rub and sauce recipes in this book call for lemon pepper. With good reason! The flavors of lemon and pepper make an irresistible combination—the former perfumed and fruity, the latter pungent and spicy. What makes lemon pepper so beguiling is that you get all of the fragrant fruit flavor of the lemon and none of the citrusy tartness. You can buy commercial lemon pepper, but brands vary widely in quality and are often artificially flavored. Besides, it's easy to make your own.

The zest is the oil-rich outer peel of the lemon. Use a vegetable peeler to remove it from the fruit. (Remove only the yellow outer peel, not the bitter white pith beneath it.) For best results, choose plump, firm lemons.

2 lemons   ½ cup black peppercorns

1. Preheat the oven to 250°F.
2. Scrub the lemon under hot water and blot dry. Using a vegetable peeler, remove the zest in thin strips. Arrange the strips on a baking sheet and place in the oven. Bake until dry, about 1 hour.
3. Place the lemon zest and peppercorns in a spice mill. (Don't overcrowd the spice mill—work in several batches if necessary.) Grind the lemon and pepper to a coarse powder. Transfer to a jar, cover, and store away from heat and light. The lemon pepper will keep for several weeks.

Makes ½ cup

SIX PEPPER BLEND

TRY THIS!

Use as you would regular pepper— not just on grilled foods. It's better.

When I was growing up, pepper was, well, pepper. How times have changed! The spicy black dust of yester-year has given way to a veritable rainbow of peppercorns: white, black, pink, green, and the handsome reddish hue of Sichuan pepper. There's more to this diversity than mere color. Each of the true peppercorns has a distinct flavor: the earthy pungency of black peppercorns; the clean, sharp heat of white pepper; the herbacious, almost fruity tang of green peppercorns.

Pink peppercorns and Sichuan peppercorns aren't real-ly pepper at all, but the berries of exotic shrubs. The for-mer has a lovely fragrant floral quality, while the latter possesses a piney freshness that makes me think of a walk in the woods. As for hot pepper flakes, they belong to the capsicum family and are here in all their tongue-blasting glory. Put them together and you get a pepper blend that's long on flavor and bound to make people sit up and take notice.

2 tablespoons Sichuan peppercorns
½ cup black peppercorns
2 tablespoons white peppercorns
2 tablespoons green peppercorns

1 tablespoon pink peppercorns
1 tablespoon hot pepper flakes

1. Heat a small dry heavy skillet over medium heat. Add the Sichuan peppercorns and toast, stirring occasionally, until fragrant and just beginning to darken, 2 to 4 minutes. Transfer the peppercorns to a bowl to cool. Stir in the remain-ing ingredients.

2. Grind the pepper mixture in a pepper or spice mill. If using a spice mill, work in small batches to ensure an even grind. Transfer to a jar, cover, and store away from heat and light. The pepper blend will keep for several months.

Makes ¾ cup

AMERICAN RUBS

BASIC BARBECUE RUB

Here's the grand-daddy of all barbecue rubs, but don't let its simplicity fool you. There's a heap of flavor in this simple rub—the sweetness of the brown sugar, the heat of the black pepper, the mellow earthiness of the paprika, and the slow burn of the cayenne. Use this basic formula as a springboard for your own creativity. To make a New England rub, for example, substitute maple sugar for the brown sugar. For a Santa Fe–style rub, add chili powder (I'd use chipotle chili powder) and cumin. The possibilities are limited only by your imagination.

TRY THIS!

Sprinkle this rub on pork, beef, chicken, or even robust fish, like salmon. You can cook the meat at once or, for an even richer flavor, let it marinate for 2 to 4 hours first.

¼ **cup coarse salt (kosher or sea)**
¼ **cup (packed) dark brown sugar**
¼ **cup paprika**
3 **tablespoons freshly ground black pepper**

1 **tablespoon garlic powder**
1 **tablespoon dried onion flakes**
½ **to 1 teaspoon cayenne pepper**
½ **teaspoon celery seeds**

Combine all the ingredients in a bowl and stir or whisk to mix. Transfer to a jar, cover, and store away from heat and light. The rub will keep for several months.
Makes 1 cup

HOW TO CRACK BLACK PEPPERCORNS

Grillers love gutsy flavors. Like tongue-tingling chunks of black peppercorns, also known as cracked pepper. To crack peppercorns in a pepper mill, set the mill on the largest grind. To crack peppercorns by hand, wrap a couple of tablespoons of peppercorns in a dish towel and crush them with a heavy object, like a rolling pin or the bottom of a cast-iron skillet. A heavy-duty mortar and pestle work well, too. The French call cracked black peppercorns *mignonnettes* and use them to make steak *au poivre*. Any sort of steak or chop, as well as grilled bread and seafood, tastes better with a sprinkling of cracked black pepper.

KANSAS CITY SWEET AND SMOKY RUB

TRY THIS!

Sprinkle on ribs, pork shoulders, briskets, and chicken 30 minutes to 2 hours before smoking. If desired, sprinkle more rub on during cooking and give a final hit just before serving.

This Kansas City rub is the most universal of all barbecue seasonings. Sweet rather than salty, flavorful rather than fiery, it contains mustard in the style of a Memphis rub and chili powder and cayenne in the style of Texas, but considerably less of each. This open-mindeness reflects KC's central geographic location. Beef and pork are equally popular here and sauces and seasonings tend to be mild and sweet, rather than strongly flavored or spicy.

A well-mannered rub, this recipe—from my friends at the Kansas City Barbecue Society (KCBS), the source of so much good information about barbecue—will produce the sort of sweet, fall-off-the-bone tender ribs most of us would identify as perfect barbecue. Even the timid of taste will find it mild enough to enjoy as a seasoning. Note the use of smoked salt to add a smoky dimension to the rub. You can make your own or use a good commercial brand.

⅔ cup (packed) light brown
   sugar

⅔ cup granulated sugar

½ cup paprika

¼ cup seasoned salt,
   preferably Basic Seasoned
   Salt (page 16), or a good
   commercial brand, such
   as Lawry's

¼ cup Smoked Salt (page
   17), or use a good
   commercial brand

¼ cup onion salt

¼ cup celery salt

2 tablespoons freshly ground
   black pepper

2 tablespoons pure chili
   powder (not a blend)

2 teaspoons mustard powder

1 teaspoon poultry
   seasoning

1 teaspoon ground ginger

½ teaspoon ground allspice

½ teaspoon cayenne pepper

Combine all the ingredients in a bowl and stir or whisk to mix. Transfer to a large jar, cover, and store away from heat and light. The rub will keep for several months.

Makes about 2½ cups

POWDERPUFF RIB RUB

TRY THIS!

This rub was designed for ribs, but it's also great on pork shoulders and chicken.

If you've always thought of barbecue as a guy thing, this recipe will make you think again. Powderpuff BBQ was a Kansas City barbecue team run by a great pit master named Janeyce Michel-Cupito. After winning several state championships, she has temporarily retired. But her ribs are legendary, in large part because of a simple but tasty rub redolent with garlic, celery, and paprika.

½ cup celery salt

⅓ cup paprika

⅓ cup dried garlic flakes

3 tablespoons freshly ground
   black pepper

Combine all the ingredients in a bowl and stir or whisk to mix. Transfer to a jar, cover, and store away from heat and light. The rub will keep for several months.

Makes 1 cup

POWDERPUFF RIBS

Simple doesn't have to mean simple-minded. In 1993, Powderpuff won first place in the KC Royal rib competition for these smoky, mahogany-colored ribs. This is all the more remarkable because Janeyce served them Memphis-style (dry) in a city that loves a sweet, sticky barbecue sauce.

    4 racks baby back pork ribs
        (4 pounds)
    Vegetable spray cooking oil
    ¾ cup Powderpuff Rib Rub
        (page 25)

    SPECIAL EQUIPMENT
    2 cups applewood chips,
        soaked in 2 cups
        apple cider, then
        drained

Remove the papery skin on the back of each rack of ribs by pulling it off in a sheet with your fingers. (Use a corner of a dish towel to secure your grip, or ask your butcher to do it.) Spray the ribs on both sides with cooking oil. Generously sprinkle the rub on both sides of the ribs, patting it in with your fingers. Cover and marinate in the refrigerator for 1 hour.

Smoker Method: Preheat the smoker to 225°F.

Place the ribs in the smoker and smoke-cook until tender and the meat pulls away from the bones, about 4 hours.

Charcoal Grill Method: Set up the grill for indirect grilling, following the directions on page 5, and preheat to 325°F. Toss half the chips on the coals. Place the ribs in the center of the grate (ideally in a rib rack, if you have one), away from the fire. Smoke-cook the ribs until tender and the meat pulls away from the bones, 1½ to 2 hours. Turn the racks and replenish the charcoal and chips after 1 hour.

Gas Grill Method: Set up the grill for indirect grilling following the directions on page 5. Place the chips in the smoker box and preheat the grill to 325°F (you'll need to preheat some grills to high before you see smoke. Then lower the heat to 325°F). Place the ribs in the center of the grate (ideally in a rib rack, if you have one), away from the fire. Smoke-cook the ribs until tender and the meat pulls away from the bones, 1½ to 2 hours. Turn the racks after 1 hour.

Serves 4

LONE STAR STEAK RUB

Beef is the logical destination for this lip-searing rub, especially steak, roasts, and brisket. But don't overlook its use on chicken, pork, and even seafood. As for grilled vegetables, well, it's great there, too—if you can distract a Texan long enough to put some on the grill.

If you want a rub with plenty of heat and not a lick of sugar, this bad boy is your ticket. Lean. Mean. And as quick on the draw as a gunslinger. There are some foods God never meant to be sweetened, among them the steaks (especially T-bones) and briskets of which Texans are so rightfully proud. Use this rub whenever big flavors are called for—without sweeteners—and don't use more than you mean to. It burns.

½ cup coarse salt
  (kosher or sea)
½ cup cracked or coarsely
  ground black pepper
¼ cup paprika
3 tablespoons pure chili
  powder (not a blend)

2 tablespoons cayenne
  pepper
2 tablespoons garlic powder
1 tablespoon ground cumin
1 tablespoon dried oregano
1 tablespoon dried thyme

Combine all the ingredients in a bowl and stir or whisk to mix. Transfer to a large jar, cover, and store away from heat and light. The rub will keep for several months.
  Makes 1¾ cups

TEXAS SPRINKLE

This offbeat rub is the brainstorm of my friend, Tex-Mex food impresario Matt Martinez. He uses it to invigorate the grilled steaks and game served at his restaurants, which include the Rancho Martinez and Matt's No Place in Dallas. The garlic powder is predictable; so are the thyme and white, red, and black peppers. (Note the absence of sugar. Texans don't go in for a lot of sugar in their rubs.) What's unusual here is the addition of cracker meal, which fosters the formation of a crisp crust on meats and helps blunt the bite of the peppers.

TRY THIS!

Use this rub on any type of meat, from beef, pork, and lamb to game and poultry. Lightly sprinkle the rub on the meat; it works especially well with steak and chops.

¼ cup garlic powder

3 tablespoons cracker meal

2 tablespoons coarse salt (kosher or sea)

2 tablespoons freshly ground black pepper

1 teaspoon freshly ground white pepper

½ teaspoon cayenne pepper

½ teaspoon dried thyme

Combine all the ingredients in a jar, cover, and shake to mix. You can use the sprinkle right away, but it will taste better if you let it ripen overnight at room temperature to allow the cracker meal to absorb the spice flavors. Store in the jar away from heat and light. The rub will keep for several months.

Makes ½ cup

FAILPROOF FISH CURE

I've probably made this fish cure a thousand times, yet it never fails to amaze me how such a simple concoction can so radically improve the flavor of smoked fish. The sugar and salt impart a sweet briny flavor, with an edge of pepper for heat. The salt also dehydrates the fish partially, firming up its consistency and concentrating its flavor. My favorite fish for smoking is salmon. I cure it for 4 hours, then smoke it on the grill or in a stovetop smoker. The kipper-style salmon that results is some of the best smoked fish you'll ever taste. Even a beginner will have great results.

TRY THIS!

Sprinkle some fish cure on the bottom of a glass baking dish. Place the fish fillets on top and sprinkle more cure over it. Cover the fish with plastic wrap and cure in the refrigerator for 4 hours. Wipe or wash the cure off the fish and blot dry. Smoke the fish, using the indirect grilling method or a stovetop smoker.

1 cup (packed) dark brown sugar

½ cup coarse salt (kosher or sea)

2 tablespoons cracked or ground black pepper

1 tablespoon dried dill

1 teaspoon ground coriander

Combine all the ingredients in a bowl and mix with your fingers, breaking up any lumps of brown sugar. Transfer to a large jar, cover, and store away from heat and light. The cure will keep for several weeks.

Makes 1½ cups

PASTRAMI RUB

TRY THIS!

Sprinkle a layer of rub in the bottom of a baking dish or roasting pan just large enough to hold the meat. Place the meat on top and generously sprinkle more rub on top. Press the rub into the meat with your fingertips. Marinate, covered, in the refrigerator, turning the meat once or twice, for at least 24 hours or as long as 2 days. (The longer you marinate, the more pronounced the pastrami flavor will be.) The size of the meat determines how long you need to marinate it; thus a 1-pound salmon fillet needs 3 to 4 hours of marinating; a 2-pound turkey breast, 12 to 24 hours; a 5-pound brisket, 1 to 2 days. Once marinated, the meat should be smoke-cooked using the indirect method.

Remember pastrami? That beefy sandwich staple and mainstay of the delicatessen? Pastrami has gone upscale these days, as contemporary chefs dish up turkey pastrami, duck pastrami, and even salmon pastrami. This isn't quite as strange as it seems, for pastrami originated in Asia Minor, where it's known as *basturma* and where it's still sometimes made with camel or even horse meat. As it turns out, what makes pastrami pastrami is less the cut of meat than the seasonings—an invigorating interplay of sweet (sugar), spicy (mustard and peppercorns), perfumed (coriander), and pungent (sweet and hot paprika), with breath-wilting doses of garlic.

3 tablespoons coriander seeds
2 tablespoons black peppercorns
1 tablespoon white peppercorns (or additional black peppercorns)

8 cloves garlic, minced
2 tablespoons yellow mustard seeds
5 tablespoons coarse salt (kosher or sea)
3 tablespoons dark brown sugar
5 tablespoons paprika

Coarsely crush the coriander seeds and black and white peppercorns in a mortar with a pestle or in a spice mill or in a plastic bag using a heavy mallet. The idea is to crack them rather than pulverize them. Place them in a bowl and stir in the garlic, mustard seeds, salt, sugar, and paprika. You may need to use your fingers to get an even mix. Transfer to a jar, cover, and refrigerate. The rub will keep for several weeks.

Makes 1¼ cups

CAJUN CATFISH

Used to be that catfish was adored in the South and reviled just about everywhere else. Thanks to the advent of farm-raised catfish, this mild, sweet fish is sold everywhere. The boneless fillets are great for grilling. Here's a simple catfish recipe that fairly explodes with Louisiana flavors. Besides, it lets you test-drive two other recipes in this book: Ragin' Cajun Rub and Cajun Swamp Sauce.

4 catfish fillets, about ¾ inch thick (6 to 8 ounces each)
2 to 3 tablespoons Ragin' Cajun Rub or to taste (this page)
4 tablespoons (½ stick) unsalted butter, melted
1 cup Cajun Swamp Sauce (page 229)

1. Sprinkle the catfish fillets on both sides with half of the rub. Cover and marinate in the refrigerator for 30 minutes.

2. Preheat the grill to high. If you have a fish grate, preheat it as well. When the grill is hot, oil the grate or fish grate.

3. Coat each piece of fish on both sides with melted butter, using a pastry brush, then sprinkle with the remaining rub. Or place the melted butter in a shallow bowl and dip each piece of fish in it to coat evenly.

4. Place the fish on the grate or fish grate and grill until cooked through, 4 to 6 minutes per side, turning with a spatula. Transfer it to plates or a platter and spoon the sauce on top.

Serves 4

RAGIN' CAJUN RUB

Zydeco. Mardi Gras. Sun-scorched days and steamy nights. No other region in North America has a more soulful spirit or strong culinary sense of place than New Orleans, Louisiana. Not surprisingly, robust seasonings are the backbone of Louisiana cooking. Consider the following rub, which was inspired by the Cajun spices used for pan-blackening. Cayenne and black pepper give it gumption, but there's more to the rub than heat. You'll need to know about one special ingredient here: filé powder, or ground dried sassafras leaves. It is often used as a thickener in gumbos. Look for it in gourmet shops and most supermarkets. But don't worry if you can't find it; the rub will still be very tasty without it. So put on some Zydeco music and *laissez les bon temps roulez!*

TRY THIS!

This rub will give a Cajun accent to just about any food you grill or barbecue. It's especially good on seafood, but you can rub it on chicken, turkey, or pork. For that matter, there's no reason not to use Ragin' Cajun Rub on beef or even lamb.

½ cup coarse salt
  (kosher or sea)
¼ cup paprika
3 tablespoons freshly ground
  black pepper
1 tablespoon cayenne
  pepper, or to taste
1 tablespoon dried thyme

1 tablespoon onion powder
1 tablespoon garlic powder
1 tablespoon filé powder
  (optional)
2 teaspoons freshly ground
  white pepper
1 teaspoon ground bay leaf

Combine all the ingredients in a bowl and stir or whisk to mix. Transfer to a jar, cover, and store away from heat and light. The rub will keep for several months.

Makes 1 cup

VARIATION
For a sweeter rub, add 1 teaspoon fennel seeds. Grind the seeds in a spice mill before adding them to the rub. This fennel variation goes particularly well with fish.

FAJITA RUB

Like any great barbecue, fajitas begin with a rub—in this case a fragrant blend of chili powder, paprika, and cumin. The meat is marinated long enough to let the spice flavor sink in, then it is smokily charred over a hot fire. Of course, what makes fajitas so much fun is the do-it-yourself approach to the fixin's: the tortillas, grilled vegetables, salsa (on pages 251 to 258 you'll find a great selection), guacamole, sour cream, grated cheese, and scallions that you assemble at the table. The following recipe was inspired by a spice maven in Boston named Stacy Staub.

There are several possibilities for chili powder: ancho or New Mexican chili powder for mild fajitas; chipotle chili powder for something spicier. Whatever you use, be sure it's pure chili powder, not a blend.

¼ cup paprika

3 tablespoons coarse salt
   (kosher or sea)

2 tablespoons pure
   chili powder (not a
   blend)

2 tablespoons cracked
   black pepper

2 tablespoons garlic
   powder

1½ tablespoons sugar

1 tablespoon onion powder

1 tablespoon dried cilantro

1½ teaspoons ground
   cumin

½ teaspoon ground allspice

FAJITAS

This Tex-Mex favorite takes its name from the Spanish word for girdle. The undergarment in this case is an inexpensive, somewhat stringy, but exceptionally flavorful cut of beef called a skirt steak. (It comes from the underbelly of the steer—hence the name girdle.) Fajitas make a great party dish because you set out a stunning spread of grilled meat and vegetables, salsas, garnishes, and tortillas and let your guests have the fun of assembling them. Use the following recipe as a broad guideline, customizing it to suit your taste.

Fajitas are traditionally served on noisily sizzling skillets. To achieve this sort of drama, preheat a cast-iron skillet on the grill or in a 450°F oven for 20 minutes. Just before serving, transfer the beef and vegetables to the skillet; they will immediately start sizzling.

Warn your guests not to touch the skillet. And be sure to have the fixin's all ready in attractive bowls before the meat comes off the grill.

THE FAJITAS

2 pounds skirt steak

2 tablespoons olive oil

2 to 3 tablespoons Fajita Rub
   (page 31)

½ cup fresh lime juice

1 bunch scallions (about 6), trimmed

1 large onion, cut crosswise into
   ½-inch slices

1 poblano chili or green bell pepper

1 red bell pepper

1 yellow bell pepper

18 small flour tortillas

THE FIXIN'S

1 recipe Basic Mexican Salsa (page
   251)

Rub this spice mixture into skirt steaks, chicken breasts, or whatever other food you plan to grill for the fajitas. Cover and marinate in the refrigerator for 30 minutes to 2 hours before grilling.

Combine all the ingredients in a bowl and mix with a fork or your fingers. Transfer to a jar, cover, and store away from heat and light. The rub will keep for several months.
Makes 1 cup

VARIATION
To make a wet rub, add 3 tablespoons Worcestershire sauce and 3 tablespoons olive oil to the rub and stir to make a thick paste. Spread this mixture on the meat and marinate in the refrigerator for 1 hour before grilling.

1 recipe Flame-Charred Salsa Verde (page 252)
1 recipe Smoky Two-Chili Salsa (page 256)
1 large ripe tomato, seeded and finely diced (see box, page 246)
1 large red onion, finely diced
1½ cups coarsely chopped fresh cilantro
1½ cups sour cream

1. Arrange the skirt steak in a glass baking dish and toss with the oil. Sprinkle the meat on both sides with the rub, patting the spices in with your fingers. Cover and marinate the meat in the refrigerator for 1 to 2 hours. Add the lime juice and let marinate for 30 minutes more.

2. Preheat the grill to high.

3. Place the vegetables on the grate and grill until nicely charred, 2 to 4 minutes per side for the scallions; 4 to 6 minutes per side for the onion slices; 3 to 4 minutes per side (12 to 16 minutes in all) for the chili and peppers. Arrange the onions and scallions on a large platter. Stem and seed the peppers, slice into strips, and arrange on the platter.

4. Place the skirt steak on the grate and grill to taste, 4 to 6 minutes per side for medium. Thinly slice the steak across the grain on the diagonal and arrange on the platter with the grilled vegetables.

5. Warm the tortillas on the grill until soft and pliable, 10 to 20 seconds per side. Place the tortillas in a cloth-lined basket and cover to keep warm.

6. Set out attractive bowls of all the fixin's.

7. To serve, have each guest place sliced beef and grilled vegetables on a tortilla. Spoon the salsas, diced tomato, diced onion, cilantro, and sour cream on top. Roll the tortilla into a neat bundle for eating.
Serves 6

JAKE'S BOSS BARBECUE RUB

TRY THIS!

Jake sprinkles this rub on everything: ribs, pork shoulders, chicken, turkey, even the barons (whole hindquarters) of beef for which he's so famous on the Boston barbecue circuit. For a richer flavor, rub the meat the night before grilling and let it cure in the refrigerator. For a more spontaneous effect, sprinkle it on steaks, chops, and chicken breasts just prior to grilling.

Kenton "Jake" Jacobs is a quiet man with a lot to say about barbecue. The Boston pit master has won dozens of barbecue cook-offs and his funky Boston restaurant is one of the few smoke houses that belong to the James Beard Foundation. (You can't mistake his dining room: There's a bigger-than-life sculpture of a steer's head bursting through one wall.) Jake worked long and hard to develop his house rub, which he uses on everything, be it hoofed, feathered, or finned. Perhaps the reason that it works so well is that it contains something for every taste bud: brown sugar and cinnamon for sweetness, lemon pepper for heat and acidity, dried herbs and allspice for fragrance, and even a shot of MSG to sharpen all the taste buds. Not everyone likes MSG, so I've made it optional. This should be obvious by now (given the secrecy of most pit bosses), but this isn't *exactly* how Jake makes his rub. For one thing, he uses freeze-dried molasses rather than brown sugar. I also suspect the presence of dried Worcestershire sauce. (For a source see page 281. But don't worry if you can't get it; the rub will still be delicious.) So, here's my interpretation; it works like the real McCoy.

1¼ cups (packed) dark brown sugar
¼ cup coarse salt (kosher or sea)
½ cup paprika
3 tablespoons dried parsley
2 tablespoons dried basil
2 tablespoons dried oregano
2 tablespoons dried thyme
2 tablespoons dried onion flakes

1½ tablespoons dried Worcestershire sauce (optional)
1½ tablespoons Lemon Pepper, homemade (see page 21), or use a good commercial brand
1 tablespoon garlic powder
1 tablespoon MSG (optional)
1 teaspoon ground allspice
1 teaspoon ground cinnamon

Combine all the ingredients in a bowl and stir or whisk to mix. Transfer to a large jar, cover, and store away from heat and light. The rub will keep for several months.

Makes 2 cups

SALT-FREE LEMONADE CHILI RUB

TRY THIS!

Use this rub any way you would use a conventional barbecue rub, which is to say, on anything. Because it contains no salt, you can rub the meat up to a day ahead to maximize flavor without drying out the meat.

Most barbecue rubs are loaded with salt, which is good for creating flavor but bad if you're watching your sodium intake. (Another disadvantage of a high-sodium rub is that, with prolonged exposure, it tends to dehydrate the meat.) Kansas City barbecue guru Paul Kirk devised the following rub to blast food with flavor without the sodium. I doubt you'll miss the salt for a second. Note the presence of one unexpected ingredient: lemonade powder. This is the secret ingredient in a lot of Midwest barbecue rubs, prized for its citrusy tartness.

½ cup sugar

3 tablespoons New Mexico chili powder, or other good-quality pure chili powder (not a blend)

1 tablespoon lemonade powder

1 tablespoon dried parsley

1 tablespoon garlic powder

1 tablespoon onion powder

2 teaspoons freshly ground black pepper

1 teaspoon celery seed

1 teaspoon dried basil

1 teaspoon dried marjoram

1 teaspoon dried sage

1 teaspoon ground cumin

1 teaspoon mustard powder

1 teaspoon dried dill

Combine all the ingredients in a bowl and stir or whisk to mix. Transfer to a jar, cover, and store away from heat and light. The rub will keep for several months.

Makes 1 cup

ROSEMARY-MUSTARD LAMB RUB

John Darrick, owner of the Dirigo Spice Corporation, is one of the nation's foremost spice merchants. John does custom blending for some of the best chefs in the business.

TRY THIS!

Sprinkle the rub over a rack or leg of lamb and pat it in with your fingers. Let marinate for 4 to 6 hours, or overnight, then grill using the indirect method or on a rotisserie. You can also sprinkle the rub on lamb chops and steaks. Although this is a lamb rub, it's also exceedingly good on chicken and pork.

When John creates a rub, he thinks about not only taste but texture. He's a big fan of cracked black peppercorns, for example, and he prefers to crush mustard seeds coarsely with a rolling pin or in a blender rather than grind them to a fine powder in a spice mill. Often he adds a little liquid—oil, wine, or fruit juice, for example—to turn his rubs into fragrant pastes that adhere to the meat. According to John, these wet rubs foster better spice absorption and a richer overall flavor. When I asked John to create a recipe for this book, he obliged with a wonderful, coarse-textured seasoning for lamb. Rosemary, oregano, and garlic give it a Mediterranean accent, while the cracked mustard seeds and dry mustard turn up the heat.

1 tablespoon whole yellow mustard seeds
¼ cup dried rosemary
3 tablespoons dried garlic flakes
2 tablespoons coarse salt (kosher or sea)

1 tablespoon cracked black pepper
1 tablespoon dark brown sugar
2 teaspoons mustard powder

1. Place the mustard seeds in a zip-lock bag and crack them by rolling over them with a rolling pin. Or coarsely grind them in a blender, running the blender in short bursts.

2. Place the rosemary in a bowl and crumble it between your fingers. Add the cracked mustard seeds, garlic, salt, pepper, sugar, and mustard powder and mix with a fork or your fingers. Transfer to a jar, cover, and store away from heat and light. The rub will keep for several months.

Makes ¾ cup

VARIATION
To make a wet rub, stir 2 tablespoons Worcestershire sauce and 2 tablespoons olive oil into the rub. Smear the resulting paste over the lamb and let marinate for several hours before cooking. Transfer any excess wet rub to a jar, cover, and refrigerate.

INTERNATIONAL RUBS

JAMAICAN JOLT

Here's a West Indian spice mix that will light up your taste buds like a Fourth of July sky. It's based on Jamaica's notorious jerk seasoning (page 85). Sometimes you don't want to wait overnight for your meat to marinate. This incendiary blend of allspice, pepper, ginger, onion, garlic, and Scotch bonnet chilies will give you the skull-rattling spiciness of traditional jerk in a rub you can shake on at the last minute. To be strictly authentic, you'll need Scotch bonnet chili powder or its kissing cousin— habanero chili powder. Gourmet and spice shops sell both, or you can use one of the mail-order sources on page 281. I've given a range for the Scotch bonnet chili powder; don't use more than you mean to!

⅔ cup (packed) dark brown sugar
½ cup coarse salt (kosher or sea)
¼ cup freeze-dried chives
2 tablespoons freshly ground black pepper
2 tablespoons onion powder
2 tablespoons garlic powder
1 to 4 teaspoons pure Scotch bonnet or habanero chili powder, or to taste

1 tablespoon dried thyme
2 teaspoons ground allspice
2 teaspoons ground coriander
1 teaspoon ground cinnamon
2 teaspoons dried ginger
½ teaspoon ground cloves
½ teaspoon ground nutmeg

Combine all the ingredients in a bowl and whisk to mix. Transfer to a large jar, cover, and store away from heat and light. The rub will keep for several months.
Makes 2 cups

HOW TO USE
SPICES

Smoke may be the soul of barbecue, but spices make it sizzle. Rubs and sauces would pale without them. Spice use has skyrocketed in the United States in the last decades, as Americans discover what grill jockeys the world over have known for centuries: A generous hand with spices turns ordinary grilling into barbecue of truly awesome dimensions.

Alas, not all spices are the same. Nor should they be used in the same way. It's fine to buy most spices preground, but some suffer in the processing. Anyone who's ever been on the receiving end of a pepper mill knows the extraordinary difference between freshly ground and preground black pepper. What is more, when you buy whole spices, you can toast them in a skillet before grinding, boosting the flavor even more.

You probably have a lot of spices in your spice rack already. Some you may have owned since the Reagan administration. This brings us to Raichlen's first rule of spice handling: If it doesn't smell, throw it out. If you want to be an ace sauce maker, the first thing to do is to open all your spices and smell each one. If you aren't greeted with a strong, pleasant aroma, the spice is useless. Saffron, coriander, even paprika start to lose their aroma and flavor after a year or so—even sooner if you store your spices on a rack over the stove. Always store spices away from heat and light.

When you shop for spices, don't buy more than you will use in a year. Turning your inventory frequently ensures freshness. I try to buy my spices at ethnic markets, especially Indian and Middle Eastern. In these cultures, spices are central to the cuisine, so ethnic markets tend to have better quality. They also tend to be cheaper. Another good source for spices is a natural foods store, where you can buy spices in bulk. Besides getting a better deal, you can smell the spices before purchasing to be sure they're fresh and potent. Or you may wish to use one of the mail-order sources on page 281.

In many cultures spices are toasted

before using. In some instances, the spices are actually charred to give them a smoke flavor. Toasting intensifies the flavor by heating the essential spice oils. The traditional way to toast spices is in a dry heavy skillet. Toast the spices over medium heat, shaking the pan to ensure even toasting. Have a bowl handy and transfer the spices to it when toasted. If you leave them in the skillet, they'll continue to toast, even once the pan is off the heat. Let the spices cool after toasting, particularly if you are going to grind them.

The final technique for maximizing the flavor of spices is to grind them just before using. I keep a couple of coffee grinders on hand for this purpose. I never use them for coffee. Most spice mixtures stay aromatic for several months when stored in a tightly covered jar, away from heat and light, but the sooner you use them the more flavorful they'll be.

One last bit of advice. Some people believe that if a little is good, more is better. This may be true when it comes to money, but it's definitely not the case with spices. The surest way to ruin a rub or sauce is to overseason it. Too much is too much, no matter how you cut it.

Follow the steps above and you'll wind up using less of a particular spice but actually getting more flavor.

Spices that can help make you a barbecue champ include:

ALLSPICE: Small, dark, round berries native to the Caribbean, which the early explorers mistook for pepper. Sweet and spicy, allspice is one of the defining flavors of Jamaica's jerk seasoning (page 85) and it's used throughout the Caribbean and Middle East for flavoring grilled meats and seafood.

ANISE SEED: A tiny brown seed with a dulcet, licoricey flavor. Occasionally added to sauces and rubs for sweetness.

CARDAMOM: A tan pod the size of a coffee bean with a fragrant scent and haunting flavor. Beloved by grill jockeys in the Near and Far East, from Cairo to Cochin. Adds a sweet, exotic accent to marinades, rubs, and sauces (see Jake's Coffee-Cardamom Brisket Rub on page 83). Sold in pod form, as black seeds, and ground. Cardamom is expensive: For the best deal buy it at an Indian or Middle Eastern market.

CINNAMON STICKS: Like its cousin cassia, cinnamon comes from the fragrant bark of tropical trees. It's enjoyed by cooks around the world, especially in Mexico, Morocco, India, and the Republic of Georgia. Cinnamon sticks most commonly turn up in marinades, but you can also sew them into the cavities of spit-roasted

ducks and chickens. One great use for cinnamon sticks is Georgian Tabaka (page 67).

CLOVES: Sweet, fragrant, and highly aromatic. A hallmark seasoning in ketchup and many barbecue sauces, as well as in Jamaican jerk seasoning. The clove takes its name from the French word for nail, which it resembles.

CORIANDER: The small, round, ridged seed of the plant that gives us fresh cilantro. A very popular barbecue spice in the West as well as Asia. It's hard to imagine a food that doesn't benefit from its sweet, aromatic flavor.

CUMIN: A small, sickle-shaped seed with a strong earthy aroma. Greatly appreciated by Texans, who put it in their rubs and barbecue sauces. Also popular in Mexico, South America, the Caribbean, North Africa, the Middle East, and India. Use sparingly: Cumin quickly becomes overpowering.

FENNEL SEED: Another sweet, licoricey spice, which you've probably enjoyed in Italian sausage. Used in moderation, it can add a sweet touch to a rub.

GALANGAL (A.K.A. GALANGA): This cousin of ginger is used in Southeast Asian spice pastes. Galangal looks like ginger, but with zebra-like stripes on the skin. It possesses the peppery hotness of ginger but not the sweetness. Galangal is sold fresh and frozen at Asian markets. Dried galangal is a popular seasoning in Indonesia, where it goes by the name of *laos*. Fresh ginger mixed with black pepper makes an acceptable substitute.

MACE: The lacy membrane surrounding a nutmeg, which it resembles in aroma and flavor, though it's a little sweeter. Mace is sold in blades (twisted orange-tan chips) and powdered and is a key ingredient in Chesapeake Bay seafood seasoning.

MUSTARD SEED: Tiny round seeds that are ground or crushed to make mustard. The three main varieties in ascending order of hotness are white (or yellow), brown, and black. In addition to their use in mustard, the seeds are often added to rubs.

NUTMEG: A fragrant, oval, brown nut whose musky aroma hints at cinnamon and vanilla. For the best results, buy a whole nutmeg and grate it fresh as you need it. An important ingredient in Jamaican jerk seasoning.

PAPRIKA: This sweet, earthy, reddish brown powder is one of the world's most popular spices—an essential ingredient in rubs and barbecue

sauces too numerous to mention. Paprika comes both mild (sweet) and hot—the latter with a bite that ranges from pleasantly piquant to incendiary. Paprika is made all over the world: The best comes from Hungary and Spain, so you should make an effort to find an imported brand. Unless I call for hot paprika in a recipe, you should always use the mild (regular) variety.

SAFFRON: The fragrant, rust-colored stigmas of a crocus that grows in Spain, Iran, and India. It's a popular marinade ingredient in all three countries. Saffron is the world's most expensive spice: It takes 70,000 flowers—picked by hand—to make a single pound. Always buy saffron in threads, not powder—the latter is easier to adulterate. To activate the saffron, soak the threads in a tablespoon of hot water. Try the Persian Saffron Yogurt Marinade on page 70 and the Saffron Butter Baste on page 107.

SICHUAN PEPPERCORNS: This reddish peppercorn lookalike, with its hair-thin stems and open ends, is native to China. Actually, it's not in the pepper family, nor is it particularly hot. The flavor is aromatic and woodsy, which makes Sichuan peppercorns a good seasoning for grilled poultry.

STAR ANISE: A star-shaped spice from southwest China and Vietnam. It adds a distinctive smoky licoricey flavor to the marinades of this region (see the Basic Chinese Marinade on page 76).

SUMAC: A purplish berry with a tart, lemony flavor from the Middle and Near East. Ground sumac is the preferred barbecue seasoning in this part of the world: The purple powder appears in tiny bowls on the table for sprinkling over any type of grilled meat, poultry, or seafood.

TURMERIC: A fragrant, orange-fleshed cousin of ginger used widely for seasoning barbecue in Indonesia and Southeast Asia. Turmeric is also a key ingredient in curry powder and a coloring agent for ballpark mustard.

WASABI: This is the hot green paste (it looks like a gob of toothpaste) that accompanies sushi. Often described as Japanese horseradish, wasabi is actually a light green, parsnip-shaped root known as mountain hollyhock. To reconstitute dried wasabi, combine equal parts powder and water and stir to mix. Let the paste stand for 5 to 10 minutes to allow the heat to build. Then watch out! Try it in the Wasabi-Horseradish Butter on page 132.

PUERTO RICAN PIG POWDER

TRY THIS!

Use as you would any seasoned salt. Pork, chicken, and steak are the most predictable choices, but I use it pretty much on everything.

No pit boss in Puerto Rico would dream of making *lechón asado* (pit-roasted pig) or even grilling steaks or chicken without first sprinkling them with a seasoned salt called *sazón* (sometimes called adobo). The basic ingredients include salt, pepper, cumin, and garlic powder, but each cook brings his own special touch. You can buy bottled *sazón* at ethnic markets and most supermarkets, but the commercial brands are loaded with MSG. Here's a quick *sazón* that's bursting with Spanish Caribbean flavors, yet versatile enough to season anything.

⅓ cup coarse salt
    (kosher or sea)
2 tablespoons freshly ground
    white pepper
2 tablespoons freshly ground
    black pepper

2 tablespoons dried parsley
1½ tablespoons ground
    cumin
1 tablespoon dried oregano
1 tablespoon garlic powder
1 tablespoon onion powder

Combine the ingredients in a bowl and stir or whisk to mix. Transfer to a jar, cover, and store away from heat and light. The *sazón* will keep for several months.

Makes ¾ cup

HERBES DE PROVENCE

The French aren't particularly big on rubs, but there's one seasoning they'd never dream of being without: herbes de Provence. This fragrant blend of rosemary, thyme, basil, oregano, and other spices is indispensable for grilled lamb; pork and fish taste naked without it. So popular is the seasoning that clay jars and tiny burlap bags of it turn up at food markets not just in Provence but all over

TRY THIS!

Sprinkle the mix on grilled lamb—steaks, chops, rack, and leg. It's also good on seafood, pork, chicken, and even beef. To make a wet rub, combine equal parts herbes de Provence and extra virgin olive oil in a bowl and stir to form a thick paste.

France, not to mention in kitchens throughout the United States. Herbes de Provence contain one ingredient you don't normally think of as a seasoning for barbecue—lavender. The purplish flower adds a floral aroma that makes herbes de Provence unique in the world of seasoning.

¼ cup dried basil

¼ cup dried rosemary

2 tablespoons dried oregano

2 tablespoons dried summer savory (optional)

2 tablespoons dried thyme

2 teaspoons dried lavender

2 bay leaves, finely crumbled

1 teaspoon freshly ground white pepper

1 teaspoon ground coriander

⅛ teaspoon ground cloves

Combine all the ingredients in a bowl and mix with your fingers, crumbling any large rosemary leaves. Transfer to a jar, cover, and store away from heat and light. The mix will keep for several months.

Makes 1 cup

TWO TUSCAN ROSEMARY RUBS

Once a week or so, my wife and I treat ourselves to veal chops. We love the velvety texture of grilled veal and how the delicate white meat soaks up the smoke flavor. This particular rub was born in my kitchen, but its roots lie deep in the Tuscan countryside, where rosemary, sage, and garlic are considered essential flavorings for grilled meats. Sometimes, I'll combine these ingredients in dry form for a true rub; other times, I'll mix fresh rosemary and other herbs with olive oil, which makes more of a wet rub or spice paste.

TRY THIS!

Use on veal, pork, beef, chicken, or even fish. Brush the meat with olive oil, then sprinkle with rub, patting the rub into the meat with your fingertips. If desired, squeeze some lemon juice over the rub. Marinate, covered, in the refrigerator for 30 to 60 minutes before grilling.

DRY TUSCAN ROSEMARY RUB

Use this dry rub when you want to give the meat a crust. You could certainly substitute chopped fresh rosemary for the dry.

¼ cup dried rosemary

2 tablespoons dried oregano

1 tablespoon dried crumbled sage

2 tablespoons dried garlic flakes

¼ cup coarse salt (kosher or sea)

2 tablespoons cracked black pepper

Place the rosemary in a bowl and crumble the needle leaves between your fingers to break them into small pieces. Stir in the oregano, sage, garlic, salt, and pepper. Transfer to a jar, cover, and store away from heat and light. The rub will keep for several months.

Makes ¾ cup

VARIATION
For a touch of tartness, add ½ teaspoon grated lemon zest.

TRY THIS!

Spread the rub on chops and steaks, using a spatula, or spread it under the skin of chickens, squab, quail, or other birds and cook on a rotisserie. Marinate, covered, in the refrigerator for 30 minutes to 2 hours. For the best results, grill the meat or poultry over wood.

FRESH TUSCAN ROSEMARY WET RUB

Fresh herbs give a totally different effect, producing a seasoning that's more of a marinade than a rub. It's not better or worse than a dry rub, just different.

¼ cup fresh rosemary leaves

¼ cup fresh parsley leaves, rinsed and dried

2 tablespoons fresh oregano leaves

4 fresh sage leaves

2 cloves garlic, minced

2 tablespoons coarse salt (kosher or sea)

2 tablespoons cracked black pepper

½ cup olive oil

Using a chef's knife, finely chop the rosemary, parsley, oregano, sage, and garlic together. Transfer to a bowl and stir in the salt, pepper, and oil. Or chop the herbs, garlic, salt, and pepper in a food processor, then work in the olive oil. This rub tastes best used the day it's made. Cover and refrigerate until using.

Makes ¾ cup

PINCHO POWDER

TRY THIS!

To make *pinchos,* sprinkle the rub on cubes of pork, beef, lamb, or chicken and toss to mix in a mixing bowl. Stir in a little olive oil and toss again. Marinate, covered, in the refrigerator for 2 to 4 hours. Thread the meat on skewers and grill over high heat, basting with olive oil. Season with more rub before serving.

Pincho is the Spanish word for shish kebabs. These flavorful skewers turn up at tapas bars from Majorca to Madrid. An Arabic influence (don't forget, Spain was occupied by the Moors from the eleventh to the fifteenth century) is apparent in the seasonings: cumin, coriander, saffron. You can buy commercial *pincho* powder in Spain, but it's easy to make your own. Sprinkle it on any kebab meat, especially beef or pork, to give it a Spanish accent. For best results, use an imported Spanish or Hungarian paprika. Oh, and have plenty of sangria on hand.

½ teaspoon saffron threads

¼ cup Spanish paprika

¼ cup dried parsley

¼ cup freeze-dried chives

2 tablespoons coarse salt (kosher or sea)

2 teaspoons dried onion flakes

2 teaspoons dried garlic flakes

2 teaspoons hot pepper flakes

2 teaspoons ground cumin

2 teaspoons ground coriander

2 teaspoons dried oregano

2 teaspoons freshly ground black pepper

Crumble the saffron between your fingers into a bowl. Stir or whisk in the remaining ingredients. Transfer to a jar, cover, and store away from heat and light. The powder will keep for several weeks.

Makes 1 cup

BEIJING BLAST

TRY THIS!

Sprinkle Beijing Blast on grilled fish, chicken, pork, veal, vegetables, and tofu. It has so much flavor, you won't need a sauce.

A blast is a rub sprinkled on grilled food just prior to serving to give it a final blast of flavor. (Some blasts can be used for marinating as well.) The Asian roots of the rub are obvious in the sesame seeds, but it's versatile enough to accommodate a wide range of grilled dishes of the West. I developed it when my grandfather had to go on a salt-free diet. The pink peppercorns and black and white sesame seeds make this rub as pretty to look at as it is aromatic and tasty. Roasting the sesame seeds intensifies their flavor, so you don't even miss the salt. Pink and green peppercorns are available in gourmet markets.

1 cup white sesame seeds
¼ cup pink peppercorns
1½ tablespoons dried green
    peppercorns
½ cup black sesame seeds
1½ tablespoons poppy seeds

1 tablespoon hot pepper
    flakes
1 tablespoon dried garlic
    flakes

Heat a dry skillet over medium heat. Add half the white sesame seeds and toast, stirring occasionally, until fragrant and golden brown, 2 to 4 minutes. Transfer the sesame seeds to a bowl to cool. Coarsely grind the pink and green peppercorns in a spice mill and add to the sesame seeds. Add the untoasted sesame seeds and remaining ingredients and stir to mix. Transfer to a large jar, cover, and store away from heat and light. The blast will keep for several months.

Makes 2 cups

RUBBING IT IN

Ten years ago, few folks outside of the professional barbecue circuit had ever heard of rubs. Today, we can hardly cook without them. These explosively flavorful spice mixtures are turning up everywhere: on blackened fish, on golden roast chickens, on well-charred steaks and chops. The fact is that rubs are hot, and not just because they contain chilies.

Simply defined, a rub is a mixture of herbs and spices used to season meat (or seafood, tofu, or vegetables) before cooking. Many grill jockeys actually massage the seasonings into the meat with their fingers—hence the term *rubs*. Others content themselves with a light sprinkling from a shaker bottle. My own technique is to sprinkle the rub on the meat, then lightly pat it in with my fingertips.

But whether you rub these spice mixes in or not, they have the ability to transform ordinary grilled fare into barbecue of distinction. They're the essential seasonings that give it a flavorful crust, not to mention character and personality.

History is vague about when rubs first came to be used for seasoning. A good place to start might be *Cold Mountain,* Charles Frazier's stunning Civil War novel set in the Smoky Mountains. "When Ruby finally returned, she carried only a small bloody brisket wrapped in paper," writes Frazier. She fetched "salt, sugar, black pepper, and red pepper all mixed together. She opened the paper and rubbed the mixture on the meat to case it, then she buried it in the ashes of the fire." Such are the evocative powers of Frazier's writing that I have tried this recipe, using equal parts salt, sugar, black pepper, and hot paprika. It produces some of the tastiest barbecue in creation.

This simple mixture is the forerunner of the modern American barbecue rub and its ingredients suggest the basic architecture of a well-built spice mix. A good rub will have a sweet component, the sugar. A blast of heat, in this case supplied by black pepper. A fruity or earthy component, provided by the paprika. Most rubs contain salt to make your mouth water—although it's not absolutely mandatory.

The passing years have brought considerable refinements

to rubs. Pick up a typical Memphis- or Kansas City–style rub today, and you'll detect the presence of onion and garlic powder, mustard, celery seed, bay leaf, oregano, thyme, rosemary, and/or parsley. You may also get a whiff of cumin, turmeric, cinnamon, cloves, nutmeg, and even a shot of citric acid or MSG.

Like barbecue itself, American rubs remain fiercely regional. You'd never confuse a Cajun blackening mix for Chesapeake Bay fish seasoning or a Santa Fe–style chili rub. Cajun blends underscore the Louisiana fondness for onion, garlic, thyme, and cayenne. Chesapeake Bay seasoning has a Teutonic sweetness, thanks to the presence of ginger, mace, celery seed, and cardamom. (This isn't as surprising as it sounds: Baltimore's Old Bay Spice Company was founded by a German-Jewish spice merchant.)

As you move West, rubs show a Mexican influence— witness the popularity of cumin and chili powders in Tex-Mex and Southwestern rubs. The heat increases to the point where some rubs become almost painfully hot, especially when flavored with the two darlings of the new Southwestern cuisine: ground chipotle (smoked jalapeño) or habanero chilies.

But no matter how hot a rub may be, there should be a sense of balance. A rub that offers only heat isn't a rub at all—it's just fire.

Nor do North Americans have a monopoly on rubs. Puerto Ricans season their meats with a lively mixture of salt, pepper, cumin, oregano, and garlic (page 42). The Spanish spice up their *pinchos* (brochettes) with a fragrant blend of paprika, cumin, coriander, oregano, and saffron (page 45). Herbes de Provence (page 42), that fragrant mixture of rosemary, basil, savory, thyme, and lavender from the south of France, is nothing more than an herb rub with a Mediterranean accent. (And absolutely nothing tastes better on lamb.)

Whatever the ingredients, a good rub will play to every taste bud. It should certainly hit the basics: sweet, sour, salty, and bitter. There should be some deep bass tones (offered by such earthy spices as cumin), some sharp high notes (provided by the chilies and black, white, or Sichuan peppercorns). Above all, the experience should be harmonic: A good rub will remind you of a symphony, not a solo.

So how do you use a rub? There are two ways. First, you can use it as a seasoning, like salt or pepper. Sprinkle the rub on a steak, chop, or chicken breast and grill it right away. The resulting flavor will be fairly one-dimensional: When you sample the rub on the surface of the meat, it will pretty much taste like it does on its own. There's nothing wrong with this approach, and it's made me look good plenty of times when I had to make dinner in a hurry.

The other way to use a rub is as a marinade: Apply the rub several hours or even days ahead of time and leave it on to flavor the meat. (Marinate the rubbed meat in the refrigerator.) With this method, the spice flavor penetrates the meat more deeply and a transformation takes place. The intermingling of seasonings and meat juices alters the original flavor of both the rub and the meat. You wind up with a richer, more dynamic flavor that's greater than the sum of the parts. Rubs also aid in the formation of a savory crust. As you can imagine, this is how I prefer to use rubs.

The length of marinating time depends on the ingredients in the rub and the size and cut of meat. Rubs that contain lots of salt or chili powder impose their flavor more quickly than rubs that don't. A rub will penetrate a boneless chicken breast faster than it

will a whole turkey or pork shoulder. A sturdy cut of meat, like ribs, will stand up to a rub better than a thin, delicate cut, like a pork chop. And salt has a dehydrating effect on meats, which can be good up to a point (it firms up the flesh and concentrates the flavor). But curing a meat or fish with a salt-based rub for too long will make it dry or rubbery. As a rough rule, figure on 2 to 4 teaspoons rub per pound of meat, poultry, or fish.

Here are some guidelines for timing:

■ Very small foods, like shrimp: 10 to 20 minutes of marinating.

■ Thin cuts of single-serve portions of meat, like boneless chicken breasts and fish fillets: 30 to 90 minutes before cooking.

■ Thicker cuts of single-serve portions of meat, like steaks and chops: 1 to 3 hours before cooking.

■ Large or tough cuts of meat, like racks of ribs and whole chickens: 4 hours to overnight before cooking.

■ Very large or tough cuts of meats, like whole turkeys, briskets, pork shoulders, or fresh hams: Overnight to 24 hours before cooking.

Whatever you rub and however long you rub it, with the exception of fish, there's usually no need to wash off the rub before cooking.

CHINESE FIVE-SPICE POWDER

Five-spice powder is one of the most beguiling seasonings in the Chinese pantry. Star anise and fennel seed make it licoricey; cinnamon and clove add a hint of sweetness; white or Sichuan peppercorns give it a bite. Five is something of a mystical number in Chinese culture, representing the five elements: wood, metal, water, fire, and earth. You can buy five-spice powder at Asian markets, natural foods stores, gourmet shops, and many supermarkets, but it's easy to make your own.

3 star anise

2 cinnamon sticks
   (3 inches each)

3 tablespoons Sichuan
   peppercorns

2 tablespoons fennel seeds

½ teaspoon whole cloves

1. Heat a dry skillet over medium-low heat. Add the spices and toast until fragrant, 3 to 5 minutes. Transfer the spices to a bowl and let cool completely.

2. Break the star anise and cinnamon sticks into pieces. Grind the spices to a fine powder in a spice mill. Transfer to a jar, cover, and store away from heat and light. The five-spice powder will keep for several months.

Makes ⅓ cup

SWEET AND LICORICEY DUCK RUB

Kansas City meets Canton in this rub. It's a traditional American barbecue rub with a fragrant twist: five-spice powder. Use it on any

TRY THIS!

Rub this mixture onto duck, chicken, squab, and pork.

meat that can benefit from a licoricey sweetness.

½ cup coarse salt
(kosher or sea)

½ cup turbinado sugar
(Sugar in the Raw brand)

⅓ cup Chinese Five-Spice
Powder (facing page)

¼ cup freshly ground black
pepper

Combine the ingredients in a bowl and whisk to mix. Transfer to a large jar, cover, and store away from heat and light. The rub will keep for several months.

Makes 1½ cups

MARINADES WET RUBS AND SPICE PASTES

What do Jamaican jerk, Indian tandoori, and Thai saté have in common? Each achieves its bold, in-your-face flavor by means of a lengthy soak in a marinade. Marinades, like sauces, are designed to enhance the flavor of simply grilled meats and seafood. The difference is that marinades work their magic before you even light the grill.

A marinade is a seasoned liquid in which a food is soaked prior to grilling. (The term comes from the Italian *marinare,* to soak or pickle in brine.) Of all the flavor-enhancing weapons in a grill jockey's arsenal, none is as powerful as a marinade.

In this chapter I've included the world's great marinades, from garlicky Cuban adobo to the spicy saté soaks of Southeast Asia. I cover wet rubs and spice pastes— the rubs being somewhat thicker than a conventional marinade, the pastes so thick you spread them on the meat with a spatula. Your grilling will never taste bland again.

MARINADES

THE ONLY MARINADE YOU'LL EVER NEED

TRY THIS!

This marinade goes great with everything, and I mean everything: poultry, seafood, veal, pork, lamb, and vegetables. The larger the piece of meat, the longer you should marinate it (see box, page 57).

If I could use only one marinade for the rest of my life, it would be this one. Redolent with garlic, piquant with fresh lemon juice, and fragrant with extra virgin olive oil, it instantly transports you to the Mediterranean. I can't think of a single food that doesn't taste better bathed in it. You can use it as both a marinade and a basting sauce. If marinating poultry, meat, or seafood, simply set a portion aside for basting.

¼ cup fresh lemon juice
½ teaspoon hot pepper flakes
½ teaspoon cracked black pepper
½ teaspoon coarse salt (kosher or sea), or to taste
4 strips of lemon zest
3 cloves garlic, crushed with the side of a cleaver or minced

¼ cup coarsely chopped fresh parsley
¼ cup coarsely chopped fresh basil, cilantro, dill, oregano, or a mix of all four
½ cup extra virgin olive oil

Combine the lemon juice, hot pepper flakes, cracked pepper, and salt in a nonreactive (glass, ceramic, or stainless steel) bowl and whisk until the salt crystals are dissolved. Add the lemon zest, garlic, parsley, and basil. Stir or whisk in the olive oil. The virtue of this marinade is its freshness: Use it within 1 to 2 hours of making. Stir again before using.

Makes 1 cup

THE LOWDOWN ON LEMONS

Lemons pop up at every stop on the world's barbecue trail—fresh lemon wedges for squeezing over grilled seafood, lemon juice for souring barbecue sauce, lemon zest for adding a clean lemon flavor to marinades. Lemon provides the grill jockey with two very different types of flavor.

The zest (the oil-rich outer rind) is loaded with highly aromatic oils, which offer the bright, fresh, fruity lemon flavor without any acidity. Many recipes in this book call for lemon zest. The easiest way to remove lemon zest is in broad thin strips with a vegetable peeler, taking only the oil-rich outer rind, not the bitter white pith beneath it. You can also use a lemon zester, a tool with a rec-tangular blade with tiny holes at the leading edge. Drag the holes over the lemon to remove thin strands of zest. Finally, you can grate fresh lemon zest with a box grater. One neat trick is to sandwich a piece of parchment paper between the lemon and grater before grating. The zest will stay on the paper when you lift it off and the grater will be easy to clean.

When juicing lemons, soak them in a bowl of hot water for 10 minutes first. Then blot dry and roll on the work surface, pressing the top of the lemon with the palm of your hand. The heat and pressure help release the juices from the lemon pulp. When you cut the lemon open, the juice will come gushing out.

P.D.T.'S SOURPUSS LEMON CHICKEN MARINADE

The moment I tasted this lemony marinade, I knew that P.D.T. lived up to its name. The letters stand for Pretty Damn Tasty—the perfect moniker for this marinade from a husband-and-wife barbecue team from Lenexa, Kansas. Donna and Ted McClure have been competing on the American barbecue circuit since 1982, and their attention to detail, not to mention Donna's unerring taste buds when it comes to concocting sauces and marinades, has won them prizes too numerous to mention. The following marinade—sweet with butter and bracingly tart with sliced whole lemon—makes some of the best barbecued chicken you've ever tasted. Donna serves the chicken with the Honey-Pepper Barbecue Sauce on page 140, but it's really P.D.T. just with this marinade.

TRY THIS!

This marinade was designed for chicken. Cut the bird into pieces (or use thighs, as the McClures do) and arrange in a glass baking dish. Stir the marinade well to mix, then pour it over the bird. Marinate, covered, in the refrigerator overnight. The next day, remove the chicken from the marinade, drain, and season generously with salt and pepper before grilling using the indirect method.

As a change of pace, try this marinade with turkey and pork.

1 large lemon
8 tablespoons (1 stick) unsalted butter, melted
½ cup cider vinegar
½ cup (packed) dark brown sugar
¼ cup Worcestershire sauce

1 medium onion, thinly sliced
4 cloves garlic, thinly sliced
1 jalapeño chili, thinly sliced
½ teaspoon coarse salt (kosher or sea)
½ teaspoon freshly ground black pepper

1. Soak and roll the lemon as described in the box on page 55. Cut the lemon crosswise into ¼-inch slices, working over a bowl to catch the juices. Using the tines of a fork, remove any seeds from the lemon slices and place the slices in the bowl.

2. Place the butter, vinegar, brown sugar, Worcestershire sauce, onion, garlic, chili, salt, and pepper in a nonreactive saucepan and bring to a simmer over medium heat, stirring with a wooden spoon, until the sugar is dissolved, 3 to 5 minutes. Pour the mixture into the bowl with the lemon and stir to mix. Cool to room temperature. Use the marinade within an hour of making. Stir before using to mix in the melted butter.

Makes 2 cups; enough for 1 whole chicken or 2 pounds chicken thighs

RED WINE MARINADE FOR RIBS

As a rule, when it comes to ribs, I'm more a rub guy than a marinade guy. This simple red wine–rosemary marinade is the exception that makes the rule. Marinate the ribs overnight in this mix, then smoke or indirect grill as you would any ribs. Once tasted, you'll be willing to keep making exceptions, too.

TRY THIS!

Marinate pork or beef ribs, covered, in the refrigerator for 3 to 4 hours, then smoke or indirect grill.

2 cups dry red wine
2 cups water
½ cup coarse salt
   (kosher or sea)

½ cup (packed) light brown
   sugar
1 tablespoon chopped fresh
   rosemary leaves

Combine all the ingredients in a bowl and whisk until the salt and sugar are dissolved. The marinade will keep, covered, in the refrigerator for up to 1 week.

Makes 4 cups; enough for 3 pounds of ribs

MARINATING TIMES

How long should you marinate a chop or fish fillet before putting it on the grill? It's an easy question with a complicated answer, because the marinating time depends on the strength of the marinade, the particular food to be marinated, and the size and cut of the meat. For example, shrimp and chicken breasts obviously require less marinating than a whole chicken or whole fish; a light herb marinade takes longer to work than a strong marinade fiery with Scotch bonnet chilies and spices.

The following list will provide a rough guideline to marinating times. When in doubt, see the instructions in a particular recipe. Note: You can speed up the marinating time by making deep slashes in the sides of whole fish or chicken pieces.

■ Very large pieces of meat, such as brisket, prime rib, pork shoulder, leg of lamb, turkey, and capon: 12 to 24 hours.

■ Large pieces of meat, such as beef and pork tenderloins, pork loins, rack and butterflied leg of lamb, and whole chickens; large whole fish: 6 to 12 hours.

■ Medium-size pieces of meat, such as porterhouse steaks, double-cut pork chops, and chicken halves or quarters; small whole fish: 3 to 8 hours.

■ Medium-to-small pieces of meat, such as steaks, pork and lamb chops, and bone-in chicken breasts or legs; fish steaks, tofu, portobello mushrooms and other vegetables: 1 to 3 hours.

■ Small pieces of meat, such as boneless chicken breasts; fish fillets and shrimp: 15 minutes to 2 hours.

SMOKED CHILI MARINADE

This pugnacious marinade belongs to an extended family of Latino seasonings called adobo. Mexican versions contain chilies and this one owes its fiery smoke flavor to the hot-blooded presence of chipotles chilies (smoked jalapeños). I prefer the canned product over the dried because canned juices are loaded with heat and flavor. Traditionally, the marinade would be made with sour orange: To approximate the flavor of this tropical citrus fruit, I combine fresh lime and orange juice.

½ teaspoon cumin seeds
½ teaspoon peppercorns
3 ripe plum tomatoes
3 cloves garlic, peeled
½ medium onion, cut in half
½ cup fresh lime juice
3 tablespoons fresh orange juice
2 tablespoons red wine vinegar

2 to 4 canned chipotle chilies
1 to 2 teaspoons chipotle can juices
1 teaspoon dried oregano
1 teaspoon coarse salt (kosher or sea)

1. Heat a comal or dry skillet over medium heat. Add the cumin and peppercorns and toast until fragrant, 2 minutes. Transfer the spices to a blender or spice mill and grind to fine powder. Leave the spices in the blender.

2. Place the tomatoes, garlic, and onion on the comal and cook until nicely browned on all sides, turning with tongs. This will take 4 to 6 minutes for the garlic, and 10 to 12 minutes for the tomatoes and onion. Transfer the vegetables to the blender with the spices.

3. Add the lime and orange juices, the vinegar, chipotle chilies and can juices, the oregano, and salt. Run the blender in bursts to reduce the ingredients to a thick purée. Transfer to a large jar, cover, and refrigerate. The marinade will keep for several weeks.

Makes 2 cups adobo; enough to marinate 3 to 4 pounds of meat

SMOKY MARINATED PORK TENDERLOIN
WITH SPICY CORN RELISH

Mexico meets Asia in this color-ful and smoky grilled tender-loin. The pork is marinated in a classic Mexican adobo (the smoke flavor comes from the chipotles in the marinade). The salsa features traditional Mexican ingredients, but with an Asian twist—a Spicy Corn Relish. This dish is quick enough to serve as a weeknight dinner (excluding the marinating time, it can be assembled and cooked in 30 minutes). But it's also handsome and sophisticated enough to be served to company.

- 2 pork tenderloins (about 1½ pounds in all), trimmed
- 1 recipe Smoked Chili Marinade (facing page)
- 1 recipe Spicy Corn Relish (page 259)
- 3 tablespoons melted salted butter or olive oil
- 4 sprigs of fresh cilantro, for garnish

SPECIAL EQUIPMENT
- 1 cup of your favorite wood chips (optional), soaked for 1 hour, then drained

1. Arrange the pork tenderloins in a glass baking dish and pour the mari-nade over them. Cover with plastic wrap and marinate in the refrigerator for at least 8 hours, preferably overnight, turning the tenderloins a few times, so they marinate evenly. Not more than 1 hour before you plan to serve the pork, prepare the relish.

2. Preheat the grill to high. Toss wood chips on the coals using a charcoal grill, or place in the smoker box if using a gas grill, if a smoke fla-vor is desired.

3. Remove the pork from the marinade and place on the grate. Grill until cooked to taste, 3 to 4 minutes per side (12 to 16 minutes in all) for medium (160°F on a meat thermome-ter), basting every few minutes with melted butter or oil. Transfer the ten-derloins to a cutting board and let rest for 5 minutes, then slice on the diagonal. Fan out the pork slices on plates or a platter and mound the rel-ish in the center. Garnish each serv-ing with a sprig of cilantro.

Serves 4

ENNOBLED BY ADOBO

Spend time on the barbecue trail in Latin America and you'll hear the word *adobo*. This lively marinade is found throughout the Spanish-speaking world. I mean this quite literally. Adobo turns up in Spain, the Philippines, the Caribbean, and Central and South America. What's curious is that something that's so delicious should actually be named for a dry medieval legal term—*adobar*, literally to ennoble. (The term survives in English in the word *dub*, as in "I dub thee Sir Knight.") It's meat that's being ennobled in this case, thanks to a bath in a flavorful marinade.

Adobo varies from country to country. In Cuba, it is a refreshingly acidic marinade of lime juice, garlic, and cumin. In Mexico, adobos are thick pastes made with chilies, tomatoes, and vinegar. Vinegar and garlic characterize the adobo of the Philippines. You'll find several adobos in this book, including the Cuban adobo below and a Mexican smoked chili adobo on page 58.

ADOBO (Cuban Garlic Marinade)

Walk into a Cuban home and this marinade is what you'll smell. Garlic. Cumin. Sour orange juice. Adobo is the very lifeblood of Cuban cuisine. Traditionally, the ingredients are combined in a mortar with a pestle. But acceptable results can be obtained with a blender.

TRY THIS!

Adobo is a versatile marinade, equally delectable with chicken, pork, beef, lamb, shellfish, and fish. Marinate the food, covered, in the refrigerator for between 1 and 6 hours, depending on the size of the cut. For instance, a fish fillet or chicken breast would marinate 1 to 2 hours, a pork butt, the full 6 hours.

5 cloves garlic, coarsely chopped
1½ teaspoons coarse salt (kosher or sea)
1 teaspoon ground cumin
1 teaspoon dried oregano
½ teaspoon freshly ground black pepper

1 cup fresh sour orange juice (see box, page 174) or ¾ cup fresh lime juice and ¼ cup fresh orange juice

Place the garlic, salt, cumin, oregano, and pepper in a mortar and pound with a pestle to a smooth paste. Gradually work in the sour orange juice. Or place all the ingredients in a blender and blend to a smooth purée. Adobo tastes best used within a few hours of making.

Makes 1 cup; enough for 2 pounds of meat

FRENCH WEST INDIAN CHILI-LIME MARINADE

Whenever my wife and I visit Guadaloupe, the first thing we do is head for a roadside shack for grilled chicken. The French of the West Indies do some of the tastiest grilling in the Caribbean. Their secret? A pungent marinade made with garlic, Scotch bonnet chilies, fresh thyme, allspice, and lime juice or vinegar. The ingredients are commonplace, and yet I know of no better way to set the stage for grilling.

TRY THIS!

Spoon one third of the marinade over the bottom of a glass baking dish. Arrange the food to be marinated on top. If using chicken pieces or whole fish, make deep slashes in the meat to the bones. Pour the remaining marinade over the food. Cover and marinate in the refrigerator for at least 2 or up to 6 hours, turning the pieces of food a couple of times to ensure even marinating.

4 cloves garlic, minced

½ to 1 Scotch bonnet chili, seeded and finely chopped

1 teaspoon coarse salt (kosher or sea)

½ teaspoon freshly ground black pepper

¾ cup fresh lime juice or white wine vinegar or a mixture of the two

1 bunch of chives or 4 scallions (white and green parts), trimmed and finely chopped

2 shallots, thinly sliced

1 small onion, thinly sliced

3 tablespoons finely chopped flat-leaf parsley

4 sprigs of fresh thyme, stripped, or 1 teaspoon dried thyme

2 bay leaves

4 allspice berries

2 whole cloves

¼ cup peanut or canola oil

Place the garlic, chili, salt, and pepper in a bowl and mash to a paste with the back of a spoon. Add the lime juice and stir until the salt crystals are dissolved. Stir in the remaining ingredients. The marinade tastes best used within a few hours of making.

Makes 1 cup marinade; enough for 1 cut-up chicken; 2 pounds beef, pork, lamb, goat, or fish steaks; or 4 small (1 pound) fish; or use it for grilled lobster

HOW TO HANDLE A SCOTCH BONNET CHILI

Scotch bonnets (and their cousins, Mexican habaneros) are the world's hottest chilies—50 times hotter than fresh jalapeños. As you can imagine, handling these babies can wreak havoc with the skin on your fingertips and your eyes if you touch them. The easiest way to protect yourself is to wear rubber or plastic gloves when handling any chilies. French West Indians use an even simpler method: Hold the chili with the tines of a fork and cut it in half. Scrape out the seeds with the knife tip, then, holding each half with the fork, cut it into thin crosswise slivers, then finely chop.

BRAZILIAN GARLIC-LIME MARINADE

Brazilians use this *tempeiro* marinade whenever they grill pork or chicken. (Beef is considered a "noble" meat, so it's grilled in its natural state.) A simple version might contain only lime juice, salt, and garlic—*lots* of garlic. A more elaborate *tempeiro,* like this one, might contain fresh herbs, wine, and even hot sauce. Your tongue will be dancing the samba by the time you've finished with this one!

TRY THIS!

Use this marinade for pork, chicken, or lamb. Marinate thin cuts of meat (steaks, chops, and chicken breasts), covered, in the refrigerator for 1 to 2 hours; larger cuts of meat, such as pork loins or shoulders, for 6 to 8 hours, or even overnight.

6 cloves garlic, finely chopped
2 teaspoons coarse salt (kosher or sea)
¾ cup fresh lime juice
¼ cup dry white wine
1 tablespoon red wine vinegar
1 to 2 teaspoons Piri-Piri Sauce (Brazilian hot sauce; page 245), Tabasco sauce, or your favorite hot sauce
3 tablespoons finely chopped fresh flat-leaf parsley
2 scallions (white and green parts), trimmed and finely chopped
1 tablespoon chopped fresh rosemary or mint

Place the garlic and salt in a bowl and mash to a paste with the back of a spoon. Add the lime juice, wine, vinegar, piri-piri sauce, parsley, scallions, and rosemary and stir until all the salt is dissolved. The marinade tastes best used within a few hours of making.

Makes 1 cup; enough to marinate 2 to 3 pounds of meat

BELGIAN BEER MARINADE

TRY THIS!

This marinade goes best with robust meats, like beef, pork, and chicken. You could also use it with rich, oily fish, like salmon and kingfish. Marinate large pieces of meat (whole chickens and roasts) overnight; medium-size pieces of meat (steaks, chops, and chicken pieces) for 4 to 6 hours; and smaller cuts (boneless chicken breasts and cubed meat for shish kebabs) for 2 to 4 hours, covered, in the refrigerator.

Barbecue without beer would be like, well, life without breathing. Hyperbole, perhaps, but beer is *the* beverage of choice among most of the world's barbecue cultures and an essential ingredient in countless marinades, bastes, and barbecue sauces. There's good reason for its popularity; beer adds a unique malty sweetness and a pleasantly bitter hint of hops. You can vary the potency of this marinade by your choice of beer: A light ale or pilsener will give you a mild beer flavor, while a dark beer, like stout or porter, will really make you aware of its presence.

2 cups of your favorite beer
¼ cup honey mustard
¼ cup canola oil
1 teaspoon coarse salt (kosher or sea)
1 teaspoon freshly ground black pepper
1 medium onion, thinly sliced
½ green or red bell pepper, stemmed, seeded, and finely chopped

4 scallions (white and green parts), trimmed and chopped
4 cloves garlic, flattened with the side of a cleaver
2 slices fresh ginger (each ¼ inch thick), flattened with the side of a cleaver
1 tablespoon pickling spice
1 tablespoon paprika
½ teaspoon caraway seeds

Combine the beer, mustard, oil, salt, and pepper in a nonreactive mixing bowl and stir or whisk until the salt crystals are dissolved. Stir in the remaining ingredients. Transfer to a large jar, cover, and refrigerate. The marinade will keep for 3 days.

Makes 2½ cups; enough for 2 to 3 pounds of meat

THE MYSTIQUE OF
MARINADES

When it comes to boosting the flavor of grilled meats, nothing can beat a marinade. This simple truth is appreciated around the world, from the Jamaican jerk master to the Indian tandoori boss. Marinades lend grilled foods a unique ethnic identity. They also help tenderize tough meat fibers, and keep foods moist during cooking. The latter function is particularly important for grilling, as the strong heat of live fire tends to dry out the meat.

Most marinades have three components: acids, oils, and aromatics. The acids help break down tough muscle fibers, tenderizing the meat. The oil coats the exterior of the meat, keeping it from drying out during cooking. The aromatics, which can include chopped vegetables, fresh or dried herbs, ground or whole spices, and/or condiments, such as Tabasco sauce, add cannon blasts of flavor. Put them together, and there isn't a food in creation that can resist their transforming powers.

The acids can include vinegars of all kinds (wine, cider, rice, distilled, and balsamic), fruit juices, and cultured milk products, like yogurt. Lemon juice is a popular souring agent in the Mediterranean basin and Central Asia; lime juice in Latin America and the Far East; pomegranate juice in the Near East. Dairy marinades include the yogurt and yogurt cheese mixtures of India, Iran, Iraq, and Afghanistan.

The oils in a marinade seal in flavor and keep foods moist during grilling. Olive oil is the preferred oil in California and the Mediterranean. (Use a good, fruity olive oil for marinating.) Sesame oil imparts a pleasing nutty flavor to the marinades of the Far East. (Be sure you buy a dark, fragrant sesame oil, one made from toasted sesame seeds, for your marinades; you'll find it at an Asian market, not a natural foods store.) Walnut, hazelnut, and pistachio oils (available at gourmet shops) work especially well

with delicately flavored poultry and seafood. If you want the moisturizing benefits of oil without a distinct flavor, use a bland oil, like canola or peanut.

The aromatics are the soul of a marinade. Classic French marinades start with a *mirepoix*, diced onion, celery, and carrot. The Chinese Holy Trinity is ginger, scallion, and garlic. Dried, fresh, and roasted chilies lie at the heart of Mexican marinades, like the Smoked Chili Marinade on page 58. Herbs and spices add high notes of character and flavor. (On page 88, you'll find a complete discussion of the herbs and on page 38 the spices used in marinades.) As for condiments, they can be as commonplace as soy sauce or Tabasco or as exotic as fish sauce.

Marinades are generally liquid, but some can be as thick as paste. These would include wet rubs, like the Tex-Mex Tequila-Jalapeño Wet Rub on page 81, and true spice pastes, like the Berber mixture on page 95. Pesto makes a memorable marinade for poultry, beef, and fish.

The flavorings for a marinade are limited only to your imagination. Nonetheless, over the course of time, certain flavorings have come to be associated with specific foods. Seafood is well served by the fragrant tartness of lemon juice, olive oil, and fresh herbs. Lamb positively shines in a marinade of lemon juice, onion, and yogurt. My favorite marinade for beef is an Asian blend of soy sauce, sesame oil, rice wine, fresh ginger, garlic, and scallions.

Most marinades are used raw, but in some instances, they are cooked. The French marinate game in a mixture of boiled red wine and juniper berries. Besides increasing flavor, boiling has the added advantage of reducing the marinating time. Mexicans often roast onions and garlic to give their spice pastes a rich smoky flavor. If you cook a marinade, be sure to let it cool to room temperature before using.

Food should be marinated in a nonreactive container—glass, porcelain, ceramic, or stainless steel. Zip-top plastic bags make great vessels for marinating. Avoid aluminum and cast iron, which react with the acids in the marinade. It is not necessary for the food to be completely submerged in liquid, but it should be turned several times. Cover the pan or bowl with plastic and refrigerate the food while it's marinating. Drain meats well before placing them on the grill: Wet meat tends to stew rather than grill. If you want to use the marinade for basting, bring it to a rapid boil in a saucepan first to kill any bacteria. Marinades should not be reused.

Be careful not to marinate foods for too long. Meats can become mushy when marinated for longer than 24 hours. In some cases, the acids in a marinade will "cook" the food, particularly a delicate food like fish. On page 57, you'll find a guide to marinating times.

CINNAMON-ORANGE MARINADE

This marinade comes from the Caucasus Mountains in the Republic of Georgia, where it's used to flavor a game hen dish called *tabaka*. I first sampled it at a wonderful imperial Russian restaurant in the Boston of my youth called The Hermitage and while I've eaten it many times since then, I've never had a *tabaka* I liked quite as much. The traditional way to cook *tabaka* is by panfrying, but the cinnamon-orange marinade—heated with ginger and hot pepper flakes—makes an exotic seasoning for grilling.

3 oranges

2 limes

1 lemon

¼ cup dry white wine

2 cinnamon sticks
   (3 inches each)

3 cloves garlic, peeled and
   crushed with the side of
   a cleaver

3 slices (each ¼ inch thick)
   fresh ginger, crushed with
   the side of a cleaver

½ teaspoon cracked black
   pepper

1 medium onion, thinly
   sliced

3 tablespoons paprika

1 tablespoon light brown
   sugar

½ teaspoon coarse salt
   (kosher or sea), or to
   taste

½ teaspoon hot pepper
   flakes

¼ teaspoon freshly grated
   nutmeg

½ cup extra virgin olive oil

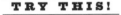

TRY THIS!

Arrange the meat or fish in a glass baking dish. Pour the marinade over the meat, cover, and marinate in the refrigerator for as little as 6 hours or as long as overnight (the longer the better), turning once or twice.

1. Using a vegetable peeler, remove 1 strip of orange zest, 1 strip of lime zest, and 1 strip of lemon zest and set aside. Juice the oranges, limes, and lemon.

2. Place the citrus juice and zest, the wine, cinnamon, garlic, ginger, and pepper in a heavy nonreactive saucepan and bring to a boil over high heat. Reduce the heat to medium and simmer, uncovered, until the mixture is reduced to 1 cup, about 10 minutes.

3. Remove the pan from the heat and cool to room temperature. Stir in the onion, paprika, sugar, salt, hot pepper flakes, nutmeg, and oil. Use right

away or transfer to a large jar, cover, and refrigerate. The marinade will keep for up to 5 days.

Makes 2 cups; enough for 4 Cornish game hens,
1 chicken, or 2 pounds of pork

TABAKA (GRILLED GAME HENS)

Tabaka is one of the glories of Georgian gastronomy: butterflied boned game hens cooked under a weight to compact the meat and crisp the skin. Tradition calls for the birds to be panfried, but I like the robust smoke flavor achieved by grilling.

4 Cornish game hens (1 pound
    each), rinsed and patted dry
1 recipe Cinnamon-Orange Marinade
    from the Caucasus (facing page),
    cooled
6 tablespoons (¾ stick) unsalted
    butter, melted
Coarse salt (kosher or sea) and
    freshly ground black pepper
1 small onion, thinly sliced
½ cup coarsely chopped cilantro
1 recipe Tkemali (page 196), for
    serving

SPECIAL EQUIPMENT
4 bricks wrapped with aluminum foil

1. Spatchcock the game hens. To do this, cut out the backbone of each hen, using poultry shears. Open the hens as you would a book and flatten them with the side of a cleaver. Arrange the game hens in a glass baking dish and pour the marinade over them. Cover with plastic wrap and marinate the hens in the refrigerator for at least 6 hours, preferably overnight. Turn 2 or 3 times to ensure even seasoning.

2. Preheat the grill to medium-high.

3. Remove the hens from the marinade, brush with melted butter, and place them on the grate, skin side down. Place a brick on top of each to flatten it. Grill the hens until cooked through, 8 to 10 minutes per side. Baste again with melted butter when you turn the birds. Move birds as needed to prevent flareups. Season with salt and pepper.

4. To serve, arrange the hens on a platter and sprinkle with the onion and cilantro. Serve the *tkemali* on the side.

Serves 4

WILD GAME MARINADE WITH JUNIPER AND GIN

The year was 1976; the place, the La Varenne cooking school in Paris. A nice Jewish guy from Baltimore (yours truly) was about to have his first taste of wild game. Our instructor, Chef Fernand Chambrette, had secured a haunch of wild boar, and he prepared a traditional marinade of red wine and juniper berries to heighten its gamy flavor. A shot of gin reinforced the woodsy flavor of the juniper. If I'd known game could be this good, I would have tried it a lot sooner. You'll be amazed by the power of this simple marinade to turn tame supermarket pork, beef, and even lamb into "wild" game.

3 cups dry red wine
½ cup balsamic vinegar
½ cup extra virgin olive oil
2 tablespoons gin
1 medium onion, thinly sliced
1 carrot, thinly sliced
1 rib celery, thinly sliced
2 cloves garlic, flattened
   with the side of a cleaver
3 tablespoons chopped
   fresh parsley
2 teaspoons juniper berries
2 teaspoons black
   peppercorns

2 bay leaves
2 whole cloves
2 sprigs of fresh thyme,
   stripped, or ½ teaspoon
   dried thyme

TRY THIS!

If using a large cut of meat, like a leg of wild boar, haunch or saddle of venison, or a pork shoulder, marinate the meat, covered, in a large earthenware or stainless steel bowl or even in a clean plastic garbage bag in the refrigerator for 24 hours, turning several times. If using small cuts of meats, such as steaks or chops, marinate for 2 to 4 hours. The longer you marinate, the stronger the flavor will be.

Combine all the ingredients in a saucepan and bring to a boil over medium-high heat. Cool to room temperature. Use right away or transfer to jars, cover, and refrigerate. The marinade will keep for several days.

Makes 4 cups; enough for 3 pounds of meat

TURKISH GARLIC YOGURT MARINADE

TRY THIS!

Garlic yogurt mari-
nade was designed
for lamb, either cubed
to make shish kebabs
or in chops or a whole
rack for grilling. It's
also tasty with chick-
en and beef. Marinate
the meat, covered, in
the refrigerator for at
least 6 hours, or as
long as overnight.

Travel the world's barbecue trail and you'll find yogurt marinades in Greece, Turkey, Iran, Iraq, Afghanistan, and India. As you move east, the spicing becomes more extravagant, reaching its apotheosis in northern India. The idea behind a yogurt marinade is both ancient and practical: The acids in the yogurt served to preserve meat in the age before refrigeration and to break down tough muscle fibers, a function it still serves today. Yogurt marinades give meats a delectable sourish tang and soft, tender texture. Add onion and garlic, as is done throughout the region, and you'll wind up with some of the tastiest kebabs on the planet. Here's a simple, garlicky Turkish yogurt marinade, followed by a Persian saffron marinade and Indian tandoori.

For best results, use whole milk yogurt, which is available in natural foods stores.

2 cups plain whole milk
    yogurt
½ cup extra virgin olive
    oil
3 tablespoons fresh lemon
    juice
1 onion, finely chopped
3 cloves garlic, minced

1 teaspoon coarse salt
    (kosher or sea)
½ teaspoon freshly ground
    black pepper
½ teaspoon hot pepper
    flakes, or to taste

1. Place the yogurt in a strainer lined with paper towels. Set the strainer over a large bowl and allow the yogurt to drain for 2 hours in the refrigerator. You can save the resulting whey for drinking. (If you're in a hurry, you can omit this step—the marinade will be very nearly as rich.)

2. Place the drained yogurt in a bowl and stir in the remaining ingredients. The marinade works best used within a few hours of making.

Makes 2 cups; enough to marinate 2 to 3 pounds of meat

PERSIAN SAFFRON LAMB CHOPS

When it comes to grilling lamb, no one can beat the Iranians. The kebab was invented in what is now called Iran. (Kebab is an old Persian word for meat.) Iranians use complex marinades of yogurt and lemon and fragrant basting sauces of butter and saffron to create some of the most spectacular grilled lamb in the world. This recipe works equally well with other foods, including chicken, beef, and even seafood.

> 8 loin lamb chops (4 to 5 ounces
>   each) or 12 rib lamb chops
>   (3 ounces each)
> 1 recipe Persian Saffron Yogurt
>   Marinade (see below)
> 1 recipe Saffron Butter Baste
>   (page 107)
> 1 small sweet onion, such as Vidalia
>   or Walla Walla, thinly sliced
> 8 sprigs of fresh flat-leaf parsley

1. Arrange the lamb chops in a glass baking dish and pour the yogurt marinade over them. Turn the chops a few times, cover with plastic wrap, and marinate in the refrigerator for 12 to 24 hours, the longer the better.

2. Preheat the grill to high.

3. Remove the chops from the marinade, place on the grate, and grill, basting with the saffron butter baste, until cooked to taste, about 4 minutes per side to cook rib chops to medium, about 6 minutes per side to cook loin chops to medium. Place the chops on a platter and arrange the sliced onion on top. Garnish with parsley and serve.

Serves 4

PERSIAN SAFFRON YOGURT MARINADE

Iran is one of the great grilling capitals of the world. Indeed, the term *kebab* comes from the ancient Persian word for meat. Iranians use a variety of marinades—some yogurt based, some olive oil based—to make succulent

TRY THIS!

This is one of the best marinades I know of for grilled chicken, Cornish game hens, and quail, and it makes terrific lamb or beef shish kebabs. Marinate the meats, covered, in the refrigerator for at least 6 hours and preferably overnight.

shish kebabs of extraordinary succulence and flavor. I've never met anyone who tasted kebabs made with this aromatic marinade and didn't love them. To enjoy the full effect of this marinade, you must use whole milk yogurt and saffron in thread form, not powder.

2 cups plain whole milk
    yogurt
½ teaspoon saffron threads
1 tablespoon hot water
2 medium onions, thinly
    sliced
2 cloves garlic, finely
    chopped

2 strips of orange zest
½ cup fresh lemon juice
2 teaspoons coarse salt
    (kosher or sea)
1 teaspoon freshly ground
    black pepper

1. Place the yogurt in a strainer lined with paper towels. Set the strainer over a large bowl and allow the yogurt to drain for 2 hours in the refrigerator. You can save the resulting whey for drinking. (If you're in a hurry, you can omit this step—the marinade will be almost as rich.)

2. Crumble the saffron threads between your thumb and forefinger and place in a small bowl with the hot water. Let the saffron infuse for 10 minutes.

3. Place the drained yogurt in a bowl and stir in the saffron mixture and the remaining ingredients. The marinade tastes best used within a few hours of making.

Makes 2 cups; enough for 2 cut-up chickens or 2 to 3 pounds of meat

TANDOORI MARINADE

India's contribution to the world of barbecue is tandoori: meats, seafood, or vegetables marinated to a Mercurochrome orange in a pungent paste of yogurt, aromatic vegetables, and spices, then grilled on vertical skewers in a blazing hot clay barbecue pit, known as a tandoor.

A good tandoori balances the tartness of the lemon juice with ginger and spices, the fire of chilies with the soothing coolness of yogurt. I've made the food coloring optional, but know that no self-respecting Indian barbecue buff would dream of making tandoori without it.

For an even richer marinade, start with 4 cups of yogurt. Drain it in a strainer lined with paper towels set over a large bowl to catch the whey. Place in the refrigerator overnight. This is what tandoori masters do in India to make a marinade of incomparable richness.

TRY THIS!

To make chicken tandoori, use skinless chicken pieces. Cover and marinate in the refrigerator for at least 6 hours and preferably overnight. Marinate lamb the same way. Marinate seafood for 2 to 4 hours, depending on the size of the pieces (marinate bigger pieces longer than smaller pieces).

2 teaspoons coriander seeds
1 teaspoon black peppercorns
1 teaspoon cumin seeds
1 teaspoon mace blades
½ teaspoon fennel seeds
4 cardamom pods
2 whole cloves
1 piece (1 inch) cinnamon
   stick
½ teaspoon saffron threads
1 tablespoon hot water
1 small onion, coarsely
   chopped
6 cloves garlic, coarsely
   chopped

6 slices (each ¼ inch thick)
   peeled fresh ginger,
   coarsely chopped
2 jalapeño chilies,
   preferably red, seeded
   and coarsely chopped
3 tablespoons fresh lemon
   juice
3 tablespoons vegetable oil
2 cups plain whole milk
   yogurt
2 teaspoons coarse salt
   (kosher or sea)
2 to 4 drops orange food
   coloring (optional)

1. Heat a dry skillet over medium heat. Add the coriander, peppercorns, cumin, mace, fennel, cardamom, cloves, and cinnamon and toast, shaking the pan, until fragrant, 3 minutes. Transfer the spices to a bowl to cool. Grind to a fine powder in a spice mill.

2. Crumble the saffron threads between your thumb and forefinger and place in a small bowl with hot water. Let the saffron infuse for 10 minutes.

3. Combine the onion, garlic, ginger, chilies, lemon juice, and oil in a blender or mini-processor and purée to a smooth paste. You may need to add a tablespoon of water or so to obtain a paste.

4. Combine the yogurt, spices, onion paste, saffron mixture, salt, and food coloring, if using, in a bowl and stir to mix. Use right away or transfer to a large jar, cover, and refrigerate. The marinade will keep for up to 3 days.

Makes 2 cups; enough to marinate 1 cut-up chicken or 2 pounds of lamb or seafood

TANDOORI SHRIMP

Tandoori shrimp are one of the glories of Indian gastronomy. They're exceedingly quick and easy to make, but to get the full effect you should serve the shrimp with a kaleidoscopic assortment of side dishes. A bare minimum would include the Raita on page 200 and Tomato Chutney on page 277. The more people you have, the more elaborate your spread should be. In India, the shrimp would be cooked in a tandoor, an urn-shaped clay barbecue pit. But this recipe also works well with the shrimp cooked over a high flame on a conventional American grill.

2 pounds jumbo shrimp, peeled and deveined

1 recipe Tandoori Marinade (see page 71)

4 tablespoons (½ stick) unsalted butter, melted

1 small red onion, thinly sliced

½ cup fresh cilantro sprigs

1 lemon, cut into wedges

1 recipe Raita (page 200)

1 recipe Tomato Chutney (page 277)

1 recipe Fresh Mango Chutney (page 275)

1. Place the shrimp in a glass baking dish and pour the marinade over them. Cover with plastic wrap and marinate for 4 to 6 hours in the refrigerator. Stir a couple of times to coat evenly.

2. Preheat the grill to high.

3. Remove the shrimp from the marinade and thread them onto skewers. Place on the grate and grill until firm, pink, and cooked through, 2 to 3 minutes per side, basting with melted butter.

4. Transfer the shrimp to a platter and sprinkle the onion slices and cilantro sprigs on top. Garnish with lemon wedges and serve with bowls of raita, tomato chutney, and mango chutney. Basmati rice would make a good accompaniment.

Serves 6 as an appetizer; 4 as a main course

SWEET SESAME-SOY MARINADE

This marinade is simplicity itself, yet I never met anyone who didn't adore it. The hardest part will be assembling the ingredients, but most can be found at your local supermarket. You may need to go to an Asian market for sesame oil, five-spice powder, and oyster sauce. The marinade reflects several Asian grilling cultures: the Korean fondness for sesame oil and sesame seeds; the Japanese yen for soy sauce and ginger; the Chinese love of five-spice powder and garlic; and the Thai enthusiasm for chili sauce. Put them all together and you get a marinade that turns poultry, meat, seafood, and even tofu into championship barbecue.

You must use Asian sesame oil for the marinade: Some of the oils sold at health food stores aren't roasted, so they lack the rich nutty taste.

TRY THIS!

This marinade goes great with everything—shrimp, fish, chicken, beef, pork, lamb, tofu. Marinate small pieces, like shrimp, for 30 minutes; chicken breasts and fish fillets for 2 to 4 hours; ribs and whole chickens for 6 to 8 hours; and large cuts of meat, like leg of lamb, for 1 to 2 days, covered, in the refrigerator.

⅓ cup Asian sesame oil
⅓ cup rice wine or dry sherry
⅓ cup soy sauce
3 tablespoons oyster sauce (optional)
3 tablespoons light brown sugar
2 cloves garlic, minced

1 tablespoon minced fresh ginger
2 scallions (white and green parts), minced
2 strips of lemon zest
1 to 2 jalapeño chilies, seeded and chopped
1 tablespoon toasted sesame seeds (see box, page 105)
½ teaspoon Chinese five-spice powder, preferably homemade (page 50), or use a good commercial brand

Combine all the ingredients in a bowl and stir or whisk to mix. Use right away or transfer to a large jar, cover, and refrigerate. The marinade will keep for up to 3 days.

Makes 1½ cups; enough for 2 pounds of food

SESAME GRILLED TOFU

Tofu is hardly the life of the party at a North American barbecue, although, thanks to its health benefits, it's slowly gaining acceptance. But in Japan, grilled tofu is a delicacy, enjoyed at fancy *robata-yaki* (grill) restaurants, at the stalls of street vendors, and just about everywhere in between. This recipe plays the flavors of soy sauce and honey against the nutty fragrance of sesame oil and sesame seeds. It's guaranteed to turn skeptics into believers.

Black sesame seeds *(kuro goma)* are available at Japanese shops and natural foods markets.

2 pounds extra firm tofu
1 recipe Sweet Sesame-Soy Marinade
     (page 74)
1 tablespoon toasted sesame seeds
     (see box, page 105)
1 tablespoon black sesame seeds
     (optional)
2 scallions (green parts
     only), finely
     chopped

1. Rinse the tofu under cold water. Place it on a gently sloping cutting board in the sink. Place a heavy plate or frying pan on top of it and let stand for 1 hour. (Pressing the tofu this way extracts the excess water and firms up the tofu for grilling.)

2. Cut each block of tofu horizontally into 2 broad thin rectangles. Cut each rectangle in half crosswise. Arrange the tofu pieces in a glass baking dish and pour the marinade over them. Cover with plastic wrap and marinate in the refrigerator for 2 to 4 hours, turning twice.

3. Remove the tofu from the marinade to a platter. Strain the marinade into a saucepan and boil over high heat until thick and syrupy, 3 to 4 minutes.

4. Preheat the grill to high. Oil the grate well. (Tofu tends to stick to the grate.)

5. Place the tofu pieces on the grate and grill until nicely browned, 2 to 4 minutes per side, brushing with the boiled marinade and carefully turning with a spatula. Transfer the tofu to a platter and spoon any remaining glaze over it. Sprinkle with the toasted sesame seeds, black sesame seeds, if using, and scallion greens and serve at once.

Serves 8 as an appetizer; 4 as a light main course

BASIC CHINESE MARINADE

Grilling plays a relatively minor role in Chinese cooking, but the Chinese have developed a marinade that lends itself to an endless variety of grilled dishes. At its heart is the basic Asian flavor dialectic of sweet and salty, the former in the form of sugar and cinnamon, the latter in the form of soy sauce. The cool smoky licorice flavor of star anise is a good counterpoint to the Asian heat of ginger, garlic, and scallion. Put them all together and you get a marinade that's symphonic in its complexity, but that can be made in a matter of minutes.

Rice wine, sesame oil, five-spice powder, and star anise can be purchased at Asian markets, many gourmet shops, or from one of the mail-order sources on page 281.

or from one of the mail-order sources on page 281.

TRY THIS!

This marinade is enormously versatile, going equally well with seafood (especially shrimp and scallops), poultry (chicken, duck, and quail), meat (pork, lamb, and beef), and even tofu. Marinate small pieces (shrimp, diced chicken, etc.) for 30 to 60 minutes; thin cuts of meat (chicken breasts and steaks) for 1 to 2 hours; and large pieces of meat (whole chickens and roasts) for 4 to 8 hours or even overnight, covered, in the refrigerator.

2 slices (each ¼ inch thick) fresh ginger
2 cloves garlic, peeled
2 scallions, white parts only, trimmed (save the scallion greens for garnish)
½ cup soy sauce
½ cup Chinese rice wine, Japanese sake, or dry sherry

¼ cup honey or sugar
3 tablespoons Asian (dark) sesame oil
½ teaspoon Chinese five-spice powder, preferably homemade (page 50), or use a good commercial brand
2 star anise
2 cinnamon sticks (3 inches each)

Flatten the ginger slices, garlic cloves, and scallion whites with the side of a cleaver. Place them in a bowl with the soy sauce, rice wine, honey, sesame oil, and five-spice powder and stir or whisk to mix. Add the star anise and cinnamon. The marinade tastes best used within a few hours of making.

Makes 1½ cups marinade; enough for 2 to 3 pounds of seafood, meat, tofu, or vegetables

BASIC THAI SATE MARINADE

Satés are bite-size kebabs enjoyed throughout Southeast Asia. They probably originated in Indonesia, where literally hundreds of different types are served. As the preparation spread throughout the region, each country customized the recipe, using the local spices and seasonings in the sauce and marinade. The Thai version plays the sweetness of honey against the briny tang of fish sauce or soy sauce, with garlic and coriander for punch.

Note the addition of one ingredient you may not be accustomed to using—cilantro root. The roots of this pungent plant have an earthy aromatic flavor—the sort you might get if you crossed celery root with cilantro. Your best shot at finding bunches of cilantro with the roots still on is at an Asian or Hispanic market. But don't worry too much if you can't find it; cilantro leaves will get you pretty close to the right flavor. By the way, rinse those roots well; they tend to have quite a bit of dirt still clinging to them.

¼ cup fish sauce or soy
   sauce
¼ cup fresh lime juice
2 tablespoons honey
3 cloves garlic,
   minced

2 tablespoons chopped
   cilantro roots or leaves
1 teaspoon ground
   coriander
½ teaspoon ground
   turmeric

Combine all the ingredients in a bowl and stir or whisk to dissolve the honey. The marinade tastes best used within a few hours of making.

Makes ⅔ cup; enough for 1½ pounds of meat, chicken, or seafood

TRY THIS!

Cut the meat or seafood into strips the size of your pinkie or flat strips the size and shape of tongue depressors—the flat strips work particularly well for beef. Cover and marinate in the refrigerator for 30 to 60 minutes. Then drain, skewer, and grill.

SATE MIXED GRILL

When satés are served in Thailand, you get a tiny dish of peanut sauce and a bowl of cucumber relish. The overall effect is rather like that of chamber music: beauty on a small scale with an orchestral range of flavors. Here's how to create a spectacular Thai saté party, using simple recipes in this book.

8 ounces boneless skinless chicken thighs or breast

8 ounces pork loin or tenderloin

8 ounces beef tenderloin or sirloin

8 ounces large shrimp, peeled and deveined

2 recipes Basic Thai Saté Marinade (page 77)

1½ recipes Quick Peanut Dipping Sauce (page 209) or Rich Peanut Dipping Sauce (page 208)

2 recipes Thai Cucumber Relish (page 261)

2 to 3 tablespoons coconut milk or vegetable oil, for basting

12 sprigs of fresh cilantro

3 tablespoons chopped dry-roasted peanuts

SPECIAL EQUIPMENT
About 40 bamboo skewers (6 to 8 inches), soaked in cold water for 1 hour, then drained

1. Cut the 3 meats into strips about 3 × ½ × ¼ inch. Place each type of meat in a separate bowl. Put the shrimp in a separate bowl. Divide the marinade among the bowls and toss to mix. Cover the bowls with plastic wrap and marinate in the refrigerator for 30 to 60 minutes.

2. Meanwhile, prepare the peanut sauce and cucumber relish. Spoon the sauce and relish into separate tiny bowls or ramekins, 1 set for each guest.

3. Preheat your grill to high.

4. Remove the meat and shrimp from the marinade and thread onto the skewers. Place the satés on the grate and grill until nicely browned and cooked through, about 2 minutes per side, basting with the coconut milk. If the skewers start to burn, protect them with strips of aluminum foil. Transfer the satés to plates or a platter, garnish with cilantro sprigs and peanuts, and serve at once.

Serves 8 to 10 as an appetizer; 4 to 6 as a light main course

KOREAN HONEY-SESAME MARINADE

Of all the marinades of Asia, few are quite as inviting as the dark, nutty, sweet-salty ointment Koreans use for flavoring butterflied beef ribs and steak. No wonder Koreans make some of the best barbecue in the world. The marinade takes mere minutes to make, yet it utterly transforms meat, poultry, seafood, or vegetables once they've spent an hour or so in its company.

½ cup soy sauce
¼ cup Asian (dark) sesame oil
¼ cup sugar
¼ cup sake or dry sherry
4 cloves garlic, minced
4 scallions (white and green parts), trimmed and finely chopped
2 tablespoons toasted sesame seeds (see box, page 105)

1 tablespoon minced fresh ginger
1 teaspoon hot paprika
½ teaspoon freshly ground black pepper
1 small Asian pear or regular pear, peeled, cored, and diced

Combine all the ingredients for the marinade in a blender or food processor and blend to a smooth purée. Use within a couple of hours of making, or transfer to a large jar, cover, and refrigerate. The marinade will keep for several days.

Makes 2 cups; enough for 3 pounds of meat or seafood

TERIYAKI MARINADE

This sweet-salty-nutty blend of honey, soy sauce, and sesame oil is one of America's most popular marinades, appreciated as much for its versatility—it goes equally well

TRY THIS!

This marinade works especially well for dark meats—chicken thighs and drumsticks, pork, beef, and dark fish, like mackerel or bluefish. You can also use it on light meats (chicken breasts, white fish, shrimp, and so on), but expect a little discoloration.

Marinate large cuts of meat (whole chickens and flank steaks) for 6 to 8 hours (or even overnight); smaller pieces of meat (fish steaks and chicken breasts) for 1 to 2 hours; very small pieces of meat (shrimp or diced chicken) for 30 to 60 minutes, covered, in the refrigerator.

with meat, poultry, seafood, tofu, and vegetables—as for its simplicity—you can whip up a batch in the time it takes to read this headnote. Teriyaki doesn't really exist as a marinade in Japan. Rather, the ingredients used to make the sauce are boiled down to a thick syrup and brushed on grilled food. But I like teriyaki as a marinade and so do grill buffs throughout the United States and Canada. Mirin is sweetened Japanese rice wine: You can buy it at natural foods stores and many supermarkets. If unavailable, use sherry and a little more honey. Be sure to use dark Asian sesame oil. Warm the honey jar in a pan of hot water before measuring; this will make it easier to measure and dissolve.

½ cup tamari or other Japanese soy sauce
½ cup mirin
¼ cup honey
¼ cup Asian (dark) sesame oil
4 slices (each ¼ inch thick) fresh ginger, lightly flattened with the side of a cleaver

3 cloves garlic, lightly flattened with the side of a cleaver
3 scallions, trimmed, white parts flattened with the side of a cleaver, green parts finely chopped

Combine the tamari, mirin, and honey in a bowl and whisk until the honey is dissolved. Whisk in the remaining ingredients. The marinade tastes best used the day it's made.

Makes 2 cups; enough for 3 to 4 pounds of meat or seafood

VARIATION

Orange or Tangerine Teriyaki: Add ½ cup orange or tangerine juice when you add the tamari.

WET RUBS AND SPICE PASTES

TEX-MEX TEQUILA-JALAPENO WET RUB

TRY THIS!

Smear this paste on pork loins and tenderloins, sirloin or beef tenderloin tips, or chicken. Marinate, covered, in the refrigerator for 2 hours, then grill.

I discovered this emerald green spice paste in the best way possible—the moment that pork tenderloins that had been marinating in it came off the grill. The place was an upscale Dallas cookware emporium called Cookworks and its creator was Texas-born chef Kent West. It takes all of five minutes to prepare; what results is a spice paste of such vivid color and vibrant taste that you're tempted to eat it with a spoon. Smear it on pork, beef, or chicken; you'll love its bold Tex-Mex flavor.

1 large bunch of cilantro, washed and stemmed (1 cup loosely packed leaves)
4 to 6 jalapeño chilies, seeded and coarsely chopped
½ small onion, minced
3 cloves garlic, coarsely chopped

¼ cup fresh orange juice
¼ cup fresh lime juice
¼ cup extra virgin olive oil
2 tablespoons tequila
1 teaspoon coarse salt (kosher or sea)
½ teaspoon sugar
½ teaspoon freshly ground black pepper
½ teaspoon ground cumin

Combine the cilantro, jalapeños, onion, and garlic in a food processor and finely chop. Gradually add the remaining ingredients and purée to a paste. The rub tastes best used within 2 hours of making. It's so quick, there's really no reason to make it ahead.

Makes 1 cup; enough to marinate 2 pounds of meat

JAKE'S COFFEE-CARDAMOM BRISKET RUB

TRY THIS!

Smear the rub on a brisket on all sides and place in a roasting pan. Marinate, covered, in the refrigerator, for at least 4 hours, or as long as overnight.

Readers of my books are no strangers to my stepson, Jake Klein. A gifted chef, Jake has done recipe testing and food styling for many of my books and his ideas sometimes best the old man's. Jake has the uncanny ability to combine the most unlikely ingredients in ways that never fail to delight or astonish. Who would think of basing a barbecue rub on ground coffee? Who would think of seasoning brisket with what's essentially a spice for dessert: cardamom? It turns out that there's a method to his madness, for cardamom is used as a flavoring in Arab coffee, which Jake learned to drink when he lived in Israel. As for coffee with beef, well, don't tell cowboys gathered around a campfire that coffee doesn't go with steak. According to Jake, the coffee gives the meat a nice caramel flavor, so you don't need to resort to a lot of sugar.

½ **cup ground coffee or chicory**

½ **cup coarse salt (kosher or sea)**

½ **cup (packed) dark brown sugar**

¼ **cup hot paprika**

2 **tablespoons ground cardamom**

2 **tablespoons ground ginger**

⅓ **cup chopped fresh garlic**

½ **cup vegetable oil, or as needed**

Combine all the ingredients, except the oil, in a bowl or food processor and stir or process to mix. Stir in enough oil to make a thick paste. The rub should be used the day it is made. Cover and refrigerate until using.

Makes about 2 cups; enough for a 6- to 8-pound brisket

COFFEE-CARDAMOM BRISKET
WITH JAKE'S
3 Cs BARBECUE SAUCE

Brisket is become something of a competition dish at my house, with each family member trying to make the best. My wife favors Jewish-style brisket, braised fork-tender with dried fruits and sweet wine. I'm a Texas-style brisket guy, preferring a simple rub and a lot of wood smoke. Jake, our son, takes the most adventurous approach, seasoning the brisket with a wet rub made from coffee grounds and serving it with an offbeat but very tasty chocolate-cherry barbecue sauce. This is his version.

1 brisket (6 pounds), trimmed
1 recipe Jake's Coffee-Cardamom
Brisket Rub (facing page)
White bread for serving
1 recipe Jake's 3 C's Barbecue
Sauce (page 156)

SPECIAL EQUIPMENT
4 cups wood chips or chunks,
soaked in beer to cover for
1 hour, then drained

1. Place the brisket in a roasting pan and smear it on all sides with the rub, using a spatula. Cover with plastic wrap and let marinate in the refrigerator, for at least 4 hours, or as long as overnight.

2. Set up the grill for indirect cooking, following the instructions on page 5. Preheat to 325°F.

3. Place the brisket, fat side up, on the grate over the drip pan. If using a charcoal grill, toss one quarter of the wood chips on the coals. If using a gas grill, place the chips in the smoker box and preheat until you see smoke. Cover the grill.

4. Smoke-cook the brisket to an internal temperature of 190°F, or until tender enough to pull apart with your fingers , 5 to 7 hours. (The cooking time will depend on the size of the brisket and the heat of the grill.) If using charcoal, add 10 fresh coals and ½ cup wood chips per side every hour.

5. Transfer the brisket to a cutting board, loosely cover with an aluminum foil tent, and let rest for 15 minutes. Pull off and discard any visible fat. (Or slice it up with the meat. That's where the best flavor is anyway.) Thinly slice the meat across the grain and serve it on slices of white bread with the barbecue sauce on the side.

Serves 12 to 14

DOWN ISLAND SEASONIN'

Every island in the Caribbean has its version of seasonin', from Cuba's tangy adobo (page 60) to Jamaica's fiery jerk (facing page) to a pungent green herb and pepper paste used in the southern Caribbean and simply known as seasonin'. It looks a little like pesto, except that the basil is replaced by such popular West Indian herbs as *escallions* (Caribbean chives), fresh thyme, and celery. Seasonin' is always flavorful, but not terribly fiery. It always contains bell peppers and may contain chilies, but the latter are used more for their aroma than their heat. Use seasonin' to flavor all manner of grilled fare, from chicken to pork to seafood. Here's how it's made in Barbados.

TRY THIS!

Place chicken pieces, pork or beef tenderloin, rack or butterflied leg of lamb, lobsters or shrimp, fish fillets or whole fish (if using the latter, make deep slashes in both sides with a knife) in a baking dish and spread the seasonin' on top with a spatula, turning the food a few times to ensure even marinating. Marinate large pieces of meat overnight, medium-size (chicken pieces, for example) for 4 to 6 hours, small pieces (chicken breasts or fish fillets, for example) for 2 hours, covered, in the refrigerator. Grill as you would normally and get ready for a taste that is out of this world.

1 green bell pepper, stemmed, seeded, and coarsely chopped

½ red bell pepper, stemmed, seeded, and coarsely chopped

2 jalapeño chilies or ½ Scotch bonnet chili, seeded and chopped

2 ribs celery, finely chopped

1 medium onion, coarsely chopped

6 cloves garlic, coarsely chopped

3 bunches of fresh chives or 2 bunches of scallions (white and green parts), trimmed and chopped

1 bunch of fresh flat-leaf parsley, stemmed and coarsely chopped (about 1 cup)

1 tablespoon fresh thyme or 1½ teaspoons dried thyme

2 tablespoons chopped fresh oregano or 2 teaspoons dried oregano

2 tablespoons chopped fresh marjoram or 2 teaspoons dried marjoram

⅓ cup vegetable oil

⅓ cup fresh lime juice

2 tablespoons soy sauce

1 tablespoon coarse salt (kosher or sea)

½ teaspoon freshly ground black pepper

½ teaspoon ground allspice

Combine the vegetables and herbs in a food processor and purée to a coarse paste. Add the oil, lime juice, soy sauce, salt, pepper, and allspice and purée until smooth. Use right away or transfer to a bowl or a large jar, cover, and store in the refrigerator. The seasonin' will keep for several days. However, the flavor is freshest and best the first day.

Makes 2 to 3 cups; enough for 2 to 3 pounds of meat, poultry, or seafood

VARIATION

Paramin Seasonin' from Trinidad: Trinidad's seasonin' owes its zingy flavor to fresh cilantro and mint—herbs that grow in profusion on the Paramin Hills outside Port of Spain. Prepare the preceding recipe, adding as well 1 bunch each of rinsed, stemmed, chopped cilantro and spearmint or peppermint.

REAL JAMAICAN JERK SEASONING

Around the time that reggae music began rocking America's airwaves, a new dish began blasting our taste buds: jerk. Invented by the Maroons (runaway slaves who lived in the hills of north-central Jamaica in the eighteenth century), this fiery Jamaican barbecue combines local seasonings (allspice, fresh thyme, Caribbean chives, and prodigious quantities of Scotch bonnet chilies) in a fiery paste that's rubbed on pork and chicken. The pit master would "jook" the meat (poke holes in it with a sharp stick) to hasten the absorption of the seasonings—the process that gives us our word jerk. The other remarkable thing about Jamaican jerk is the cooking method: open-pit barbecuing over a low smoky fire made of burning allspice wood. You may be aghast by the amount of chilies and salt in this recipe, but that's how Jamaicans make it. (The salt helped preserve the meat without refrigeration.) For a somewhat less fiery jerk seasoning seed the chilies or use a few as two Scotch bonnets.

JERK LEG OF LAMB

The traditional meat for jerk is pork, with chicken coming in a close second. But fiery jerk seasoning goes great with a robust meat, like lamb.

This recipe requires only a few minutes of actual preparation time, but you should marinate the lamb overnight to achieve the maximum flavor. The rum rids the lamb of any gamy flavor and puts you in the right mood for jerk.

½ bone-in leg of lamb
   (4 to 5 pounds)
½ cup rum
1 recipe Real Jamaican Jerk
   Seasoning (page 85)

SPECIAL EQUIPMENT
2 cups fruit wood chips, soaked for
   1 hour, then drained

1. Using the tip of a paring knife, make 24 small holes in the lamb, each about ¼ inch deep. Place the lamb in a roasting pan and rinse it on all sides with the rum. Pour off and discard the rum and let the lamb air dry for 5 minutes.

2. Smear the jerk seasoning on the lamb on all sides with a spatula or your fingers, forcing it into the holes in the meat. Cover with plastic wrap and marinate in the refrigerator for at least 8 hours, preferably overnight.

3. Set up the grill for indirect grilling, following the instructions on page 5, and preheat to 350°F. Toss the wood chips on the coals if using a charcoal grill. If using gas, place the wood chips in the smoker box and preheat until you see smoke.

4. Place the lamb on the grate and indirect grill until cooked to taste, about 1½ hours for medium. Transfer the lamb to a platter, loosely cover with an aluminum foil tent, let rest for 10 minutes, then carve and serve.

Serves 8 to 10

4 to 12 Scotch bonnet chilies, stemmed and cut in half

1 medium onion, coarsely chopped

½ cup coarsely chopped shallots

2 bunches of chives or scallions (white and green parts), trimmed and coarsely chopped

4 cloves garlic, coarsely chopped

½ cup coarsely chopped fresh flat-leaf parsley

½ cup chopped fresh cilantro

2 teaspoons chopped fresh ginger

2 tablespoons coarse salt (kosher or sea), or to taste

1 tablespoon fresh thyme or 1½ teaspoons dried thyme

2 teaspoons ground allspice

1 teaspoon freshly ground black pepper

½ teaspoon ground cinnamon

½ teaspoon freshly grated nutmeg

¼ teaspoon ground cloves

¼ cup fresh lime juice

¼ cup vegetable oil

¼ cup (packed) dark brown sugar

2 tablespoons soy sauce

¼ cup cold water, or as needed

TRY THIS!

Place the food in a glass baking dish and spread the jerk seasoning over it, turning to ensure an even coating. Marinate large pieces of meat overnight; medium-size pieces for 4 to 6 hours; and small pieces, like shrimp or fish fillets, for 1 to 2 hours, covered, in the refrigerator. Barbecue or indirect grill the meat using moderate heat and plenty of wood smoke.

Combine the chilies, onion, shallots, chives, garlic, parsley, cilantro, ginger, salt, thyme, and spices in a food processor and process to a coarse paste. Add the remaining ingredients, including the water, 1 tablespoon at a time, processing to mix to a thick but spreadable paste. Use right away or transfer to a large jar, cover, placing a piece of plastic wrap between the rim of the jar and the lid, and refrigerate. The seasoning will keep for months.

Makes 2 cups; enough for 3 to 4 pounds meat, chicken, or seafood

THE IMPORTANCE OF
FRESH HERBS

"What is an herb?" a scholar once asked Charlemagne. "The friend of physicians and the praise of cooks," the emperor replied. You don't need to be a ruler or a sage to know that fresh herbs can make all the difference between ordinary grilling and electrifying live-fire cooking. It used to be that finding fresh herbs required a trip to a specialty greengrocer. These days, you need go no further than your local supermarket. The fact is that fresh herbs will give your sauces and marinades a Technicolor brightness.

Fresh herbs add a distinct ethnic character to whatever you're grilling. Fresh cilantro, for example, is one of the defining flavors of Mexican barbecue. Fresh basil and rosemary suggest the Mediterranean, especially Tuscany and the south of France. Greek cooks would be lost without oregano and rosemary; Moroccans, without mint; Thais, without lemongrass and kaffir lime leaves. The truth is that it's hard to think of a grilled dish that doesn't taste better with fresh herbs.

Fresh herbs serve the grill meister in several ways. First, as an aromatic flavor-enhancer to marinades and spice pastes. Second, as a surface flavoring for spit-roasted meats. (Tuscan cooks, for example, place sprigs of fresh rosemary under the trussing strings when roasting chicken.) Malaysian grillers use lemongrass stalks as a basting brush. You can also use the slender stalks of many herbs, such as lemongrass and rosemary, as flavorful skewers on which to grill kebabs. Bunches of fresh herbs can be tossed on the coals just prior to grilling to create fragrant clouds of smoke. (This is a good use for wilted herbs.)

Don't fret if you can't find the particular herb a recipe calls for. Lacking cilantro, I once made a spectacular salsa with fresh mint. Another aborted shopping mission led me to the discovery of rosemary pesto.

Before talking about specific herbs, here are a few general observations about rinsing and storing fresh herbs: To rinse cilantro, basil, parsley, and other bushy herbs, fill a bowl with cold water. Holding the herbs by the stems, plunge the leaves in the water and gently agitate up and down. Pour off the dirty water, add fresh water, and continue this process until the water runs clean.

Fresh herbs will keep for longer than you might think, provided they are stored properly. Loosely wrap the herbs in a damp paper towel and place in an *unsealed* plastic bag in the refrigerator; don't seal the bag or you'll smother the herbs. Check the paper towel every few days, moistening it as needed. It should be damp, not soaking wet. Stored this way, the herbs will keep for a week to ten days.

So what about dried herbs? Contrary to what you may have been led to believe; they're not inherently evil. In fact, drying intensifies or even reconfigures the flavor of many herbs and grill jockeys from Buenos Aires to Baku would be lost without them. The first thing you need to know is which herbs dry well and which don't. The good dryers include basil, bay leaf, dill seed (but not the leaves), marjoram, mint, oregano, rosemary, and thyme. Herbs that don't have much flavor dried include cilantro, dill, parsley, and tarragon—avoid them. To freshen up the flavor of any dried herb, mince it with a little fresh parsley.

Some specific herbs that can help the griller include:

BASIL: Lends a Mediterranean accent. Purée the leaves in oils and spice pastes, like the Sweet Basil Oil on page 119. Place whole basil leaves between the various ingredients on shish kebabs. Basil goes particularly well with poultry and seafood.

BAY LEAF: A popular ingredient in marinades, especially for game and beef. On the Portuguese island of Madeira, bay leaf branches are used as skewers and whole bay leaves placed between chunks of beef on shish kebabs.

CHIVES: Great for sprinkling over grilled seafood, poultry, and vegetables when a delicate onion flavor is desired.

CILANTRO: One of the world's most popular barbecue herbs, used in marinades and for sprinkling over grilled meats in countries as diverse as Mexico, India, and Thailand. Cilantro roots are used in Southeast Asian spice pastes and barbecue sauces.

DILL: A popular flavoring in Greek, Georgian, and Central Asian grilling. The signature flavoring of the Georgian barbecue sauce Tkemali (page 196).

KAFFIR LIME LEAF: The fragrant leaf of a Southeast Asian lime tree. Adds a wonderfully aromatic flavor to spice pastes, marinades, and grilled fish.

LEMONGRASS: Has the herbal flavor of lemon without the tartness. Used throughout Southeast Asia as an ingredient in marinades, spice pastes, and even as skewers. (Fish mousse grilled on lemongrass skewers is a classic Indonesian saté.)

MARJORAM: A traditional ingredient in French herbes de Provence and in central European grilling. Used in Mediterranean marinades.

MINT: A popular barbecue seasoning in Afghanistan and Morocco. Fresh mint is also a key ingredient in Paramin seasonin' from Trinidad (page 85) and in Indian and Afghan chutneys. Great with lamb.

OREGANO: One of the defining flavors of Greek and Mexican grilling. Great with pork and lamb.

PARSLEY: Grillers can't seem to live without this commonplace herb. Argentinians use it to make Chimichurri (page 172). Turks add it to onion relish. Parsley is often paired with onion and garlic with good reason—it helps neutralize their pungency. Think of it as nature's mouthwash.

ROSEMARY: One of the quintessential flavors of the Mediterranean and an essential seasoning for lamb, beef, and poultry. Rosemary stalks make tasty skewers for kebabs.

TARRAGON: Its licoricey flavor goes well with seafood, poultry, and beef.

THYME: Popular on much of the world's barbecue trail. You taste it strongly in Jamaica's jerk, Barbados seasonin', and French herbes de Provence. Also used in wild game marinades.

THREE RECADOS (Yucatán Spice Pastes)

Americans call them wet rubs. Mexicans call them *recados*; and in the Yucatán, no one would dream of grilling a steak, spit-roasting a fish, or pit-roasting a turkey without seasoning it first with one of these pungent pastes of chilies, herbs, and spices. Yucatán grill jockeys have it easier than their North American counterparts, for they can buy *recados* ready-made at any market. If you want to enjoy their robust flavor in the United States, you'll have to make your own. This takes a little work, but the results are eminently worth it.

There are four classic *recados: rojo* (red), *verde* (green), *recado de bistec* (steak *recado*), and the most prized of all, *recado negro* (black *recado*). The first owes its bright color and taste to achiote, a rust-colored Caribbean spice known as annatto in the States. Green *recado,* made with *pepitas* (pumpkin seeds), is used more as a sauce base than as a seasoning, and so I have not included a recipe for it. Steak *recado* is a salty, fragrant, greenish-brown paste used, as the name suggests, as a seasoning for beef. Black *recado* owes its color to burnt de árbol chilies and tortillas. It is used as a seasoning for turkey and suckling pig.

The following recipes have been modified so that you can make them in a blender, but I've tried to keep the flavors as authentic as possible.

RECADO ROJO (Yucatan Red Spice Paste)

This recipe comes from Carlos Cavich, owner of a spice stall at the central market in Mérida in the Yucatán. Normally, the *recado* would be purchased as a paste and thinned to pourable consistency at home with sour orange juice and vinegar. I've incorporated that step here.

Annatto is a pungent, rust-colored Caribbean seed, sometimes called poor man's saffron. It gives the sauce a vivid orange color and a flavor reminiscent of iodine. Masa harina is a kind of cornmeal made from hulled cooked corn. (It's the main ingredient in tortillas.) Both annatto and masa harina are available in most large supermarkets. If you can't find masa, in a pinch, you could substitute cornmeal.

TRY THIS!

When cooking chicken breasts, fish fillets or steaks, pork chops or pork loins, rub the *recado* on the outside. For chicken quarters and halves and whole fish, make slashes in the sides to the bone and force a little of the *recado* mixture into the slits, then spread the remainder on the outside. For whole chickens, spread half the *recado* in the cavity. Force half of the rest under the skin and the remainder over it. Marinate thin pieces of meat for 1 to 2 hours; medium-size pieces for 4 to 6 hours; large pieces overnight, covered, in the refrigerator.

Traditionally, the onion and garlic are roasted until brown and soft on an ungreased comal, or griddle, or a cast-iron skillet, but you could also thread the onion and garlic onto bamboo skewers and grill them over a medium fire until soft and brown.

2 plum tomatoes

1 medium onion, quartered

1 head of garlic, broken into cloves and peeled

1 tablespoon annatto seeds

1 teaspoon black peppercorns

6 allspice berries or ¼ teaspoon ground allspice

4 whole cloves or ⅛ teaspoon ground cloves

1 teaspoon cumin seeds or ground cumin

1 piece (1 inch) cinnamon stick or ½ teaspoon ground cinnamon

2 teaspoons pure chili powder (not a blend) or paprika

1 teaspoon dried oregano

2 tablespoons masa harina or cornmeal

1½ teaspoons coarse salt (kosher or sea)

1 teaspoon sugar

⅔ cup sour orange juice (see box, page 174) or lime juice

2 tablespoons distilled white vinegar

2 tablespoons vegetable oil

1. Heat a comal or cast-iron skillet over medium heat. Add the tomatoes, onion, and garlic and cook, turning with tongs, until browned on all sides and soft, 4 to 6 minutes for the garlic, 10 to 12 minutes for the tomatoes and onion pieces. Do not let the vegetables burn. Transfer the vegetables to a plate to cool as they are done.

2. Combine the annatto, peppercorns, allspice, cloves, cumin, cinnamon, chili powder, and oregano in a spice mill and grind to a fine powder.

3. Place the ground spices, masa harina, salt, sugar, sour orange juice, vinegar, oil, and roasted vegetables in a blender. Purée to a thick paste, scraping down the sides of the blender with a spatula several times. Use right away or transfer to a large jar, cover, and refrigerate. The *recado* will keep for several weeks.

Makes about 1⅓ cups; use 1 to 2 tablespoons per pound of meat

RECADO DE BISTEC (Steak Recado)

Oregano and pepper give this *recado* its dark green color and distinctive aroma. It's not too sweet, which makes it perfect for seasoning grilled steak. This recipe comes from Evaristo Escamillo, a ten-year veteran spice seller at the Central Food Market in Mérida.

TRY THIS!

Rub a little of the *recado* on steaks on both sides and marinate, covered, in the refrigerator for 1 to 2 hours. Grill as you would any steak and serve with the Smoky Two-Chili Salsa on page 256.

1 medium onion, quartered
2 heads of garlic, broken into cloves and peeled
2 tablespoons dried oregano, preferably Mexican
2 teaspoons black peppercorns or freshly ground black pepper
1 teaspoon cumin seeds or ground cumin
2 whole cloves or ⅛ teaspoon ground cloves

3 tablespoons minced fresh flat-leaf parsley
1 tablespoon masa harina or cornmeal
2 teaspoons coarse salt (kosher or sea)
¼ cup distilled white vinegar
¼ cup sour orange juice (see box, page 174) or lime juice
¼ cup vegetable oil

1. Heat a comal or cast-iron skillet over medium heat. Add the onion and garlic and cook, turning with tongs, until browned on all sides and soft, 4 to 6 minutes for the garlic, 10 to 12 minutes for the onion pieces. Do not let the vegetables burn. Transfer the onions and garlic to a plate to cool as they are done.

2. Combine the oregano, peppercorns, cumin, and cloves in a spice mill and grind to a fine powder.

3. Place the parsley, masa harina, salt, vinegar, sour orange juice, oil, onion, garlic, and spices in a blender. Purée to a smooth paste, scraping down the sides of the blender with a spatula several times. Use right away or transfer to a large jar, cover, and refrigerate. The *recado* will keep for several weeks.

Makes about 1 cup; use 1 to 2 tablespoons per pound of meat

RECADO NEGRO (Black Recado)

TRY THIS!

This *recado* is the traditional seasoning for pit-roasted turkey or suckling pig. These are fiesta foods in the Yucatán, served at weddings or the anniversary of a loved one's death. To prepare a 12-pound turkey in this fashion, use ¼ to ½ cup black *recado* to season the bird, spreading some in the neck and main cavity, some under the skin, and rubbing the remainder over the skin. Marinate the turkey, covered, in the refrigerator overnight. The next day, set up the grill for indirect grilling. Roast the turkey until cooked, 2½ to 3 hours, replenishing the coals every hour, or as needed.

Otherwise, rub the *recado* on pork, chicken, or steak; marinate, covered, in the refrigerator, for several hours, then grill.

This dark, shiny, intensely aromatic paste is the most venerated *recado* of all. Like many black dishes, it probably began as an accident. My guess is that someone burned the chilies and tortillas and, rather than waste them, pounded them into a spice paste. The broad outline of this recipe comes from Carmita Uicap, a tiny woman whose hands are jet black from kneading and packaging spice pastes at her stall at the Mérida market. Her recipe may seem a little involved. It *is* involved, but it produces one of the most electrifying seasoning mixtures in Mexico, and is definitely worth the time it takes to make. Charring the chilies produces a virulent smoke, so you should only cook them outdoors on your grill.

Note: To be strictly authentic, you'd use only chilies de árbol, but the resulting *recado* would be excruciatingly fiery. To make a milder black *recado*, replace two thirds of the chilies de árbol with milder guajillo or New Mexican red chilies.

3 ounces dried chilies de árbol, stemmed, or 1 ounce de árbol and 2 ounces guajillo or New Mexican red chilies
Cold water for soaking the chilies
2 corn tortillas
1½ heads of garlic, broken into cloves and peeled
1 medium onion, quartered
4 teaspoons dried oregano
2 teaspoons annatto seeds
2 teaspoons black peppercorns
1 teaspoon cumin seeds
1 teaspoon allspice berries
½ teaspoon whole cloves
2 bay leaves
1 tablespoon coarse salt (kosher or sea)
1 teaspoon sugar
¾ cup distilled white vinegar
¼ cup vegetable oil

1. Preheat the grill to high. Place a dry comal, or griddle, or a cast-iron skillet over the hottest part of the fire.

2. Add the chilies and cook, turning with tongs, until black, 1 to 2 minutes. Don't burn the chilies, but come close to it. Keep your head away from the comal to protect your

eyes from the virulent smoke. Transfer the chilies to a large bowl and add cold water to cover.

3. Place the tortillas on the comal and cook, turning with tongs, until very dark, 4 to 6 minutes per side. Transfer to a plate. Place the garlic and onion on the comal and cook, turning with tongs, until darkly browned on all sides and soft, 4 to 6 minutes for the garlic, 10 to 12 minutes for the onion pieces. Do not let the vegetables burn. Transfer to the plate with the tortillas. Breathe a sigh of relief: The hard part is over.

4. Grind the oregano, annatto, peppercorns, cumin, allspice, cloves, and bay leaves to a fine powder in a spice mill.

5. Drain the chilies and snip in half lengthwise, using kitchen shears. Rinse the chilies under cold water to remove the seeds. Shake off the excess water and place the chilies in a blender.

6. Break the toasted tortillas into 1-inch pieces and add to the blender. Place the salt, sugar, vinegar, oil, onion, garlic, and spices in the blender. Purée to a smooth paste, scraping down the sides of the blender with a spatula several times. Use right away or transfer to a large jar, cover, and refrigerate. The *recado* will keep for several weeks.

Makes about 2¼ cups; use ½ to 1 tablespoon per pound of meat

BERBER SPICE PASTE

I first encountered this fiery, blood-red Berber seasoning at a restaurant in Boston. I've since enjoyed it at restaurants all over the United States, not to mention in its native Morocco. The distinctive blend of aromatic and fiery, of pungent and hot makes it one of the best seasonings I know of for meat, poultry, seafood, and even vegetables. It's piquant without being pushy and hot without being unpleasant. Berber spice paste is *very* flavorful. A little goes a long way.

Fenugreek is a rectangular seed with a pleasantly bitter flavor. I've made it optional; the spice paste will still be

TRY THIS!

Smear or spread the paste on chicken breasts (or under the skin of a whole chicken), lamb chops, beef or pork tenderloin, or steak. It also goes well with fish: For whole grilled fish, make slashes in both sides and spread with paste, forcing it into the slashes. For a quick weeknight dinner, spread it on tuna or salmon steaks and grill. Marinate all, covered, in the refrigerator, 1 to 2 hours for smaller cuts (chops and chicken breasts), 4 to 6 hours for larger cuts (tenderloins and whole fish).

plenty tasty without it. Fenugreek and cardamom seeds can be purchased at Indian and Middle East markets.

2 teaspoons cracked black pepper

1 teaspoon coriander seeds

1 teaspoon cardamom seeds

1 teaspoon fenugreek seeds (optional)

1 piece (1 inch) cinnamon stick

4 allspice berries

3 whole cloves

1 small onion, cut into 1-inch pieces

2 cloves garlic, coarsely chopped

1 piece (1 inch) fresh ginger, thinly sliced

⅓ cup paprika

1 tablespoon coarse salt (kosher or sea)

1 to 2 teaspoons hot pepper flakes

½ cup olive oil

3 tablespoons fresh lemon juice

1. Heat a dry skillet over medium heat. Add the pepper, coriander, cardamom, fenugreek (if using), cinnamon, allspice, and cloves and toast, stirring occasionally, until fragrant, about 3 minutes. Transfer the spices to a bowl and cool. Grind to a powder in a spice mill.

2. Place the onion, garlic, and ginger in a food processor and finely chop. Add the toasted spices and remaining ingredients and process the mixture to a fine paste. Use right away or transfer to a jar, cover, and refrigerate. The spice paste will keep for several weeks.

Makes 1 cup; enough for 3 pounds of meat

GREEN TANDOORI SPICE PASTE

I like to think of this pungent chili paste as an Indian pesto or "seasonin'" (see page 84). It produces some of the tastiest grilled chicken I know of and it's spicy without being unbearably hot. Traditionally, the meat to be grilled would be marinated twice, first in yogurt, then in the green chili spice paste. You can certainly do this if you want, but even a single dip in the chili mixture will produce exceptionally flavorful barbecue. The Indian green bell pepper is hotter than ours. A poblano makes a good substitute.

1 cup cold water

1½ teaspoons coarse salt
(kosher or sea), or to
taste

4 ounces fresh spinach,
stemmed and rinsed

2 tablespoons unsalted
butter

3 tablespoons vegetable oil

1 medium onion, finely
chopped

3 cloves garlic, minced

1 tablespoon minced fresh
ginger

1 poblano chili or ½ green
bell pepper, stemmed,
seeded, and diced

4 jalapeño chilies, seeded
and diced

¼ cup chopped fresh cilantro

½ cup plain whole milk
yogurt

3 tablespoons fresh lemon
juice, or more to taste

1 teaspoon ground coriander

½ teaspoon ground turmeric

½ teaspoon freshly ground
black pepper

1. Bring the water and ½ teaspoon of the salt to a boil in a saucepan. Add the spinach and cook until limp, 2 minutes. Drain in a colander, rinse under cold water, and drain again. Squeeze the spinach between your fingers to wring out the water. Transfer the spinach to a food processor.

2. Heat the butter and oil in a skillet. Over medium heat add the onion and cook for about 2 minutes, stirring with a wooden spoon. Add the garlic and ginger and cook until the onions are golden brown, 2 to 4 minutes more. Transfer the onion mixture to the food processor.

3. Add the remaining ingredients (including the remaining 1 teaspoon salt) to the processor and purée to a smooth paste. Correct the seasoning, adding salt or lemon juice; the paste should be highly seasoned. Use right away or transfer to a jar, cover, and refrigerate. The spice paste will keep for 4 days.

Makes 1 cup; enough to marinate 1 cut-up chicken or 1½ pounds of lamb or seafood

TRY THIS!

Green tandoori spice paste was designed for seasoning chicken, but it's also great with lamb and seafood. Marinate meats for 6 to 8 hours, seafood for 3 to 6 hours, covered, in the refrigerator. You can also serve this spice paste as a relish.

HONEY CURE

TRY THIS!

This cure was designed for fish, but I wouldn't turn my nose up at it for turkey or chicken. Cover and marinate fish steaks for 1 to 2 hours, larger fish fillets for 2 to 3 hours, and whole fish overnight in the refrigerator. Chicken breasts need 2 to 4 hours; a whole bird, overnight.

A brine is used for salting; a marinade for flavoring. Somewhere between lies a mixture that both salts and flavors—a cure. Cures are used for curing seafood, chicken, or pork before smoking. This one works especially well with salmon and turkey. The salt partially dehydrates the meat, while the spicing and seasoning provide flavor. The honey adds a floral sweetness that's offset by the tang of the lemon zest.

4 cups cold water
¾ cup honey
½ cup coarse salt
   (kosher or sea)
4 strips of lemon zest

10 whole cloves
10 allspice berries
10 peppercorns
2 bay leaves

Combine all the ingredients in a bowl and whisk until the salt and honey are dissolved. Use right away.

Makes 4 cups; enough for 2 pounds of fish, poultry, or pork

BALINESE SPICE PASTE

T he Balinese make some of the most explosively flavorful barbecue in the world. Their secret? A tongue-blasting *base* (spice paste) perfumed with garlic, galangal, lemongrass, and fresh turmeric. Like many of the great spice pastes and basting mixtures of Southeast Asia, the flavorings are pounded to a paste, in a mortar with a pestle, then fried in a wok. This softens the harsh flavors of garlic and galangal and adds color and complexity. *Base* is the starting point of two of Bali's most famous grilled dishes: *babi guling* (spit-roasted suckling pig) and *bebek betutu* (duck barbecued in banana leaves). It also makes a great marinade for saté meat.

Because some of the called-for ingredients are not easy to find, I've noted readily available substitutes. Galangal and turmeric are members of the ginger family. Galangal is a striped rhizome with peppery tan flesh. Imagine ginger without the sweetness but with the bite of freshly ground black pepper. If you can't find it, use fresh ginger instead. Most Americans are familiar with ground turmeric, which is an ingredient in ballpark mustard, but not with the fresh root, which has powdered turmeric's color and flavor with some of fresh ginger's heat. Candlenuts are oily round nuts added for texture; macadamia nuts or cashews make acceptable substitutes. Shrimp paste is a malodorous paste of fermented shrimp and salt, which tastes a lot better than it sounds. You can approximate the flavor by substituting anchovy fillets or fish sauce. The recipe sounds more complicated than it really is. Using a food processor and a wok, you can prepare the spice paste in about 15 minutes.

TRY THIS!

Use this spice paste to season a suckling pig or pork shoulder, or poultry. Marinate all, covered, in the refrigerator for the length of time noted.

■ For suckling pig, spread some of the paste in the cavity and rub the remainder over the skin. Marinate overnight.

■ For pork shoulder, make a few deep holes in the meat with a knife and force some of the paste into the holes. Spread the remaining rub over the pork. Marinate overnight.

■ For a whole duck or chicken, spread some of the paste in the cavities and some under the skin. Spread the remainder over the bird. Marinate for 8 hours.

4 to 6 shallots, quartered

6 cloves garlic, peeled and cut in half

6 candlenuts or macadamia nuts

3 to 8 Thai chilies or jalapeño chilies (depending on your tolerance for heat)

3 to 4 stalks lemongrass, trimmed and finely chopped (¼ cup), or 4 strips of lemon zest

1½ tablespoons coarsely chopped fresh ginger

1½ tablespoons coarsely chopped fresh galangal (or use more ginger)

1 tablespoon coarsely chopped fresh turmeric or ½ teaspoon ground turmeric

1 teaspoon shrimp paste or 2 anchovy fillets or 1 tablespoon fish sauce

1 tablespoon light brown sugar

2 teaspoons coarse salt (kosher or sea)

2 teaspoons ground coriander

1 teaspoon freshly ground black pepper

2 tablespoons fresh lime juice

⅓ cup vegetable oil

1. If you have a large mortar and pestle, place the shallots, garlic, candlenuts, chilies, lemongrass, ginger, galangal (if using), turmeric, shrimp paste, brown sugar, salt, corian-

LEMONGRASS

This tall, leafy herb is one of the defining flavors of Southeast Asia. Fresh lemongrass has a delicate lemon flavor, but no tartness. As you can imagine, there's no substitute for fresh lemongrass, but dried is better than nothing. Lemon zest will give you some of the lemony flavor of fresh lemongrass, but not its haunting herbal aroma.

When buying lemongrass, choose fat, heavy stalks. Examine the stalks closely: There should be a bulbous base. Some misguided merchants sell only the leafy tops, which are useless. If you press your fingernail into the core, it should feel moist. Fresh lemon-grass is available at Asian markets and at an increasing number of supermarkets.

To prepare lemongrass for cooking, cut off the green leaves, leaving a firm, 3-to-4-inch-long, slightly bulbous stalk. (You can save the leaves and tie them together to make an offbeat basting brush.) Cut off the root end and strip off the outside leaves to expose the cream-colored core. This is the edible part of lemongrass, but even so it's quite fibrous, so mince it very fine or leave the pieces large enough that you can fish them out before serving.

der, and pepper in the mortar and pound to a smooth paste with the pestle. Work in the lime juice. Or purée the ingredients through the pepper in a food processor, scraping down the workbowl several times with a spatula. Add the lime juice at the end.

2. Heat a wok or skillet over high heat to smoking. Reduce the heat to medium and swirl in the oil. Add the spice paste and fry until fragrant and shiny and the oil starts to separate out, 5 minutes. Cool to room temperature. Use right away or transfer to a large jar, cover, and refrigerate. The spice paste will keep for several months.

Makes about 2 cups; enough for 4 to 5 pounds of pork or fish or 2 chickens or ducks

VARIATION

Substitute tamarind purée for the lime juice when making this paste for seafood.

BASTES, MOPS GLAZES OILS FINISHING SAUCES AND BUTTERS

For many people, barbecue is the true religion. Like any good faith, it has its holy water and its unguents—the bastes, mops, glazes, flavored oils, finishing sauces, and compound butters that will help them turn out righteous barbecue every time.

Bastes are designed to keep foods moist and flavorful during grilling. The Garlic Butter Baste on page 103 or Saffron Butter Baste on page 107 will turn apostates into believers. The same holds true for those flavorful liquids called mops, which are traditionally applied to large quantities of ribs and pork shoulders with a clean cotton floor mop. Check out the fiery Buffalo Mop (page 109) and Cider

Squirt (page 111). You'll also meet up with the new injector sauces, which you squirt into roasts and turkeys using a hypodermic needle.

Glazes and finishing sauces are used to give grilled meats an inviting sheen before serving. Some even come with a kick, such as the Irish Whiskey Glaze (page 116) or the Black Magic Finishing Sauce (page 126). As for flavored oils, ever since grill meisters began borrowing them from cutting-edge chefs in the 1990s, barbecue has never tasted better or looked more colorful.

This brings us to the last unction of an expertly seared steak or chop: flavored butter. A golden disk of Tarragon-Lemon Butter (page 128) or Mustard-Beer Butter (page 131) can turn a piece of grilled meat or fish into a religious experience. Keep a selection of these flavorful butters in your freezer and you're only a slice away from barbecue heaven.

BASTES AND MOPS

GARLIC BUTTER BASTE

TRY THIS!

Everything is fair game for this baste, including bread (grilling is the best way I know to make garlic bread), vegetables (especially mushrooms and corn), all types of seafood, poultry, meats, sweetbreads, and starches, such as grilled polenta or grits.

Brush the baste on the food while it's grilling, using a longhandled basting brush. Take care to brush just enough baste on the meat to coat it. Don't slop it on, or the dripping butter will catch fire, resulting in flare-ups and giving a sooty taste to your food.

This aromatic concoction is, undoubtedly, the world's most popular baste for barbecue. During my travels on the world's barbecue trail, I enjoyed variations of garlicky butter in places as diverse as Brazil, India, Malaysia, France, and Turkey. Its virtue lies in its simplicity—the reek of garlic and the moisturizing sweetness of butter— yet within these simple parameters, a host of variations exist. Some cooks add parsley, or cilantro, or hot pepper flakes, or paprika, or lemon juice. Others deliberately burn the butter, at least partially, to achieve the golden brown color and distinctive nutty flavor that the French call *beurre noisette*: hazelnut butter. (Why not make a real hazelnut butter baste by adding chopped toasted hazelnuts and a shot of Frangelico liqueur?) Use the following recipe as a starting point, customizing the flavorings to suit your taste.

BASIC BASTE
8 tablespoons (1 stick)
    salted butter
3 cloves garlic, minced
½ teaspoon freshly ground or
    cracked black pepper

OPTIONAL FLAVORINGS
¼ cup finely chopped fresh
    flat-leaf parsley or cilantro
1 teaspoon sweet or hot
    paprika

½ to 1 teaspoon hot pepper
    flakes
1 tablespoon drained capers
1 tablespoon chopped
    toasted hazelnuts or
    almonds (see box,
    page 105)
2 tablespoons fresh lemon
    juice
½ teaspoon grated lemon
    zest

Melt the butter in a heavy saucepan over medium heat. Add the garlic and pepper and any of the optional flavorings (except the lemon juice), if using, and cook until the garlic pieces are translucent and fragrant, but not brown, 2 minutes. Remove the pan from the heat. Add the lemon juice. The baste can be made ahead of time, but it's so quick and easy to prepare, you might as well make it as you need it. If storing, transfer to a jar, cover, cool to room temperature, and refrigerate. The baste will keep for several weeks. Reheat to melt the butter before using.

Makes 1 cup; enough for 2 to 3 pounds of seafood or meat

VARIATIONS

■ For a milder garlic flavor, peel the cloves and gently crush them with the side of a cleaver, but do not chop. Cook them in the butter until soft, fragrant, and just beginning to brown.

■ For *beurre noisette* flavor, cook the butter over medium heat until it starts to brown. Add the garlic and continue cooking until the garlic is translucent and fragrant and the butter is golden brown.

■ For a Mediterranean accent, prepare the baste with extra virgin olive oil instead of butter. For extra flavor, add a sprig of rosemary.

SESAME-SOY BUTTER BASTE

I first tasted this savory baste at a Japanese restaurant in Jakarta. It's one of those preparations that transcend national borders, offering the dulcet richness of butter, the salty tang of soy sauce, the nuttiness of sesame plus the indispensable aroma of garlic. Seldom do so few ingredients deliver such a wallop of flavor.

TRY THIS!

Brush the baste on grilled chicken, pork, seafood, vegetables, or tofu. Serve any extra baste as a sauce.

8 tablespoons (1 stick) unsalted butter

2 tablespoons toasted sesame seeds (see box, below)

2 cloves garlic, minced

2 scallions (white and green parts), finely chopped

2 tablespoons soy sauce

½ teaspoon freshly ground black pepper

Melt the butter in a saucepan over medium heat. Add the sesame seeds, garlic, and scallions and cook until the garlic and scallions are aromatic but not brown, 3 minutes. Stir in the soy sauce and pepper. Simmer for 2 minutes. This is so quick and easy to prepare, there's no reason not to make it right before using. However, you can make it in advance. If storing, transfer to a jar, cover, cool to room temperature, and refrigerate. The baste will keep for up to 1 week. Reheat to melt the butter before using.

Makes ¾ cup, enough to baste 2 to 3 pounds of seafood, poultry, meat, or vegetables

TOASTING SESAME SEEDS AND NUTS

In many recipes in this book you'll be instructed to toast sesame seeds or nuts in a dry skillet. The reason is simple: Toasting intensifies their flavor, adding a smoky dimension as well. To toast sesame seeds or nuts, preheat a dry heavy skillet over medium heat. Add the seeds or nuts and toast, shaking the pan to ensure even toasting, until lightly colored and fragrant, 2 to 4 minutes. Immediately transfer the seeds or nuts to a bowl. (If you leave them in the pan, they'll continue to cook, and possibly burn, even after the pan is off the heat.) If you've never toasted sesame seeds or nuts, you'll be amazed at how much this simple procedure boosts the flavor.

SMOKE BASTE

TRY THIS!

Brush the baste on whenever a smoky flavor is desired. It works equally well with chicken, pork, beef, and seafood. Use it sparingly, trying to avoid drips, because the butter will cause flare-ups, which would give the food a sooty flavor.

Ifirst created smoke baste for some New York friends who wanted the smoky taste of barbecued ribs but didn't have access to a grill. (Horror of horrors—they had to cook the ribs in the oven!) I liked the baste so much, I've taken to using it to add or reinforce the smoke flavor of all sorts of grilled dishes, especially when I don't have time to use wood chips. Where there's smoke there's fire, goes the old saying; the heat in the baste comes from Tabasco sauce. Add as much as you can stand, or none at all if a nonfiery smoke flavor is desired.

4 tablespoons (½ stick) salted butter
1 clove garlic, minced

1 teaspoon Tabasco or other hot sauce (optional)
½ teaspoon liquid smoke

Melt the butter in a saucepan over medium heat. Add the garlic and cook until fragrant but not brown, 2 minutes. Stir in the Tabasco sauce, if using, and liquid smoke and cook for 1 minute. This baste is so easy, make it as you need it.

Makes ½ cup; enough for 2 pounds of meat

LIQUID SMOKE

Dr. Richard Davis, inventor of K.C. Masterpiece barbecue sauce, hit the nail on the head. "What Americans really like about barbecue isn't so much the tomatoes or vinegar or mustard. It's the smoke." This realization led the doctor to enrich his legendary Kansas City–style sauce with a few drops of liquid smoke. The rest, as they say, is history, for K.C. Masterpiece became the nation's best-selling premium barbecue sauce.

Long before the advent of refrigeration or even salting, humans preserved meats by drying them over smoky fires. Liquid smoke is a natural product, made by dissolving wood smoke in water. Some manufacturers add a little vinegar or brown sugar for flavoring and caramel for color.

Liquid smoke is a uniquely American condiment, manufactured by several companies, including Colgin and Wright's. You can now buy several flavors, including hickory and mesquite. It's strong stuff, so use it sparingly; a few drops are usually enough to give any barbecue a rich, smoky aroma. Too much will quickly overpower the sauce.

SAFFRON BUTTER BASTE

What makes Persian barbecue so extraordinary? First, there's the marinade—Iranians aren't afraid to give their meats a tenderizing bath in a yogurt or lemon juice–based marinade for a full day or even two. Then, there's the basting mixture and here butter, lemon juice, and saffron conspire to make one of the most succulent anointments ever brushed on grilled chicken, shish kebab, or lamb. Note: When buying saffron, look for threads not powder. The threads (the stamens of the saffron crocus) are harder to adulterate than saffron powder, so you're more likely to get the real McCoy.

½ **teaspoon saffron threads**
1 **tablespoon hot water**
8 **tablespoons (1 stick)**
    salted butter, melted
3 **tablespoons fresh lemon**
    juice

1 **clove garlic, minced**
½ **teaspoon freshly ground**
    black pepper

TRY THIS!

Brush this fragrant butter on grilled chicken, game hen, quail, lamb, beef, pork, and shish kebab. It also makes an awesome bruschetta (grilled bread).

1. Crumble the saffron threads between your thumb and forefinger and place in a small bowl with the water. Let the saffron infuse for 10 minutes.

2. Combine the saffron and the remaining ingredients in a saucepan and cook over low heat for a few minutes to warm the garlic. Use right away.

Makes ¾ cup; enough for 3 pounds of meat

COCONUT CURRY BASTE

Gurney Road in Penang, Malaysia, is one of the meccas of the world's barbecue trail—a broad, bay front avenue lined with hundreds of open-air food stalls that serve some of the tastiest satés in Asia. The following basting sauce is part of what makes Malaysian barbecue so succulent.

Coconut milk is available canned at Asian and Hispanic

markets and most supermarkets. Be sure to buy unsweetened coconut milk (not coconut cream).

2 tablespoons vegetable oil

3 cloves garlic, minced

1 large shallot, minced

1 stalk lemongrass, trimmed and minced, or ½ teaspoon grated lemon zest

1 tablespoon curry powder

1 cup unsweetened coconut milk

1 tablespoon fish sauce or soy sauce

1. Heat the oil in a wok or saucepan over medium heat. Add the garlic, shallot, and lemongrass and cook, stirring with a wooden spoon, until softened, 3 minutes. Add the curry powder and cook until the vegetables are golden brown, 1 to 2 minutes more. Do not burn.

2. Stir in the coconut milk and bring to a boil. Stir in the fish sauce. The baste can be made ahead and refrigerated, but it's so quick and easy, I usually make it as I need it. If made ahead, transfer to a jar, cover, cool, and refrigerate. The baste will keep for up to 5 days. Reheat before using.

Makes 1¼ cups; enough for 2 pounds of meat

TRY THIS!

Traditionally, this baste would be brushed on grilled fish and satés. You can also use it on grilled pork loin or chicken breast.

GREEK LEMON-GARLIC BASTE

TRY THIS!

Brush the baste on spit-roasted lamb, lamb or beef kebabs, grilled chicken (the high oil content makes it very good for chicken breasts), and seafood, from shrimp to fish to octopus. Brush it on with a long-handled basting brush or long sprig of

Wherever Greeks gather, you'll find a fire for grilling, and wherever you find Greeks grilling, you'll find this simple, flavorful baste. For when you combine fragrant dark Greek olive oil with fresh garlic and lemon juice, you wind up with a taste that's as ancient and soulful as Greek civilization itself.

Greek oregano has a different flavor—more minty and aromatic—than the Italian-style oregano familiar to most North Americans. So, for best results here, buy oregano at a Middle East market.

fresh rosemary. You'll need to stir the baste each time you use it to mix the oil and lemon juice. Note that the dripping oil may cause flare-ups. For this reason, set up the grill so that the fire is next to, not directly under, the food. This baste is well suited for the rotisserie.

½ cup fresh lemon juice

3 cloves garlic, minced or crushed

1 teaspoon coarse salt (kosher or sea)

1 teaspoon cracked black pepper

2 teaspoons dried oregano, preferably Greek

1 cup extra virgin olive oil

Combine the lemon juice, garlic, salt, pepper, and oregano in a bowl and stir or whisk until the salt crystals are dissolved. Stir in the oil. This baste tastes best used within 6 hours of making. Transfer any leftovers to a jar, cover, and refrigerate. The baste will keep for several days; let it come to room temperature and shake before using.

Makes 1½ cups; enough for 3 pounds of meat or seafood

BUFFALO MOP

TRY THIS!

The obvious use for Buffalo Mop is on grilled or barbecued chicken wings. Marinate the wings in half the mop in a covered baking dish in the refrigerator for at least 4 hours, preferably overnight. Use the remainder of the mop for basting, but don't start mopping until the outside of the chicken is cooked. This mop is also great on chicken breasts and thighs, turkey, and even pork.

October 30, 1964, may not be a red-letter day in history. No rocket ship blasted off for the moon, no landmark presidential speech was made, no Internet stock went public. But human happiness was immeasurably enriched on that fateful day, when Teressa Belissimo, owner of the Anchor Bar in Buffalo, New York, invented buffalo wings. Faced with an extra shipment of chicken wings and some unexpected guests, she had the idea to deep-fry them, then slather them with melted butter and hot sauce. The essence of buffalo wings is the sauce—a fiery amalgam of melted butter and Tabasco. That was the inspiration for this invigorating mop.

8 tablespoons (1 stick) salted butter, cut into 1-inch pieces

3 cloves garlic, minced

2 tablespoons tomato paste

½ cup dry white wine

2 tablespoons distilled white vinegar

¼ to ½ cup Tabasco sauce (depending on your tolerance for heat)

Melt 2 tablespoons of the butter in a saucepan over medium heat. Add the garlic and cook until fragrant but not brown, 3 minutes. Stir in the tomato paste and cook for 2 minutes. Add the wine and vinegar and bring to a boil, whisking to dissolve the tomato paste. Add the Tabasco sauce and remaining butter and simmer for 2 minutes.

I suppose you could make this mop ahead, but why bother? It takes 5 minutes to assemble on the spot.

Makes 1½ cups mop; enough for 2 pounds of meat

TABASCO SAUCE

Tabasco sauce is the world's most famous hot sauce. If you had a nickel for every bottle sold in a day, you'd have a small fortune. If you made the same deal for a year, you could probably retire.

Tabasco sauce takes its name from the Mexican state of Tabasco—itself named for an Indian word meaning humid soil. The name aptly describes the place where Tabasco sauce is produced: Avery Island, Louisiana. Located off the coast, 140 miles west of New Orleans, Avery Island has a hot, humid climate that's perfect for growing the fiery, small, red chili peppers—members of the cayenne family—that give Tabasco sauce its color and heat. As for the flavor, it comes from a unique process in which the chilies are mashed to a pulp, mixed with vinegar and local salt, placed in white oak barrels to ferment, then aged for up to 36 months. What results is a hot sauce that has a lot more going for it than heat. Tabasco sauce is hot, tart, salty, and intensely aromatic. The barrel aging gives it a complexity unique among the world's hot sauces. This complexity makes the Tabasco indispensable to sauce meisters and pit bosses.

Tabasco sauce was invented by Edmund McIlhenny, who planted his first red pepper on Avery Island in the 1860s. By 1868, he was making and selling his sauce, which he packaged in perfume bottles. Today, Tabasco is the world's best-selling hot sauce. The McIlhenny family ships more than 50 million bottles to more than 100 countries each year.

CIDER SQUIRT

One of the secrets of world-class barbecue is consistent and conscientious basting while the meat is cooking. The traditional tool for basting is literally a kitchen mop (hence the term mop sauce), but more and more pit jockeys are using spray bottles or misters. Here's a simple baste that's short on preparation time but long on flavor. The recipe was inspired by a Memphis-based barbecue team I met a few years back called Crispy Critters.

2 cups apple cider
¾ cup cider vinegar
½ cup bourbon
½ cup water

¼ cup Worcestershire sauce
¼ cup fresh lemon juice
½ teaspoon salt

Combine all the ingredients in a heavy saucepan and bring to a boil. Reduce the heat and simmer the sauce for 5 minutes. Let cool to room temperature. Transfer the squirt to a spray bottle and use right away or refrigerate. Use within 1 or 2 days of making.

Makes 4½ cups; enough for 4 pounds of meat

INJECTOR SAUCES

Welcome to grilling in the new millennium! Barbecue acquires medical precision in a device designed to produce the most succulent chickens, turkeys, pork shoulders, and rib roasts you've ever tasted: a meat injector. The theory is simple enough: The slender needle enables you to shoot a flavorful liquid deep inside the meat. Injector sauces are simple, but you should avoid chopped garlic and large flakes of herbs and spices, which risk clogging the holes in the needle. Many companies make meat injectors: One good brand is Chef William's Cajun Injector (see Mail-Order Sources, page 281). Below are three injector sauces that guarantee a succulent turkey or roast every time.

BASIC BUTTER INJECTOR SAUCE

TRY THIS!

Place the sauce in the injector and inject it in several places into the deepest part of the meat.

Here's my homemade version of what makes a commercial buttery turkey buttery. Ideally, you'd use unsalted homemade chicken broth. Canned broth is quite salty, so if you use it, the butter should be unsalted.

1 cup unsalted chicken broth, preferably homemade

4 tablespoons (½ stick) salted butter

2 tablespoons fresh lemon juice

½ teaspoon garlic powder

Coarse salt (kosher or sea), to taste

½ teaspoon freshly ground white pepper

Combine all the ingredients, except for the salt, in a nonreactive saucepan and warm over medium heat just until the butter melts and the salt crystals dissolve. Correct the seasoning, adding salt if needed. Cool to warm room temperature (the butter should remain liquid), then put it in the injector and fire away.

Makes 1½ cups; enough for 4 chickens or 1 to 2 turkeys or roasts

CAJUN INJECTOR SAUCE

Most of the commercial injector sauces are manufactured in Louisiana, so I thought it only fitting to offer a recipe for a Cajun variation. Use the Ragin' Cajun Rub from this book or your favorite commercial brand.

TRY THIS!

Use as described on the facing page. The injector sauce goes particularly well with turkey or chicken.

TRY THIS!

Use as described on the facing page. This sauce goes especially well with chicken or pork.

1 cup unsalted chicken broth, preferably homemade

4 tablespoons (½ stick) salted butter

2 tablespoons white wine or dry vermouth

4 tablespoons Ragin' Cajun Rub (page 30) or a good commercial brand

½ teaspoon freshly ground white pepper

Coarse salt (kosher or sea), to taste

Combine all the ingredients, except the salt, in a nonreactive saucepan and warm over medium heat just until the butter melts and the salt crystals dissolve. Correct the seasoning, adding salt if needed. Cool to warm room temperature (the butter should remain liquid), then put it in the injector and fire away.

Makes 1½ cups; enough for 4 chickens or 2 turkeys

ASIAN INJECTOR SAUCE

Based on a traditional Chinese dish called master sauce chicken, this sauce lends a sweet, anisey Asian accent to whatever you happen to be grilling.

1 cup unsalted chicken broth, preferably homemade

3 tablespoons sesame oil

2 tablespoons rice wine or dry sherry

2 tablespoons soy sauce

2 tablespoons honey

½ teaspoon Chinese Five-Spice-Powder, preferably

homemade (page 50), or use a good commercial brand

½ teaspoon garlic powder

½ teaspoon onion powder

½ teaspoon freshly ground white pepper

½ teaspoon ground cinnamon

½ teaspoon coarse salt (kosher or sea)

Combine all the ingredients, except the salt, in a nonreactive saucepan and warm over medium heat just until the butter melts. Correct the seasoning, adding salt if needed. Cool to warm room temperature (the butter should remain liquid), then put it in the injector and fire away. This should be used as soon as it is ready.

Makes 1½ cups; enough for 4 chickens or 2 turkeys

GLAZES AND OILS

NOT-JUST-FOR-HAM GLAZE

TRY THIS!

The first logical use for this glaze is ham, either a whole fresh or cooked ham (smoked using the indirect grilling method; see page 5) or a ham steak charred directly over the coals. Pork loin or chops benefit from the clove-scented sweetness of this glaze; so do chicken, turkey, and quail. It is also delicious on grilled sweet potatoes.

This sweet-spicy glaze was inspired by traditional American ham, that mustard-painted, brown sugar–crusted, clove-studded glory that graces many a holiday table. To make a glaze, I combined these ingredients with just enough rum and butter and boiled them to a thick syrup. What results is good enough to eat right off a spoon. It's so good, you won't want to limit it just to ham.

½ cup (packed) dark brown
   sugar
8 tablespoons (1 stick)
   unsalted butter, cut into
   1-inch pieces
½ cup dark rum

3 tablespoons Dijon mustard
1 tablespoon cider vinegar
1 scant teaspoon ground
   cloves
¼ teaspoon freshly ground
   black pepper

Place all the ingredients in a heavy nonreactive saucepan and bring to a boil over high heat, whisking steadily. Reduce the heat to medium and simmer the mixture until thick and syrupy, about 5 minutes. Use right away.

Makes 1¼ cups; enough for 4 pounds of meat or poultry

PINEAPPLE GARLIC GLAZE

We don't normally link pineapple and garlic in North America, but elsewhere in the world, especially in Southeast Asia, these flavorings are often combined to make a barbecue sauce or relish that plays the brassy acidity of the fruit against the aromatic earthiness of the fried garlic. Frying the garlic heightens this earthy quality, adding a nutty flavor component, too. The smoky flavor is reinforced by the Scotch whisky. The net result is heaven sent for seafood, poultry, and pork.

TRY THIS!

You can use this tasty glaze on anything, but my first choice would go to a light meat, like chicken, turkey, Cornish game hens, fish, lobster, scallops, or pork. Start brushing it on the last 5 to 10 minutes of cooking.

4 tablespoons (½ stick)
   unsalted butter
4 cloves garlic, thinly sliced
1 cup (packed) dark brown
   sugar
1 cup Scotch whisky

½ cup pineapple juice
½ cup ketchup
3 tablespoons fresh lemon
   juice
½ teaspoon freshly ground
   black pepper

1. Melt the butter in a heavy nonreactive saucepan over medium heat. Add the garlic and cook until the slices turn the palest gold, 3 to 4 minutes.

2. Stir in the remaining ingredients and simmer over medium heat until thick and flavorful, about 5 minutes. Use right away.

*Makes 2 cups; enough for
2 to 3 pounds of meat or seafood*

TANGERINE LACQUER GLAZE

This sauce was inspired by the culinary lacquers of Japan and China—sweet, soy-based glazes traditionally brushed on chicken and duck to give them a shiny, lacquered appearance. I decided to make one with the most delicious of all Florida citrus fruits: fresh tangerine. The result is a glaze that pits the briny tang of the soy sauce against the perfumed sweetness of honey and tangerines. Add sesame oil, garlic, scallion whites (save the greens for garnishing the finished dish) and ginger and everyone comes out a winner. When tangerines aren't in season, I use oranges.

The best way to remove the zest from the tangerines is with a vegetable peeler. Star anise is a star-shaped spice with a distinctive smoky licoricey flavor; you can find it at Asian markets and gourmet shops, or simply omit it.

½ cup soy sauce

½ cup fresh tangerine juice

⅓ cup honey

3 tablespoons Asian (dark) sesame oil

5 strips (½ inch each) tangerine zest

3 cloves garlic, peeled and lightly crushed with the side of a cleaver

3 scallions (white parts only), trimmed, lightly crushed with the side of a cleaver

3 slices (¼ inch thick each) fresh ginger, lightly crushed with the side of a cleaver

1 cinnamon stick (3 inches)

1 star anise (optional)

Place all the ingredients in a heavy saucepan and bring to a boil over medium heat. Reduce the heat slightly and simmer, uncovered, until the mixture is thick and syrupy, 6 to 8 minutes. Strain the glaze into a bowl. Use right away.

Makes 1½ cups; enough for 3 pounds of meat or seafood

IRISH WHISKEY GLAZE

This silky glaze owes its kick to a generous dose of Irish whiskey and its good manners to a mellowing shot of Baileys Irish Cream.

½ cup (packed) dark brown sugar

½ cup Irish whiskey (preferably Bushmills)

¼ cup Baileys Irish Cream

¼ cup soy sauce

¼ cup ketchup

4 tablespoons (½ stick) unsalted butter

3 tablespoons of soy sauce

2 tablespoons heavy (or whipping) cream

2 tablespoons fresh lemon juice

1 teaspoon garlic powder

½ teaspoon freshly ground black pepper

Combine all the ingredients in a heavy saucepan and bring to a simmer over medium heat. Briskly simmer until thick and flavorful, about 5 minutes. Use right away.

Makes about 2 cups; enough for 3 pounds of meat

THREE VARIATIONS ON A THEME OF GARLIC OIL

Barbecue without garlic is a little like grilling without fire. I can't think of a single culture that *doesn't* use this odoriferous bulb as a seasoning. One of the easiest ways to endow grilled breads, seafood, chicken, and vegetables with a sit-up-and-take-notice flavor is to brush or baste them with garlic oil. There are three ways to make garlic oil. The first will give you the strongest garlic taste, but it's also the most perishable. The second, fried garlic oil, will give your food a soulful Portuguese accent; while the third, roasted garlic oil, highlights the earthy sweetness of garlic. Whichever oil you make, start with whole fresh heads of garlic, not the prechopped garlic you can buy in jars in the supermarket.

FRESH GARLIC OIL

If you like garlic, you'll love this odoriferous oil. Just be sure your date eats some, too!

TRY THIS!

Brush this fragrant elixir on anything—bread, seafood, poultry, vegetables, beef. Use it before or during grilling. Don't serve it as a sauce.

3 to 6 cloves garlic, chopped

1 cup extra virgin olive oil or canola oil

Combine the ingredients in a blender or food processor. Process until the garlic is puréed. This oil tastes best used within a few hours of making. Cover and store any extra in the refrigerator, but use it within 2 days. After that it will take on a heavy flavor. Bring it to room temperature before using.

Makes 1 cup; enough for 3 to 4 pounds of meat, seafood, or vegetables

VARIATIONS

Add other flavorings to this essential oil as you wish, including fresh herbs (especially basil), spices (black pepper or cumin goes well), chilies (fresh or dried), lemon or orange zest, or even a combination of flavorings.

FRIED GARLIC OIL

One of the best restaurants in Brazil is a fish house called Candidos, located in a seaside village a couple of hours south of Rio. What gives the food here its haunting flavor is a seasoning that's as old as the Portuguese heritage of the restaurant's owner, Carmen Sousa Sampaio: fried garlic oil.

TRY THIS!

Fried garlic oil is great for marinating and basting but even better as a condiment for spooning over grilled fare once on the table. It goes especially well with grilled seafood, vegetables, and pork.

2 heads of garlic, broken into cloves and peeled	1 cup extra virgin olive oil, preferably Portuguese

1. Finely chop the garlic by hand or in a mini-processor. Heat the oil in a heavy saucepan over medium heat. Add the garlic and cook until light golden brown, 6 to 8 minutes. Don't burn the garlic; it will become bitter. Immediately, transfer the garlic and oil to a heatproof bowl.

2. Use right away or transfer to a jar, cover, and store in the refrigerator. The oil will keep for several weeks. Bring it to room temperature before using.

Makes 1 cup; enough for 3 to 4 pounds of meat, seafood, or vegetables

HOW TO PEEL AND SMASH GARLIC

Forget about using a garlic press. When I went to cooking school in Paris, I learned a simple way to pulverize garlic, which I use to this day. To peel garlic, lightly flatten each clove with the side of a chef's knife or cleaver. Once cracked, the skin will slip off easily. To smash the garlic, cut it crosswise into ¼-inch-thick slices. Stand each slice on end on a cutting board near the edge. Place the side of the knife or cleaver on top of it, blade angled downward slightly, and slam the top of the blade with the heel of your hand. The garlic will be reduced instantly to an aromatic purée.

ROASTED GARLIC OIL

TRY THIS!

This precious oil is too subtle to use as a marinade, although it makes a nice baste for delicate grilled fare, like seafood or poultry. Roasted garlic oil tastes best spooned or drizzled over grilled food once it's brought to the table.

As we Americans discovered in the 1980s, roasting transforms garlic from a taste bud bully to a culinary sophisticate. Specifically, it eliminates the nose-jarring pungency, bringing out an earthy, aromatic sweetness you'd never expect garlic to possess. This truth is known to anyone who has spread a roasted garlic clove on a crostini. Over the years, I've experimented with lots of ways to roast garlic and I've found that poaching it in oil works best.

2 heads of garlic, broken into cloves and peeled

1 cup extra virgin olive oil

1. Place the garlic and oil in a heavy saucepan and cook over medium-low heat. Roast until the garlic cloves are soft and golden, 10 to 15 minutes. Do not let burn. Transfer the garlic and oil to a heatproof bowl and let cool to room temperature.

2. Use right away or transfer the garlic cloves and oil to a jar, cover, and refrigerate. The oil will keep for several weeks. Bring it to room temperature before using.

Makes 1 cup; enough for 3 to 4 pounds of meat, seafood, or vegetables

SWEET BASIL OIL WITH GARLIC

I like to think of this oil as Provence in a bottle. It's wonderfully aromatic and it looks as good as it tastes. You can certainly use basil oil for marinating and basting, which you should, and you can also drizzle it over grilled food the moment you're ready to serve it. When the cool oil hits the hot meat or fish, a burst of Mediterranean flavor is released. Even if you miss the food, the oil looks cool in telegraphic dashes or dots on the white part of the plate.

I give two methods for making basil oil.

FRESH BASIL OIL

The uncooked version of this oil gives you the most direct basil taste, but the flavor fades fairly quickly.

1 bunch fresh basil,
   stemmed (2 cups loosely
   packed basil leaves)
½ cup (loosely packed) fresh
   spinach leaves, stemmed

1 clove garlic, chopped
2 cups extra virgin olive oil

   1. Rinse the basil and spinach in cold water and blot or spin the leaves dry. Place the basil, spinach, garlic, and oil in a blender and blend until very finely chopped. Transfer the oil to a bowl and let steep for 4 hours at room temperature.

   2. Strain the oil through a fine-mesh strainer into a large jar. The oil tastes best used within 2 or 3 days of making. Cover and refrigerate, but let it come to room temperature before serving.

Makes 2 cups

BLANCHED BASIL OIL

Blanching the basil produces a brighter, cleaner tasting, longer lasting oil. Make a batch as the summer basil season winds down so that you have some to take you through the fall.

1 tablespoon coarse salt
   (kosher or sea)
1 bunch fresh basil,
   stemmed (2 cups loosely
   packed basil leaves)
½ cup (packed) fresh
   spinach leaves, stemmed

2 cups extra virgin olive oil
3 cloves garlic, peeled and
   crushed with the side of
   a cleaver

TRY THIS!

The beauty of this oil is that you can use it as a sauce, baste, or marinade. Seafood, poultry, pork, veal, grilled polenta, and all manner of grilled vegetables seem to come alive in its presence. To make a simple marinade, combine 2 parts basil oil with 1 part fresh lemon juice.

---

1. Bring 2 quarts water and the salt to a rapid boil in a large saucepan. Have ready a large bowl of ice water.

2. Rinse the basil and spinach, add to the boiling water, and blanch for 15 seconds. Drain in a colander, then plunge the greens into the ice water. Drain well, then squeeze the greens in the palm of your hand to wring out all the water.

3. Heat ¼ cup of the oil in a small frying pan over medium heat. Add the garlic and cook until golden brown, about 4 minutes. Remove the pan from the heat.

4. Transfer the garlic and oil to a blender with the blanched basil and spinach and the remaining oil and blend until very finely chopped. Transfer the oil to a bowl and let steep for 4 hours at room temperature. Strain the oil through a fine-mesh strainer into a large jar. Use right away or cover and store in the refrigerator, but let it warm to room temperature before serving. The oil will keep for several weeks.

Makes 2 cups

TRY THIS!

Use as you would the uncooked oil.

LEMON PEPPER OIL

This simple oil brings together my three favorite flavors for grilling: lemon, extra virgin olive oil, and black pepper. You can buy precracked black peppercorns, but you'll get more bang for the buck if you crack whole peppercorns yourself (see page 24)—especially if you use the Talamanca peppercorns imported from Honduras by my friends Bill and Danny Brugger.

2 large lemons, scrubbed and dried
3 tablespoons cracked black pepper

1 cup extra virgin olive oil
1 cup grapeseed or canola oil

1. Using a vegetable peeler, remove the zest of the lemon in broad thin strips. Place these strips in a small frying pan with the peppercorns and grapeseed oil. Place the

TRY THIS!

Lemon pepper oil works best with delicate grilled foods: shellfish (especially shrimp and scallops), white fish, chicken breasts, quail, pork chops, and veal. It's fantastic on grilled vegetables, from asparagus to zucchini. You can use it as a marinade, baste, or sauce.

pan over medium-low heat and cook until the peppercorns sizzle and the lemon zest strips just begin to brown, 8 to 12 minutes. Transfer the mixture to a heatproof bowl.

2. Add the remaining olive oil. Cool to room temperature, then grind the mixture in a blender. Let stand at room temperature for 4 hours. Strain the oil through a fine-mesh strainer into a large jar. Use right away or cover and refrigerate. The oil will keep its brisk flavor for up to 1 month. Bring it to room temperature before using.

Makes 2 cups

VARIATION

Combine the ingredients in a blender, uncooked, and blend well. Infuse and strain as described above. This gives you a great-tasting lemon oil without any cooking.

CURRY OIL

I love this oil—its golden color, its fragrant scent, its pungent flavor. Cooking mellows the taste of the curry powder, so even if you don't normally fancy curry, you may still find this oil to your liking.

TRY THIS!

Curry oil works equally well as a marinade, baste, or sauce. It goes great with seafood, poultry, pork, and veal, and it's robust enough to stand up to lamb and beef. It's also delicious drizzled over grilled vegetables, especially eggplant, and tofu.

2 cups canola oil
1 medium onion, minced
3 cloves garlic, minced

1 tablespoon minced fresh
   ginger
2 tablespoons pure curry
   powder (not a blend)

1. Heat the oil in a frying pan over medium heat. Add the onion, garlic, ginger, and curry powder and cook until the ingredients are golden brown, 2 to 3 minutes. Remove the pan from the heat and let cool.

2. Transfer the mixture to a blender and blend until very finely chopped. Transfer the oil to a bowl and let stand for 4 hours at room temperature. Strain the oil through a fine-mesh strainer into a large jar. Use right away or cover and refrigerate. The oil will keep for several months. Bring it to room temperature before using.

Makes 2 cups

CHINESE FIRE OIL

TRY THIS!

The Chinese use this fiery oil the way we would a good hot sauce, that is drizzled over every imaginable type of main dish, not to mention over appetizers and salads. A few teaspoons will enliven any marinade. The oil is probably too fiery to use for basting. (That doesn't mean that some chili head out there won't try it!)

I first encountered this fiery oil in, of all places, Paris. The year was 1976; the place, the La Varenne cooking school; and its creator was my friend Nina Simonds, just back from a culinary apprenticeship in Taipei. Nina heated some peanut oil in a wok and tossed in a handful of fiery, tiny, dried red chilies. The smoke that billowed through the room burned our eyes, savaged our throats, and made our teeth clench with discomfort. Now *that* was chili oil! Over the years, I've used this oil to invigorate everything from grilled tofu to spare-ribs and I've varied the chilies and flavorings, adding black or Sichuan peppercorns, garlic, ginger, scallions, or other seasonings. Which is to say that you should consider the following recipe as a broad outline, not a formula to be followed to the letter.

The best way to remove the zest from the tangerines is to use a vegetable peeler.

Note: Run the exhaust fan over your stove at high speed when preparing this oil. Better still, prepare it on the side burner of your grill. It generates a lot of smoke.

1 cup peanut oil

½ to 1 cup small dried Chinese chilies or other dried chilies (the more you use, the hotter the oil will be)

2 tablespoons Sichuan peppercorns or black peppercorns

4 scallions (white parts only), trimmed and crushed with the side of a cleaver

4 slices (each ¼ inch thick) fresh ginger, crushed with the side of a cleaver

4 cloves garlic, peeled and crushed with the side of a cleaver

4 strips of tangerine or orange zest

1 cup Asian (dark) sesame oil

1. Place the peanut oil in a wok or deep, heavy saucepan and heat over high heat to 375° on a deep-fry thermometer. Add the remaining ingredients, except for the sesame oil, fry for 10 seconds, then remove the wok or pan

from the heat. Transfer to a heatproof bowl, stir in the sesame oil, and let the oil steep at room temperature for 1 to 2 hours.

2. Pour the oil through a fine-mesh strainer into a large jar. Use right away or cover and refrigerate. The oil will keep for several months. Bring it to room temperature before using.

VARIATION:

To make an interesting dipping sauce, combine equal parts chili oil, soy sauce, rice wine, and rice vinegar, adding sugar or honey to taste for sweetness.

Makes 2 cups

MEXICAN CHILI OIL

Give fire oil a Mexican accent by preparing the preceding recipe using dried Mexican chilies. Pequins or de árbol chilies will give you a ferocious back-of-the-throat heat. Dried chipotles will give you an interesting smoke flavor. For a milder chili oil, you could use guajillo or dried New Mexican red chilies. Run the exhaust fan over your stove on high or prepare outdoors for this one as well.

TRY THIS!

This baby makes a great drizzle for *carnitas* and fajitas. Use it in Mexican or Tex-Mex marinades. Sprinkle it on quesadillas.

2 cups canola or peanut oil
½ to 1 cup dried Mexican chilies or other dried chilies (the more you use, the hotter the oil will be)
1 tablespoon black peppercorns

1 teaspoon cumin seeds
½ medium onion
2 cloves garlic, peeled and crushed with the side of a cleaver
4 strips of orange zest

1. Place the oil in a wok or deep, heavy saucepan and heat over high heat to 375° on a deep-fry thermometer. Add the remaining ingredients, fry for 10 seconds, then remove the wok or pan from the heat. Transfer to a heatproof bowl and let stand at room temperature for 1 to 2 hours.

2. Pour the oil through a fine-mesh strainer into a large jar. Use right away or cover and refrigerate. The oil will keep for several months. Bring it to room temperature before using.

Makes 2 cups

TRUFFLE OIL

Undoubtedly, this will be the most expensive flavored oil you've ever made. But it's worth every penny, because nothing captures the splendor of Italy's Piedmont region in the fall like olive oil flavored with the highly perfumed, mystical white truffle.

Truffles are aromatic fungi that grow beneath oak and other trees. Italians use specially trained dogs to find them, often hunting truffles in the dead of night to keep their location secret from competitors. Truffles are ugly, resembling misshapen lumps of tan or gray clay, with a powerful musky smell. They're hideously expensive—even in bad years. (White truffles can cost as much as $1,600 per pound!) So why on earth would anyone bother to buy them? The simple fact is that white truffles possess a haunting aroma and flavor unique in the world of food. As with fine brandy or aged cheese, what initially seems off-putting quickly becomes addictive.

Truffle oil is a great way to capture the flavor of fresh truffle; it's also a way of making a little go a long way.

Fresh truffles can be found at gourmet shops from October to January or ordered by mail from one of the sources on page 281.

1 cup extra virgin olive oil	½ ounce fresh white truffle
1 cup grapeseed or canola oil	

Place the oils in a large jar and shake to mix. Cut the truffle into paper-thin slices. (Cookware shops sell special truffle cutters for this purpose. If you're investing in truffles, you might as well invest in a cutter. They're worth buying, for the thinner a slice of truffle, the more aromatic it will be.) Add the truffle slices to the oil. Cover and let the truffle oil stand at room temperature for 1 day. At that point, it's ready to use. Store any extra, covered, in the refrigerator. The oil will keep for several months. However, the flavor will fade as time passes. Bring it to room temperature before using.

Makes 2 cups

TRY THIS!

During truffle season in the Italian truffle city of Alba, I ate one of the most memorable meals of my life—a simple grilled veal chop drizzled with truffle oil and sprinkled with shavings of fresh white truffle. Grilled chicken, scallops, and shrimp are also ennobled by its presence. Another treat is grilled asparagus, mushrooms, endive, or other vegetables drizzled with fresh truffle oil.

FINISHING SAUCES AND BUTTERS

BLACK MAGIC FINISHING SAUCE

TRY THIS!

Brush or squirt this sauce on steaks, chops, roasts (it works equally well for pork, beef, and lamb), and chicken as they grill. The sauce goes on the meat after it's been browned by the fire, in the last 5 minutes of cooking. Cook until the sauce evaporates: The flavor will pass right through to the meat.

Matt Martinez is a fourth-generation Mexican-American and acclaimed expert on Tex-Mex cuisine. I pulled into one of his restaurants—Matt's No Place in Dallas—late one night and was greeted by kickass margaritas (cayenne and salt on the glass rim), irresistible swamp-bottom frog legs (smothered with poblano chilies and onions), and "smoked bob," a fiendishly tasty combination of shredded smoked beef tenderloin, salsa, guacamole, tortillas, and *queso fundido* (melted cheese).

Matt attributes the lip-smacking succulence of his meats to his Black Magic Finishing Sauce—a piquant blend of soy sauce, vinegar, and red wine, which he brushes or squirts on the meats while they're grilling. The vinegar "breaks the seal" (the seared crust), explains Matt, allowing the heady flavors of the wine and soy sauce to be absorbed by the meat. Black Magic is a finishing sauce—you use it to flavor the meat during cooking, rather than serve it at the table. It works equally well on grilled meats and true barbecue.

Matt uses Kikkoman light soy sauce and a mixture of vinegars. But you'll get highly acceptable results with ½ cup of one type of vinegar.

1 cup Kikkoman light soy
 sauce
½ cup dry red wine
3 tablespoons red wine
 vinegar

3 tablespoons cider
 vinegar
2 tablespoons rice
 vinegar

Combine all the ingredients in a bowl and stir to mix. Transfer to a large jar or squirt bottle and use right away. Store any extra in the refrigerator. The sauce will keep for several months.

Makes 2 cups; use 2 to 3 tablespoons per pound of meat

FAT BOYS FINISHING SAUCE

TRY THIS!

Brush the sauce over brisket, pork, and other meats after slicing but before serving.

Can a finishing sauce make a winning brisket? Ask Danny Mikes of the Fat Boys barbecue team from Temple, Texas. Danny has won first place numerous times in the brisket competition at the Kansas City Royal. His secret? Well, first, there's the rub. Then, the long, slow smoking over the right blend of hard woods. But the one thing that makes Danny's brisket unique is the finishing sauce, a mixture of ketchup, lemon juice, and bean juice that goes on the meat between the mop sauce and the final slather of barbecue sauce.

Bean juice is the cooking liquid Danny's wife saves whenever she cooks pinto beans. Danny swears that the starches in the bean juice lock in the flavor and keep the meat from drying out. You'd never mistake this finishing sauce for a barbecue sauce: It doesn't taste particularly good by itself, but it goes a long way toward producing an award-winning brisket.

¼ cup bean juice (the cooking liquid from any freshly boiled beans)

¼ cup ketchup
1 tablespoon fresh lemon juice

Place all the ingredients in a nonreactive saucepan and warm over medium heat, whisking to mix. Do not let the sauce boil. Use right away.

Makes ½ cup; enough for 3 to 4 pounds of sliced meat

GRILLED GARLIC BREAD WITH
TARRAGON AND LEMON

Grilling is the best way I know to make garlic bread. The fire crisps the bread and imparts an irresistible smoke flavor. Especially when coupled with the bright licoricey taste of fresh tarragon.

1 baguette
1½ recipes Tarragon-Lemon Butter (see below), at room temperature
3 cloves garlic, minced

1. Preheat the grill to high.
2. Cut the bread sharply on the diagonal into ½-inch-thick slices. Arrange the slices on a baking sheet. Place the tarragon butter and garlic in a bowl and stir or whisk to mix. Using a spatula, spread the garlic butter on both sides of the bread slices.
3. Grill the bread until golden brown on both sides, 1 to 2 minutes per side. Don't take your eyes off the grill for a second, as the bread will burn quickly. Serve at once.

Serves 8 to 10

TARRAGON-LEMON BUTTER

TRY THIS!

Unwrap the roll and cut it crosswise into ½-inch-thick slices. Place these slices on steaks, chops (especially veal and lamb), fish fillets, or vegetables hot off the grill.

Here's a twist on the classic French *maître d'hôtel* butter (parsley-lemon butter). The bright licorice tang of fresh tarragon goes equally well with beef, poultry, and seafood.

3 tablespoons finely chopped fresh tarragon leaves
1 clove garlic, minced
½ teaspoon finely grated lemon zest
A few drops of fresh lemon juice

8 tablespoons (1 stick) salted butter, at room temperature
Freshly ground white or black pepper, to taste

Place the tarragon, garlic, lemon zest, lemon juice, butter,

and pepper in a mixing bowl and stir or whisk until light and fluffy. Or do the stirring with a mixer or in a food processor. Wrap, roll, and store the butter as described in the box on page 130.

Makes ½ cup; enough for 8 servings

WALNUT-GORGONZOLA BUTTER

Toasted walnuts and gorgonzola cheese give this butter a northern Italian accent. (Gorgonzola comes from Lombardy.) The brash, salty tang of blue cheese and the earthiness of roasted walnuts go particularly well with grilled meats.

TRY THIS!

When I first created this butter, I thought how good it would be on grilled veal and beef. And it is. But there's no reason not to serve it on a grilled salmon steak or even a plate of grilled vegetables. Unwrap the roll and cut it crosswise into ½-inch-thick slices. Place the slices on the hot grilled food.

¼ cup toasted walnut pieces (see box, page 105)
8 tablespoons (1 stick) salted butter, at room temperature

2 ounces gorgonzola cheese, at room temperature
½ teaspoon freshly ground black pepper, or to taste

1. Place the nuts in a food processor and coarsely chop, running the machine in short bursts. Add the butter, gorgonzola, and pepper and process until creamy and smooth.

2. Wrap, roll, and store the butter as described in the box on page 130.

Makes ¾ cup; enough for 12 servings

BACON-ONION BUTTER

If you like bacon, you'll love smoky flavors of this butter, which contains caramelized onions for sweetness and a touch of mustard for bite. Wait until you taste this baby on burgers!

TRY THIS!

This butter screams hamburger. Unwrap the roll and cut it crosswise into ½-inch-thick slices. Place a slice on top of a well-charred burger. Better still, place a disk of the bacon butter in the center of the burger meat before grilling. Close the meat around the butter and grill. You could also serve bacon onion butter on steaks, chicken, grilled mushrooms, and even robust fish, like grilled wahoo or bluefish.

8 tablespoons (1 stick) salted butter, at room temperature
3 strips of lean bacon, cut into ¼-inch slivers
1 medium onion, very finely chopped

2 teaspoons mustard, preferably brown or Dusseldorf style, or more to taste
½ teaspoon freshly ground black pepper, or more to taste

1. Melt 1 tablespoon of the butter in a skillet over medium heat. Add the bacon and cook until the fat begins to render. Add the onion and sauté until the bacon crisps and the onions are golden brown, about 5 minutes. Do not let the bacon burn. Transfer the bacon mixture to a mixing bowl and cool to room temperature.

2. Add the remaining butter, the mustard, and pepper and beat the mixture with a wooden spoon until light and fluffy. Correct the seasoning, adding more pepper or mustard if needed.

3. Wrap, roll, and store the butter as described in the box below.

Makes ½ cup; enough for 8 servings

MAKING AND STORING COMPOUND BUTTER ROLLS

Arrange a 12-inch square piece of plastic wrap or parchment paper on your work surface and mound the butter in the center. Roll it up into a cylinder 1¼ inches in diameter, twisting the ends of the wrap to compact the butter. Store the butter in the refrigerator for up to 5 days or in the freezer for up to 3 months.

MUSTARD-BEER BUTTER

Mustard goes to finishing school in this recipe, inspired by a classic barbecue combination: sausage, mustard, and beer. To reinforce the mustard flavor, we use three types: seed, powder, and prepared. The choice of the prepared mustard is up to you: A sharp French mustard will give you a very different flavor than a sweet honey mustard.

Black mustard seeds are available at Indian markets or from one of the mail-order sources on page 281. If unavailable, use more yellow mustard seeds.

TRY THIS!

Mustard-beer butter goes well with grilled pork and pork products, especially sausages. That's not to rule out grilled chicken or fish. Unwrap the roll and cut it crosswise into ½-inch-thick slices. Place a slice on the hot grilled food.

2 teaspoons yellow mustard seeds
2 teaspoons black mustard seeds (or additional yellow mustard seeds)
¼ cup finely chopped shallots
½ cup dark beer

2 teaspoons wine or distilled white vinegar, or to taste
2 teaspoons mustard powder
2 tablespoons prepared mustard, or more to taste
8 tablespoons (1 stick) salted butter, at room temperature

1. Place both mustard seeds, the shallots, vinegar, and beer in a small saucepan and bring to a boil over high heat. Reduce the heat to medium and simmer until most of the beer has evaporated and the mixture is thick and syrupy, 6 to 8 minutes. Remove the pan from the heat and let cool to room temperature.

2. Place the mustard powder, prepared mustard, and butter in a mixing bowl and stir or whisk until light and fluffy. Stir in the mustard-beer mixture. Correct the seasoning, adding more prepared mustard or vinegar if needed.

3. Wrap, roll, and store the butter as described on the facing page.

Makes ¾ cup; enough for 10 to 12 servings

WASABI-HORSERADISH BUTTER

TRY THIS!

Imagine a whole roast beef, the ends seared and crusty, the meat sanguine and juicy. (If this is your idea of paradise, take your imagination no further than to my book, *Barbecue! Bible*, where you'll find a great recipe for cooking prime rib on the grill.) Or imagine a bible-thick tuna steak, charred on the outside and sushi-rare in the center. Those are two great uses for wasabi-horseradish butter, but don't overlook grilled chicken, veal, or trout. Unwrap the roll and cut it into ½-inch-thick slices. Place a slice on each portion of meat or fish.

The English fondness for horseradish with beef is well documented, as is the Japanese love for a fiery, pale-green, horseradish-like root called wasabi with tuna. Put them together and you get a butter that fires a double-barrel blast of flavor.

1 tablespoon wasabi powder
1 tablespoon rice wine vinegar or distilled white vinegar
8 tablespoons (1 stick) salted butter, at room temperature

1 tablespoon prepared white horseradish
½ teaspoon freshly ground black pepper

1. Place the wasabi and vinegar in a small bowl and stir to mix into a paste. Let stand for 5 minutes.

2. Place the butter in a mixing bowl and stir or whisk until light and fluffy. Add the wasabi paste, horseradish, and pepper.

3. Wrap, roll, and store the butter as described in the box on page 130.

Makes ½ cup; enough for 8 servings

AMERICAN BARBECUE SAUCES

Not long ago, I was discussing barbecue with the celebrated chef Thomas Keller. "Where I come from, the sauce *is* the barbecue," explained the owner of the French Laundry restaurant in the Napa Valley. It's a sentiment that may make a few thousand pit masters on the professional barbecue circuit cringe. (For the purist, what really makes barbecue barbecue is the long, slow, smoky cooking in the pit.) But Keller has a point: For many Americans, the essence of barbecue lies in the sauce.

But which sauce? Well, that's easy. Isn't barbecue sauce the store-bought thick, red, sweet, smoky stuff you pour from a K.C. Masterpiece bottle? Sure, that's one type of barbecue sauce and it's certainly a popular one. But even in Kansas City, barbecue sauces range from the vinegary Bubba-lina (page 169) to a brash, peppery, briskly acidic red sauce that's kept people lining up at Arthur Bryant's for half a century.

Leave the confines of Kansas City and the sauce question becomes even more confusing. Serve a typical North Carolina vinegar sauce to most Americans, and they'll wonder why you left out the ketchup and molasses. Offer an Alabama white sauce and you might just be asked if it's barbecue sauce or salad dressing? The truth is that while we Americans love barbecue sauce, we can't agree on what it is. This chapter will help you navigate through America's favorites.

SWEET-AND-SMOKY BARBECUE SAUCE

TRY THIS!

Use as you would any barbecue sauce, that is to say, brushed on pork, ribs, and chicken toward the end of cooking and poured freely at the table.

Ask most Americans to describe the perfect barbecue sauce and they'll evoke a thick, sweet, red, ketchup-based sauce with a zing of vinegar and a whiff of liquid smoke. In short, the sort of sauce Kansas City barbecue buffs have slathered on ribs and briskets for decades. The following recipe comes from the Kansas City Barbecue Society. (Motto: "Barbecue—it's not just for breakfast.")

6 tablespoons (packed) dark
    brown sugar
½ cup cider vinegar
¼ cup molasses
¼ cup honey
¼ cup Worcestershire sauce
2 tablespoons dark rum
2 tablespoons yellow mustard
1 tablespoon liquid smoke
1 tablespoon pure chili
    powder (not a blend)

2 teaspoons freshly ground
    black pepper
2 teaspoons garlic powder
1 teaspoon ground allspice
¼ teaspoon ground cloves
4 cups ketchup
Coarse salt (kosher or sea)
    and freshly ground black
    pepper

    1. Combine all the ingredients, except for the ketchup, in a large, deep, heavy, nonreactive saucepan and bring to a simmer over medium heat. Cook, uncovered, until all the ingredients are dissolved, stirring constantly, about 5 minutes. Stir in the ketchup and bring to a boil, stirring well, as the ketchup has a tendency to spatter. Add salt and pepper to taste.

2. Reduce the heat slightly and gently simmer the sauce, uncovered, until dark, thick, and richly flavored, about 30 minutes, stirring often. Use right away or transfer to jars, cover, cool to room temperature, and refrigerate. The sauce will keep for several months.

Makes 5 cups

RIGHTEOUS RIBS

Eating these ribs can be almost a religious experience, especially when coupled with Sweet-and-Smoky Barbecue Sauce. I like the succulence and tenderness of baby back ribs, but you could certainly use spare ribs if you prefer. You'd need to increase the amount of rub and sauce for the latter.

**6 racks baby back ribs
    (6 pounds)**
**¾ cup Basic Barbecue Rub
    (page 23)**
**2 cups Sweet-and-Smoky Barbecue
    Sauce (facing page)**

**SPECIAL EQUIPMENT
2 cups wood chips, preferably
    applewood, soaked in 2 cups
    apple cider for 1 hour, then
    drained**

1. Remove the papery skin on the back of each rack of ribs by pulling it off in a sheet with your fingers (using a corner of a dish towel to secure your grip, or ask your butcher to do it). Sprinkle the ribs on both sides with two thirds of the rub, patting it in with your fingers. Cover and marinate in the refrigerator for 1 hour.

2. Set up the grill for indirect grilling, following the instructions on page 5. If using a charcoal grill, toss the chips on the coals. If using a gas grill, place the chips in the smoker box. Don't grill until you see smoke.

3. Place the ribs in the center of the grate (ideally in a rib rack, if you have one), away from the fire. Indirect grill for 1 hour.

4. Brush the ribs with half the barbecue sauce and continue indirect grilling until done. When done, the meat will be very tender and will have pulled back from the ends of the bones, 15 to 30 minutes more. Transfer the ribs to a platter. Sprinkle with the remaining rub and serve the remaining sauce on the side.

Serves 6

B.B.'S LAWNSIDE SPICY APPLE BARBECUE SAUCE

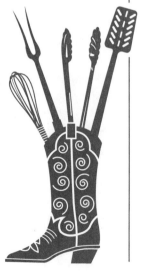

The quintessential Kansas City barbecue joint, B.B.'s Lawnside is a rough-and-tumble roadhouse on the outskirts of the city, which specializes in the three Bs of the Kansas City good life: blues, beer, and barbecue. The barbecue emerges finger-licking good and fall-off-the-bone tender from a brick pit fueled with blazing hickory. Rib tips (the meaty trimmings of spareribs) are the house specialty and the gumbo (made with home-smoked meats) rivals anything you'll taste in Louisiana.

B.B.'s proprietor, Lindsey Shannon, is a die-hard blues enthusiast and his club/restaurant hosts some of best blues acts in the Midwest. As for his sweet, suave barbecue sauce, it owes its fruity finish to apple cider. It's thick enough to stick to ribs and versatile enough to accompany pork, beef, chicken, turkey, and vegetables.

1 bottle (14 ounces) ketchup (Lindsey uses Hunt's)
1 cup apple cider
2 tablespoons Worcestershire sauce
1 tablespoon molasses
1 tablespoon cider vinegar
1 tablespoon soy sauce
½ teaspoon liquid smoke

1½ tablespoons dark brown sugar
1 tablespoon granulated sugar
1 teaspoon cayenne pepper
½ teaspoon freshly ground black pepper
½ teaspoon celery seed
½ teaspoon ground cinnamon
⅛ teaspoon ground cloves

Combine all the ingredients in a large, heavy, nonreactive saucepan and stir or whisk to mix. Bring the sauce to a boil over medium heat. Reduce the heat to low and gently simmer the sauce, uncovered, until thick and richly flavored, stirring often to prevent scorching, 30 minutes. Use right away or transfer to jars, cover, cool to room temperature, and refrigerate. The sauce will keep for up to several months.

Makes about 3 cups

PRESERVING
SAUCES AND CONDIMENTS
FOR THE LONG RUN

Throughout this book, you're instructed to store barbecue sauces and chutneys in the refrigerator. Our ancestors would have found this a curious practice, as would a lot of Third World grill jockeys. The fact is that by following a few time-honored principles of canning and preserving, you can store many sauces and chutneys without refrigeration for months. The procedure involves sterilizing the jars and lids, which adds an extra step and 20 to 30 minutes to the cooking time. I've omitted this procedure in the individual recipes, but it's easy to preserve any barbecue sauce or chutney that's boiled in the process of cooking. (Storage time given in a recipe is for a sauce stored in a clean jar, not a sterilized one.)

The first step is to trim off the soft spots or blemishes of any fruits and vegetables you may be using.

The next step is to sterilize the containers and cooking equipment. To sterilize jars or bottles place them, uncovered and open end up, in a large pot with water to cover by at least 3 inches. (Hold the jars under the surface until they completely fill with water.) You can place a circular rack or folded towel on the bottom of the pot to keep the jars from rattling. Boil the jars,

caps, and lids for at least 15 minutes. Dip the tongs and ladle in the boiling water to sterilize them as well. Leave the jars and equipment in the hot water until you're ready to use them.

Remove the jars from the water with tongs and drain well. (If you like, invert them on a clean cake rack.) Add the hot barbecue sauce or chutney to within ¼ inch of the top of each jar. Place the flat lid on top, plastic side down. Tightly screw on the cap. Invert the filled jar for 10 minutes, then turn right side up and let cool. As the sauce cools, it will shrink, creating a vacuum seal.

It's very important to test this seal before putting the jars in your pantry or giving them as gifts. When the jar is properly sealed, the lid will be slightly concave. Press it in the center with your finger: If the lid pops up, the jar isn't properly sealed. Another test is to unscrew the screw band around the ball jar and gently lift the jar by the lid. If the lid comes off, the jar wasn't properly sealed. Should you doubt the integrity of the seal, refrigerate the sauce until using.

Sauces and chutneys that contain a lot of sugar, salt, and/or vinegar keep the best. Stored in a cool dark place, they will keep for months.

LEAN-AND-MEAN TEXAS BARBECUE SAUCE

Texans take the same bold no-nonsense approach to barbecue sauce that they do to beef. Little or no sugar and plenty of vinegar and chili hellfire. Consider this sauce, which is inspired by the one served at the legendary Sonny Bryan's in Dallas. (It isn't the actual sauce served at Sonny Bryan's, but you can taste a family resemblance.) This tart hot slather is everything a Texas barbecue sauce should be and there isn't a brisket in creation that wouldn't be proud to wear it. For an added measure of authenticity, serve it warm in an empty beer bottle.

1 bottle (14 ounces) ketchup
1 cup cider vinegar
½ cup Worcestershire sauce
2 tablespoons yellow mustard
2 tablespoons fresh lemon juice
½ teaspoon liquid smoke
¼ cup pure chili powder (not a blend)
2 tablespoons paprika
1 teaspoon hot pepper flakes, or to taste
1 teaspoon freshly ground black pepper
1 teaspoon dark brown sugar (optional)
⅓ cup brisket or bacon drippings (optional)
3 cups water

Combine all the ingredients in a large, heavy, nonreactive saucepan and stir or whisk to mix. Bring the sauce to a rolling boil over high heat. Reduce the heat slightly and briskly simmer the sauce, uncovered, until thick and richly flavored, stirring often to prevent scorching, 20 minutes. Use right away or transfer to jars, cover, placing a piece of plastic wrap under the lid, cool to room temperature, and let ripen for 2 to 3 days in the refrigerator before serving. The sauce will keep for several months.

Makes about 6 cups

WORCESTERSHIRE
SAUCE

What's the ingredient most frequently used in barbecue sauces? If you answer ketchup, you're close. But I'd put my money on a condiment that comes in a paper-wrapped bottle: Worcestershire sauce.

This thin, brown, sweet-sour condiment turns up in barbecue sauces of all stripes and types—from the tomato-based sauces of Kansas City to the butter sauces of New Orleans to the vinegar sauces of North Carolina. The reason is simple: Worcestershire sauce contains something for everyone—sweetness in the form of corn syrup and molasses, acidity in the form of tamarind and vinegar, saltiness in the form of soy sauce and anchovies, with garlic and shallots for aroma and a pinch of cloves for spice.

Like mushroom ketchup and A.1. Steak Sauce, Worcestershire was born in the heyday of the great English table sauces, when a condiment maker's larder was limited only to his imagination. According to David Burton, author of *The Raj at Table: A Culinary History of the British in India,* the recipe originated in India and was brought back to England by a former governor of Bengal, Lord Marcus Sandys.

In 1835, Lord Sandys brought his recipe to the chemist shop of John Lea and William Perrins on Broad Street in Worcester and asked them to brew up a batch. The resulting mixture was so fiery, it "almost blew the heads off Mssrs. Lea and Perrins," according to Burton. They deposited the barrel in a back corner of the cellar and promptly tried to forget it. The chemists stumbled upon it a few years later, and, morbidly curious, they tried it again. With age, the Worcestershire had mellowed into an extraordinary sauce. The recipe was hastily purchased from Lord Sandys and in 1838, commercial Worcestershire sauce was born.

According to Adrian Bailey and Philip Dowell, authors of *Cooks' Ingredients,* the original Lea & Perrins recipe contained walnut and mushroom ketchups, sherry, brandy, and even pork liver, which has been eliminated from the American formula. Today the sauce is enjoyed all over the world. Many companies manufacture Worcestershire sauce today, but no one makes a better one than Lea & Perrins. This is the sauce you should use for the recipes in this book.

Many American rub makers add a freeze-dried Worcestershire sauce to their spice mixes. This flavorful powder is available from Pendery's (see Mail-Order Sources, page 281).

HONEY-PEPPER BARBECUE SAUCE

TRY THIS!

Use pretty much as you would any barbecue sauce, that is, brushed on ribs, pork, chicken, and even beef during the last few minutes of cooking. Serve the remaining sauce on the side.

Honey-flavored barbecue sauces have a tendency to be too cloying. Not this one, a specialty of a Kansas State barbecue team called P.D.T. (short for Pretty Damn Tasty). To cut the sweetness, pit masters Donna and Ted McClure "fry" the peppers and onion in honey before adding them to the sauce. The honey melts and mellows the sharp onion and pepper flavors, while the vegetable juices seem to tone down the sweetness of the honey. The "lemon" flavor comes from the 7UP. What results is the sort of mild, mellow, finger-lickin' good barbecue sauce that keeps you coming back for taste after taste to figure out why it's so damn tasty.

¼ **cup honey**

¼ **cup diced green bell pepper**

¼ **cup diced red bell pepper**

¼ **cup diced yellow bell pepper**

1 small onion, finely chopped

1 jalapeño chili, seeded and finely chopped (for a spicier sauce, leave the seeds in)

1½ cups ketchup

¾ **cup cider vinegar, or more to taste**

½ **cup 7UP or Sprite, or more as needed**

2 tablespoons dark brown sugar, or more to taste

2 tablespoons apple juice

1 teaspoon liquid smoke

½ **teaspoon freshly ground black pepper**

Coarse salt (kosher or sea), to taste

Pour the honey into a heavy nonreactive saucepan. Add the peppers, onion, and jalapeño and "sauté" over medium heat until the peppers are soft and the onion translucent, about 5 minutes. Stir in the remaining ingredients and simmer the sauce, uncovered, until thick and richly flavored, 15 minutes. Transfer the sauce to a blender and purée until smooth.

Correct the seasoning, adding salt, vinegar, or brown sugar if needed; the sauce should be sweet, smoky, and tangy. If the sauce is too thick, thin with a little more 7UP. Use right away or transfer to a large jar, cover, cool to room temperature, and refrigerate. The sauce will keep for several months.

Makes 2 cups

TEXAS JACK SAUCE

TRY THIS!

Start brushing the sauce on barbe-cued chicken or pork during the last 10 minutes of cooking. Brush it again once the meat is cooked. Transfer the remaining sauce to a bowl or squirt bottle and serve it with the meat on the table.

Lola and James Rice are legends in the competition bar-becue circuit, the first team ever to win the Grand Championship at the Kansas City Royal for two consecutive years. Not bad for a team that's been competing for barely a decade. The Rices created Texas Jack Sauce to go with barbecued chicken, but it also goes great with pork and even brisket. The sauce has something for everyone: Tabasco sauce and mustard for hotheads; molasses and maple syrup for sweet tooths. Lola classes Texas Jack as a hybrid: She uses it both as a finishing sauce and as a dip-ping sauce for the table. This baby has quite a kick. The tender of tongue may wish to cut back on the Tabasco sauce.

2 cups ketchup
¼ cup Tabasco sauce (must be Tabasco sauce)
¼ cup Dijon mustard
¼ cup Jack Daniel's whiskey
¼ cup molasses

2 tablespoons dark brown sugar
1 tablespoon Worcestershire sauce
1½ teaspoons garlic powder
¼ teaspoon liquid smoke

Combine all the ingredients in a deep, heavy, nonreac-tive saucepan over medium heat and bring to a boil. Reduce the heat slightly and simmer the sauce, uncovered, until thick and richly flavored, 15 to 20 minutes. Correct the sea-soning, adding any ingredient you fancy. Use right away or transfer to jars, cover, cool to room temperature, and refrig-erate. The sauce will keep for several months.

Makes about 3 cups

HOW TO BUILD A GREAT
BARBECUE
SAUCE

Barbecue sauces can contain literally dozens of different ingredients. I've seen sauces flavored with everything from coffee to cranberry sauce to cough syrup! But whether you're making a simple North Carolina–style vinegar sauce or a Kansas City–style everything-but-the-kitchen-sink sauce, there's one ingredient you simply can't do without: balance. The goal of any good sauce is to bring the contrasting elements— sweet, sour, salty, aromatic, hot—into equilibrium.

Here's a look at the essential building blocks you need to construct a great barbecue sauce. Master them and you'll become a sauce maker extraordinaire.

THE BASE: The base is the starting point, the foundation for any great barbecue sauce. A red sauce is based on ketchup or tomato sauce. A mustard sauce is based, logically, on mustard; a vinegar sauce, on vinegar. Here are some common bases for barbecue sauce: ketchup, tomato sauce/tomato purée/tomato paste, fresh tomatoes, chili sauce, mustard, vinegar, chicken or beef stock, and mayonnaise.

THE SWEETENERS: Most barbecue sauces have an element of sweetness. Kansas City–style sauces are the sweetest, but even a western North Carolina vinegar sauce contains a little sugar to blunt the edge of the vinegar. Here are some common sweeteners:

Granulated sugar: Merely sweet

Turbinado sugar (Sugar in the Raw brand): Sweet with a light molasses flavor

Light or dark brown sugar: Sweet with a strong molasses flavor

Piloncillo (unrefined Mexican brown sugar; sold in pyramids or cones): Sweet with a rich, earthy, malty, molasses flavor

Sucanat (freeze-dried sugar-cane juice; sold in natural foods stores): Sweet with a malty flavor

Honey: Sweet with a floral flavor

Molasses: Sweet and bitter

Cane syrup: Sweet with a rich mouthfeel

Corn syrup (light or dark): Less sweet than sugar, with a rich mouthfeel

Maple sugar/maple syrup: Less sweet than sugar, with a haunting maple flavor

Rice syrup (sold in natural foods stores): Less sweet than sugar, with earthy malt flavors

Jams and jellies: Sweet, fruity flavor

THE SOURING AGENTS: Every great barbecue sauce contains a souring agent to help keep the sweetness in check. Here are the most commonly used souring agents:

Distilled vinegar: Just plain sour

Cider vinegar: Tart with a fruity finish

Wine vinegar: Tart with a complex wine flavor

Balsamic vinegar: Tart with a fruity sweetness

Lemon juice: Tart with a fruity flavor; often whole lemons are added to a sauce, contributing a bitter element as well as tartness

Lime juice and sour orange juice: Work in the same way as lemon juice

Tamarind: Sour-sweet, smoky flavor

Pickle juice: Need I say more?

THE SEASONINGS: Every barbecue sauce needs a touch of salt to balance the acidity and sweetness.

Salt: In particular, kosher salt or sea salt (see page 18)

Soy sauce: Salt with an Asian accent

Miso: Fermented soy bean paste (available in many colors and flavors)

Hoisin sauce: A thick Chinese condiment that's both salty and sweet

Anchovy fillets/paste: An ingredient in many steak sauces

Capers: The pickled buds of a Mediterranean flower

Olives: Especially salty olives, like Kalamata or Sicilian

Sun-dried tomatoes: Dried or oil-packed, your choice

HEAT: The defining element in many barbecue sauces (particularly those from Texas and the American Southwest). Here are some of the ingredients that can help set your sauce on fire.

Hot sauces: Particularly Tabasco, which owes its sharp, distinctive flavor to lengthy aging in barrels; Crystal hot sauce and Texas Pete possess heat without the benefit of aging; among Caribbean-style hot sauces, Matouk's from Trinidad is king

Fresh chili peppers: Range from the relatively mild jalapeño to the tongue-torturing Scotch bonnet; pickled chilies, such as pickled jalapeños, add an acidic element as well

Black and white pepper: Grind it fresh for extra flavor

Cayenne pepper and hot pepper flakes: These are hotter than you think. Start easy until you know your tolerance level.

Fresh ginger: Minced or grated

Mustard: Either prepared or powder

Horseradish: Either freshly grated or prepared; add it at the last minute, as cooking makes it sweet and destroys its heat

Wasabi: Japanese "horseradish"; dissolve it in a little cold water to form a thick green paste and add it at the last minute, as cooking diminishes its heat

THE AROMATICS: Aromatics give barbecue sauce its personality and sex appeal. Use them decisively but with restraint; a lot of people think that if a little is good, more is better. But any aromatic becomes offensive if you add too much.

Onions: Fresh (either raw or sautéed), dried flakes, or powder

Garlic: Fresh (either raw or sautéed), dried flakes, powder, or salt

Celery (also celery seed and celery salt)

Bell peppers: Especially green bell pepper

Chili powder: Indispensable in Texas

Herbs (both fresh and dried): Common barbecue sauce herbs include basil, bay leaf, chives, cilantro, dill, marjoram, mint, oregano, parsley, rosemary, and thyme

Spices: Common barbecue sauce seasonings include both the sweet spices (allspice, aniseed, cardamom, cinnamon, cloves, fennel seed, ginger, mace, nutmeg, and star anise) and the savory spices (caraway seed, coriander, cumin, curry, dill seed, mustard seed, paprika, pepper, saffron, sage, Sichuan peppercorns, and turmeric)

Liquid Smoke: Dallas's legendary barbecue emporium, Sonny Bryan's, actually smokes its barbecue sauce in the pit; the rest of us can add a few drops of this natural product to give barbecue sauce the flavor of wood smoke

Worcestershire sauce: Salty, sweet, and aromatic; contains tamarind and anchovies

Steak sauce: Salty and tomatoey, with a touch of raisin and orange

ENRICHERS: A well-built barbecue sauce not only tastes good, it feels good on your palate. That's where enrichers come in. Animal and vegetable fats will give your sauce a properly luscious mouthfeel.

Butter: Salted or unsalted, depending on the recipe

Oil: Olive, sesame, walnut, and hazelnut add flavor as well as richness; vegetable oil is merely rich

Lard: Traditional fat used for frying Mexican salsas

Bacon/bacon fat: Adds a rich smoky flavor

Meat drippings: The secret ingredient to many a sauce, including the lip-smacking sauce served at Shorty's in Miami

Beef stock/chicken stock: Adds a rich meaty flavor without fat

WILD CARDS: If you want to be a great sauce master, you need two attributes of creative genius: inspiration and fear-lessness. The former leads to the juxtaposition of unexpected flavors. The latter allows you to try adding anything. Some of the stranger sauce ingredients I've seen include:

Coffee: Adds a roasted, caramelized, wake-up flavor

Soda: Cola, root beer, ginger ale, lemon-lime, and orange are but a few of the flavors of soda that are added for sweetness and flavor

Wine: Adds a pleasing acidity

Booze: "Too much whiskey is just enough," observed Mark Twain; popular liquors for barbecue sauce include bourbon, Scotch, brandy, rum, and vodka

Peanut butter: Sounds strange and yet 300 million Asians can't be wrong; This is the main ingredient for Thai and Indonesian saté sauce

Vanilla extract: In the 1980s, there was a wonderful barbecue joint in Boston called the Hoodoo; their sauce owed its fragrant *je ne sais quoi* to a splash of vanilla extract

Water: Can have a powerful effect; used judiciously, it can help mellow strong flavors and knit disparate tastes into a harmonious whole

PUTTING IT ALL TOGETHER: Simply put the ingredients in a pot and bring to a boil. Then stir enough to keep it from burning. That's the beauty of barbecue sauce: You can't curdle it, scramble it, or break it.

MEMPHIS-STYLE BARBECUE SAUCE

John Willingham is a legend on the American barbecue circuit: He's a winner of dozens of grand championships, at the Memphis in May, Kansas City Royal, and Jack Daniel's Invitational barbecue competitions; he's an inventor (one of his cookers is on display at the Smithsonian Institution); a successful restaurateur; an acclaimed author; a teacher; and an irrepressible raconteur. People speak of him in reverential tones and crowd around his booth whenever he sets up shop at a barbecue festival. His disciples have opened restaurants from Louisville to Dallas.

As befits a barbecue king, Willingham calls Memphis home and his sauce—or one I watched him make—contains something for everyone: tomato sauce, steak sauce, mustard, even Coca-Cola. ("I figure with this many ingredients, everybody's bound to like something," Willingham quips.) The addition of a rub to the "wet fixin's" gives a blast of flavor typical of Memphis-style barbecue sauce. This recipe is just a rough approximation of what Willingham does, as no rib meister would share *all* his secrets with another barbecue man.

WET FIXIN'S

4 cups tomato sauce

1 cup cider vinegar

1 cup Coca-Cola, or other cola

¼ cup steak sauce (such as A.1.)

¼ cup yellow mustard

¼ cup fresh lemon juice

3 tablespoons molasses

3 tablespoons soy sauce

3 tablespoons Worcestershire sauce

1 teaspoon Tabasco sauce

½ teaspoon liquid smoke

DRY FIXIN'S

½ cup (packed) dark brown sugar

1 to 2 tablespoons Basic Barbecue Rub (page 23; John uses a rub he manufactures called W'ham)

1 tablespoon pure chili powder (not a blend)

1 tablespoon freshly ground black pepper

1 tablespoon mustard powder

2 teaspoons garlic salt

1. Combine all the wet fixin's in a large, heavy, nonreactive saucepan and slowly bring to a boil, uncovered, over medium heat.

2. Meanwhile, combine the dry fixin's in a bowl and mix with your fingers.

3. Reduce the heat and stir the dry fixin's into the sauce mixture. Gently simmer the sauce until thick, concentrated, and richly flavored, about 30 minutes. Use right away or transfer to jars, cover, cool to room temperature, and refrigerate. The sauce will keep for several weeks.

Makes 4 cups

ST. LOUIS RED

TRY THIS!

St. Louisans like to serve this sauce with grilled pork steaks, but feel free to slather it on your favorite barbecue, whatever that may be.

The thing I love best about barbecue (besides good eating) is its powers of goodwill and friendship. When I was on book tour in St. Louis, a local barbecue team/restaurant called Super Smokers showed their support by bringing samples of their award-winning 'que to a television station where I was appearing. Super Smoker founders Terry Black and Skip Steele have become friends, and when they learned I was writing a sauce book, they rushed me the recipe for this St. Louis red sauce. "St. Louis has a large Italian community, so our sauces are sweet and mild," explains Terry. "Ever-practical, St. Louisans like sauces you can make with ingredients you can grab off the grocery store shelves," adds Skip. So here's a St. Louis–style sauce that's long on character and short on preparation time (the honey, molasses, and liquid smoke are my own contributions to the recipe). It adds yet one more chapter in the story of American barbecue sauces.

4 cups ketchup

1 bottle (10 ounces) A.1.
   Steak Sauce

1 bottle (10 ounces) Heinz
   57 Sauce

1½ cups apple juice or apple
   cider

⅓ cup Worcestershire sauce

⅓ cup dark corn syrup

⅓ cup honey

¼ cup molasses

1 teaspoon liquid smoke

2 teaspoons freshly ground
   black pepper

1 teaspoon garlic powder

Combine all the ingredients in a large, heavy, nonreactive saucepan and bring to a simmer over medium heat. Continue simmering, uncovered, until richly flavored, 5 minutes, stirring or whisking to prevent scorching. Use right away or transfer to jars, cover, cool to room temperature, and refrigerate. The sauce will keep for several months.

Makes about 8 cups

STILL HOUSE BARBECUE SAUCE

TRY THIS!

Brush this sauce on ribs, chicken, or pork during the last 10 minutes of cooking. And serve plenty of it on the side. The appropriate beverage? Lynchburg lemonade (lemonade spiked with Jack Daniel's), of course!

American barbecue owes an enormous debt to the Jack Daniel's distillery in Lynchburg, Tennessee. Not just for creating one of the finest sipping whiskeys in North America—and an essential ingredient in countless barbecue sauces and marinades—but also because the distillery hosts one of the nation's most important barbecue festivals: The Jack Daniel's Invitational. Every October, fifty of America's best barbecue teams converge on this hamlet in southern Tennessee to compete in such categories as whole hog, ribs, and pork shoulders. The winners walk off with thousands of dollars in prize money.

Curiously, the one thing you won't find at the competition is whiskey, at least not publicly and certainly not for drinking. The great irony is that Lynchburg is a dry town. Contestants get around this inconvenient regulation by using their favorite whiskey as an ingredient for bastes and barbecue sauces. The following sweet, sassy barbecue sauce may be the best reason I know of for not *drinking* Jack Daniel's.

1 cup Jack Daniel's Tennessee whiskey
1 cup ketchup
1 cup cider vinegar
1 cup (packed) dark brown sugar
½ cup onion, very finely minced

2 tablespoons Worcestershire sauce
1½ tablespoons Tabasco sauce
½ teaspoon freshly ground black pepper
¼ teaspoon liquid smoke

Combine all the ingredients in a large, heavy, nonreactive saucepan and bring to a boil over high heat. Reduce the heat and briskly simmer, uncovered, until richly flavored and slightly thickened, about 20 minutes, stirring from time to time with a wooden spoon. Use right away or transfer to jars, cover, cool to room temperature, and refrigerate. The sauce will keep for several months.

Makes about 4 cups

WHODUNIT BARBECUE SAUCE

How much would the recipe for the perfect barbecue sauce be worth to you? Enough to kill for? Passions run pretty high in competition barbecue and that's what happens to one fictional Kansas City sauce meister, Pigpen Hopkins, in Lou Jane Temple's *Revenge of the Barbecue Queens.* Temple is a Kansas City mystery writer and her whodunit is the best study I know of the strange and colorful world of competition barbecue. The following recipe has been adapted from the rich apple cider, mustard, coffee, and beer barbecue sauce that one barbecue fiend found tasty enough to murder for.

2 cups apple cider

1 bottle (12 ounces) dark beer

1¼ cups ketchup

½ cup balsamic vinegar

½ cup honey mustard

½ cup yellow mustard

½ cup grainy Meaux-style mustard

½ cup honey

½ cup molasses

½ cup cane syrup, such as Stein's

½ cup brewed coffee

2 tablespoons Worcestershire sauce

2 tablespoons Tabasco sauce

2 tablespoons soy sauce

1 teaspoon celery salt

1 teaspoon freshly ground black pepper

½ teaspoon ground coriander

1 habanero chili, seeded and minced

Coarse salt (kosher or sea), to taste

TRY THIS!

Serve this off-beat sauce with barbecued chicken, pork, or shrimp. It's sweet, but not too sweet, so you could slather it on grilled sausages and lamb.

Combine all the ingredients in a large, heavy, nonreactive saucepan and stir or whisk to mix. Bring the sauce to a simmer over medium heat. Continue simmering, uncovered, until thick and richly flavored, about 30 minutes, stirring from time to time. Use right away or transfer to jars, cover, cool to room temperature, and refrigerate. The sauce will keep for several months.

Makes about 9 cups

BARBARA Q SAUCE

Every man should have his own signature barbecue sauce and so should every woman. Whenever we grill lamb or poultry, my wife, Barbara, whips up a batch of this simple sauce. It contains only three main ingredients and can be made in a matter of minutes. The sauce is sweet, but the bitter oranges in the marmalade keep it from being too sugary.

1 cup tomato-based barbecue sauce, such as Sweet-and-Smoky Barbecue Sauce (page 134)

½ cup honey

½ cup orange marmalade

½ teaspoon freshly ground black pepper

Combine all the ingredients in a heavy nonreactive saucepan and stir or whisk to mix. Bring the sauce to a simmer over medium heat and continue simmering and stirring until the marmalade is melted and the sauce is richly flavored, 5 minutes. Use right away or transfer to a large jar, cover, cool to room temperature, and refrigerate. The sauce will keep for several months.

Makes 2 cups

VARIATION

Sometimes Barbara makes this sauce with apricot jam instead of orange marmalade.

CAL'S APRICOT-HORSERADISH BARBECUE SAUCE

Cal Fussman is a journalist friend and one of the best writers in the business. You may have read his "Perfect Man" column in *Esquire* magazine. Each month Cal focuses on an area of expertise that every well-bred man should know about, then studies its fine points with a master. Most important of all, he puts his newly acquired skills to the test in the real world, chronicling his successes and failures in his column. I was flattered when Cal came to study barbecue with me and impressed that he had the courage to assay his skills at the Jack Daniel's Invitational barbecue competition in Lynchburg, Tennessee.

"Courage" is the right word here, for his co-contestants included fifty of the nation's top pit masters, most of them with decades of experience cooking on rigs that cost tens of thousands of dollars. Cal gamely set up his Oklahoma Joe smoker and turned out fork-tender smoky ribs that would do any barbecue buff proud. His sauce plays pinball on your taste buds, pitting the fruity sweetness of apricot preserves against the boozy tang of bourbon and the slow burn of Scotch bonnet chilies and horseradish. Celebrity judge Clive Cusser paid it the highest compliment, pronouncing it "better than sex."

1 cup apricot preserves
¼ cup bourbon
¼ cup tomato paste
¼ cup fresh lime juice
3 tablespoons cider vinegar, or to taste
2 tablespoons ketchup
1 tablespoon soy sauce
1 tablespoon molasses
2 teaspoons Worcestershire sauce
2 tablespoons minced fresh shallot
1 tablespoon minced fresh ginger

2 cloves garlic, minced
½ to 1 Scotch bonnet chili or other hot chili, seeded and minced
½ teaspoon hot pepper flakes
Coarse salt (kosher or sea) and freshly ground black pepper
1 to 2 tablespoons prepared white horseradish, or to taste

1. Place all the ingredients for the sauce, except for the horseradish, in a heavy nonreactive saucepan. Simmer the sauce, uncovered, over medium heat until slightly thickened and richly flavored, about 10 minutes. Correct the seasoning, adding salt and/or pepper if needed. The sauce should be of pourable consistency; if too thick, add a little water. Let the sauce cool to room temperature.

2. Stir in the horseradish to taste. Use right away or transfer to a large jar, cover, and refrigerate. The sauce will keep for several weeks.

Makes 2 cups

BLUEBERRY BARBECUE SAUCE

Crescent Dragonwagon is a woman of many talents: chef, philanthropist, former innkeeper, and an award-winning author of many cookbooks and children's books. When her

Dairy Hollow House Inn, located in Eureka Springs, Arkansas, was open, her guests included old friends Bill and Hillary Clinton. They were so impressed with her food, they invited her to cook and host a brunch for one thousand guests during Bill's first presidential inauguration. An avowed vegetarian, Crescent is broadminded enough to have created a blueberry barbecue sauce that goes well with pork, game, or chicken. It's also pretty darn good on grilled seitan or tofu. The blueberries give the sauce a fruity sweetness that makes a nice change of pace from the usual tomato-based barbecue sauce.

TRY THIS!

Because of its fruiti-ness, blueberry barbecue sauce goes especially well with turkey, chicken, or pork.

2 quarts fresh or frozen blueberries (if using frozen berries, thaw, but reserve the juices)
1½ cups finely chopped celery
1½ cups finely chopped onions
1½ cups finely chopped green bell pepper
1 carrot, minced
1 clove garlic, minced
1 cup cider vinegar, or more to taste

½ cup honey, or more to taste
2 tablespoons molasses
2 tablespoons ketchup
1 tablespoon paprika
1½ teaspoons coarse salt (kosher or sea)
1½ teaspoons freshly ground black pepper
1 teaspoon ground cinnamon
½ teaspoon mustard powder
½ teaspoon ground ginger
¼ teaspoon ground nutmeg
¼ teaspoon celery seed
¼ teaspoon cayenne pepper, or more to taste
⅛ teaspoon ground cloves

1. Purée the blueberries and any juices in a blender or food processor.

2. Combine the blueberry purée, vegetables, vinegar, honey, molasses, ketchup, and spices in a large, heavy, nonreactive saucepan. Gently simmer over medium heat until the vegetables are soft and the sauce is thick and flavorful, 15 to 20 minutes. Return the sauce to the blender and purée until smooth. The sauce should be thick but pourable; if it's too thick, add a little water.

3. Taste and correct the seasoning, adding more honey

for sweetness, vinegar for piquancy, and/or cayenne pepper for heat. Use right away or transfer to jars, cover, cool to room temperature, and refrigerate. The sauce will keep for several weeks.

Makes 5 to 6 cups

CRANBERRY BARBECUE SAUCE

So, I'm on an airplane bound for the nation's largest barbecue festival, the Kansas City Royal. I chat with the passenger next to me, and naturally our talk turns to barbecue. When Howard Bond was stationed at Offut Air Force Base in Omaha, Nebraska, thirty years ago, he pulled KP duty for an old battle-ax of a cook named Annie. He still remembers Annie's barbecue sauce, which contained an ingredient you'd expect to find on the Thanksgiving table, not at a barbecue: canned cranberry sauce. I must confess I was dubious, but one taste made me a believer. It turns out that the cranberries give the sauce just the right edge of tartness, while the pectin gives it a thick, lustrous sheen that glistens on ribs the way varnish does on an Old Master painting.

TRY THIS!

The presence of cranberry jelly in this sauce would logically lead you to barbecued turkey. Pork shoulders, ribs, and grilled chicken do well in its company, too.

1 bottle (14 ounces) ketchup
¼ cup cider vinegar
¼ cup yellow mustard
¼ cup Worcestershire sauce
2 tablespoons molasses
½ medium onion, minced
1 clove garlic, minced

¼ cup canned jellied cranberry sauce, cut into ½-inch dice
½ teaspoon coarse salt (kosher or sea)
½ teaspoon freshly ground black pepper

Combine all the ingredients in a heavy nonreactive saucepan and gradually bring to a boil over medium heat, stirring or whisking steadily to dissolve the bits of cranberry sauce. Gently simmer the sauce until thick and richly flavored, stirring often to prevent scorching, 15 to 20 minutes. Use right away or transfer to a large jar, cover, cool to room temperature, and refrigerate. The sauce will keep for several months.

Makes 2 ½ cups

GUAVA BARBECUE SAUCE

TRY THIS!

Guava barbecue sauce is one of the best slathers I know of for ribs and ham (for pork in general), and its exotic fruitiness goes well with chicken, turkey, duck, and even game. Make a double batch and keep some in a squirt bottle in the refrigerator, so you always have it on hand.

This satiny, perfumed, ruby-red sauce sure looks like a red-blooded American barbecue sauce. It sticks to ribs (and to your fingers) the way a good barbecue sauce should. But one taste and you know you're not in Kansas anymore. Guava is a highly aromatic tropical fruit that lends a Caribbean sweetness to the sauce, a sultry succulence that's reinforced by a blast of ginger and a shot of dark rum.

Guava paste is much beloved by Cuban Americans in South Florida—and by Puerto Ricans and Central and South Americans, too. Look for guava paste in the jam, canned fruit, or Hispanic foods section of the supermarket or go to a Caribbean market. It's sold in flat cans in supermarkets, as well as ethnic grocery stores. Buy the kind sold in cans, not cardboard boxes; the latter is too soft and sweet.

1 cup guava paste
6 tablespoons cider vinegar
1 cup cold water
¼ cup dark rum
¼ cup tomato paste
¼ cup fresh lime juice
1 tablespoon soy sauce
2 teaspoons ketchup
2 teaspoons Worcestershire sauce
2 tablespoons minced onion
1 tablespoon minced fresh ginger
2 cloves garlic, minced
¼ to ½ Scotch bonnet chili or other hot chili, seeded and minced
Coarse salt (kosher or sea) and freshly ground black pepper, to taste

1. Place all the ingredients in a heavy nonreactive saucepan and whisk to mix. Bring the sauce to a simmer, uncovered, over medium heat and continue to simmer until the sauce is slightly thickened and richly flavored, 10 to 15 minutes. Correct the seasoning, adding more salt or pepper if needed. The sauce should be pourable; if too thick, add a little more water.

2. Use right away or transfer to a large jar or squirt bottles, cover, cool to room temperature, and refrigerate. The sauce will keep for several months.

Makes 2 cups

JAKE'S THREE C'S BARBECUE SAUCE

TRY THIS!

Serve this sauce warm or at room temperature. It makes a great accompaniment to grilled poultry of all sorts (especially game birds), pork, and game. The sauce is also great with brisket—check out the recipe on page 83.

This may be the strangest sauce you'll ever find in a barbecue book. Cherries? Chocolate? Are we talking barbecue or dessert? Once you get beyond the initial shock, however, the sauce actually makes sense. The great wild game sauces of Europe play the tartness of vinegar or lemon against the sweetness of cherries and Port. The grand-daddy of Mexican sauces, *mole poblano,* contains chipotle chilies and a trace of chocolate, prized for its chalky bitterness. Put them together and you get an exotic yet oddly familiar sauce that goes great with poultry, pork, and game.

This recipe comes from my stepson chef, Jake Klein, who invented it one afternoon while we were testing recipes. Jake used fresh Bing cherries, but you can also use frozen or canned. For a milder sauce, seed the chipotle or use only half a chili.

3 tablespoons unsalted
  butter
½ medium onion, finely
  chopped
2 cloves garlic, thinly sliced
2 cups pitted Bing cherries,
  fresh, canned (drained),
  or frozen
2 tablespoons unsweetened
  cocoa powder
1 teaspoon pure chili powder
  (not a blend)
1½ cups Port wine
½ cup sherry vinegar
½ cup honey, or more to
  taste

4 teaspoons ketchup
2 teaspoons fresh lemon
  juice, or more to taste
1 teaspoon grated lemon
  zest
2 canned chipotle chilies,
  minced, or 2 teaspoons
  chipotle chili powder
½ teaspoon caraway seeds
½ teaspoon coarse salt
  (kosher or sea), or more
  to taste
½ teaspoon freshly ground
  black pepper

1. Melt the butter in a nonreactive saucepan over medium heat. Add the onion, garlic, and cherries and cook until the onion is soft but not brown, 3 minutes.

2. Add the remaining ingredients and bring to a boil over medium-high heat. Reduce the heat to medium and simmer the sauce, uncovered, until reduced to about 2 cups, 15 minutes, stirring occasionally. Correct the seasoning, adding salt, lemon juice, or honey; the sauce should be a little sweet, a little sour, and very flavorful. Use right away or transfer to a large jar, cover, cool to room temperature, and refrigerate. The sauce will keep for several weeks.

Makes 2 cups

TAMARIND-BANANA BARBECUE SAUCE

The notion of a tamarind-banana barbecue sauce may sound exotic, even downright strange, but it makes sense historically and geographically. Barbecue originated

TRY THIS!

The tropical roots of this sauce would suggest use with any Caribbean-style barbecue. Come to think of it, it tastes pretty good on American-style barbecue, too.

in the Caribbean; *barbacoa* was the Arawak Indian word for a grill. And tamarind and bananas are classic flavorings of the West Indies. Tamarind is a key ingredient in many commercial steak and barbecue sauces. In the following recipe, tamarind supplies the tartness provided by vinegar in a traditional American barbecue sauce, while the sweetness comes from bananas and molasses.

1½ cups tamarind purée, or more to taste (recipe follows)
1 small onion, minced
1 tablespoon minced fresh ginger
½ Scotch bonnet chili, or other hot chili, seeded and minced

½ green bell pepper, stemmed, seeded, and finely chopped
2 ripe bananas, finely chopped
¼ cup dark rum
¼ cup (packed) dark brown sugar, or more to taste
¼ cup molasses
¼ cup raisins
½ teaspoon cumin
¼ teaspoon ground allspice
¼ teaspoon cayenne pepper
Coarse salt (kosher or sea), to taste
Freshly ground black pepper, to taste

1. Thaw or prepare the tamarind purée. Combine all the ingredients in a heavy nonreactive saucepan. Bring to a simmer over medium heat and continue simmering, uncovered, until the vegetables and bananas are soft and the sauce is well flavored, 20 to 30 minutes.

2. Transfer the sauce to a blender or food processor and purée. Correct the seasoning, adding salt, brown sugar, or more tamarind purée. The sauce should be sweet, sour, and spicy. If too thick, add a little water. Use right away or transfer to jars, cover, cool to room temperature, and refrigerate. The sauce will keep for several weeks.

Makes 3 cups

TAMARIND PUREE

Tamarind is nature's sweet-and-sour sauce, boasting an acidity reminiscent of fresh lime juice and a sweetness akin to prunes. (The fruit takes its name from the Arabic words *tamr hindi,* literally Indian date.) The only tricky part about using tamarind is reducing the stringy, seed-studded pulp to a smooth purée. Ethnic markets and specialty greengrocers sometimes carry fresh tamarind pods. Look for pods with cracked dusty-brown skins, which indicate ripeness. Better yet, buy peeled tamarind pulp, which is sold in blocks at Hispanic markets and at many supermarkets. It is easier to use and there's no appreciable difference in flavor. Best of all, you may be able to buy frozen tamarind purée, in which case you can handily skip this recipe. Tamarind purée is sometimes called tamarind water.

TRY THIS!

Add 1 or 2 tablespoons tamarind purée to glazes and barbecue sauces for a refreshing fruity tartness.

8 ounces tamarind pods (8 to 10 pods) or 8 ounces peeled tamarind pulp

1½ cups boiling water

1. If using tamarind pods, peel and pry off the skin with a paring knife. If using a block of pulp, break it into 1-inch pieces. Place the tamarind in a blender with 1 cup boiling water. Let the tamarind soften for 10 minutes.

2. Run the blender in short bursts at low speed for 15 to 20 seconds to obtain a thick brown liquid. Do not overblend, or the seeds will break up. Strain the liquid into a bowl, pressing hard with a wooden spoon to extract the juices and scraping the bottom of the strainer with a spatula.

3. Return the pulp in the strainer to the blender and add the remaining ½ cup boiling water. Blend and strain the mixture into a bowl, pressing well to extract the juices. Tamarind water will keep for up to 5 days, covered, in the refrigerator and can be frozen for several months. I like to freeze it in plastic ice cube trays, so I have convenient premeasured portions on hand.

Makes about 1 cup

SQUIRT BOTTLES: BARBECUE SAUCE MEETS JACKSON POLLOCK

Remember when decorative dots, squiggles, and zigzags of sauce began decorating plates at cutting-edge restaurants? In the late 1980s, American chefs discovered a tool that fast-food operators have used for decades: squirt bottles. Once reserved for ketchup and mustard, these squeezable plastic bottles have become the paintbrushes of artistic grill jockeys. Fill them with your favorite sauce or sauces—the more colorful the better—and use them to decorate your food with Jackson Pollock-esque squiggles of flavor. Squirt bottles are available at most cookware shops.

The only tricky thing about squirt bottles is getting the sauce out. For a smooth sauce, cut off just the very tip of the nozzle. For a sauce that contains tiny bits of onion, chilies, or spices, you'll need to cut off more of the nozzle to make a wider hole. For a cool presentation at a party, make six different sauces and serve them in a cardboard beer or soda six-pack.

COFFEE BARBECUE SAUCE

Marcus Samuelsson is one of the most-talked-about culinary talents in New York, chef of a sleekly contemporary restaurant called Aquavit and a winner of the James Beard Rising Chef Award. His accomplishments are all the more remarkable given his place of birth—Sweden—and his cuisine—contemporary Scandinavian. Scandinavia may have some great food, but it isn't exactly known for world-class cuisine. "I come from a poor man's culture," explains Samuelsson. "It's my job to make it luxurious." Come to think of it: Isn't that true of American barbecue, which rou-

TRY THIS!

Samuelsson serves this sauce with a salmon-veal combination, which says a lot about its versatility. You'll be amazed how much coffee adds to a barbecue sauce.

tinely transforms the cheapest cuts of meat—ribs, chicken thighs, briskets—into morsels of epicurean glory?

Marcus serves the following barbecue sauce with a sort of Nordic surf and turf: crispy salmon with barbecued boneless veal ribs. You'll find that the chipotle and coffee add a brisk touch to a barbecue sauce that's not too sweet and will have you licking your fingers. It belongs to that branch of the barbecue sauce family tree whose members taste somewhat strange by themselves but great with food.

1 tablespoon olive oil
1 tablespoon honey
1 tablespoon dark brown
    sugar
1 medium red onion, finely
    chopped
4 ripe tomatoes, peeled,
    seeded, and diced
1 piece (3 inches) fresh
    ginger, finely chopped
1 cup brewed coffee
2 tablespoons ketchup
1 tablespoon chili
    sauce

1 tablespoon tomato paste
½ teaspoon fresh lemon
    juice
½ teaspoon Worcestershire
    sauce
1 canned chipotle chili,
    minced
2 sprigs of fresh rosemary
2 sprigs of fresh thyme
1⅓ cups cold water
Coarse salt (kosher or sea),
    to taste

1. Combine the oil, honey, brown sugar, and onion in a heavy nonreactive saucepan and cook over medium heat until the onion is caramelized (golden brown), 5 to 10 minutes, stirring with a wooden spoon.

2. Stir in the remaining ingredients, except for the salt, and bring to a simmer. Reduce the heat to medium-low and gently simmer the sauce until thick and flavorful, 20 to 30 minutes, stirring from time to time with a wooden spoon.

3. Remove the herb sprigs and transfer the sauce to a blender. Purée and correct the seasoning, adding salt or any other ingredient if needed. Use right away or transfer the sauce to a jar, cover, cool to room temperature, and refrigerate. The sauce will keep for several weeks in the refrigerator.

Makes 1¼ cups

COCA-COLA BARBECUE SAUCE

Dare to be different. That's Jim Budros's motto, and his culinary open-mindedness has won the financial advisor turned pit boss a championship at the Kansas City Royal International Barbecue Contest. What's different about his barbecue sauce is its main flavoring, an ingredient most people are more likely to drink than cook with: Coke! This isn't quite as strange as it sounds, because Coke is sweet, tart, and spicy—the flavor profile of most great barbecue sauces. Incidentally, pot roast braised in Coca-Cola is a favorite in Venezuela.

TRY THIS!

Use pretty much as you would any sauce, keeping in mind it has a strong affinity for chicken, ribs, and pork.

1 cup Coca-Cola	1 teaspoon onion flakes
1 cup ketchup	1 teaspoon garlic flakes
¼ cup Worcestershire sauce	½ teaspoon freshly ground
1 teaspoon liquid smoke	black pepper
3 tablespoons A.1. Steak Sauce	

Combine all the ingredients in a heavy nonreactive saucepan and gradually bring to a boil over medium heat. Reduce the heat slightly to obtain a gentle simmer. Simmer the sauce until reduced by a quarter, 6 to 8 minutes. Use right away or transfer to a large jar, cover, cool to room temperature, and refrigerate. The sauce will keep for several months.
Makes 2 cups

EAST-WEST BARBECUE SAUCE

Patrick Clark was one of the first Afro-American chefs to achieve superstar status. While he made his name at such high-falutin' New York establishments as Metro, Odéon, and Tavern on the Green in New York, he remained true to his roots. His menus paid homage to the foods he grew up on: corn muffins, pot pies, meat loaves, and rice puddings.

Clark had a lifelong fascination with barbecue sauce and developed dozens of cutting-edge twists on this down-home American favorite. The following sauce, for example, adds exotic Asian accents in the form of cardamom, coriander, star anise, and garlic chili paste to the familiar North American combination of ketchup, vinegar, and honey. When Patrick died at the age of forty-two, his chef friends, led by Charlie Trotter, produced a cookbook honoring Clark. (The royalties from the book will go into a college fund for his children.) This recipe has been adapted from *Cooking with Patrick Clark.*

Garlic chili paste and star anise can be found at Chinese markets, gourmet shops, and by mail order (see page 281).

(see page 281)

TRY THIS!

Clark originally created this sauce as a glaze for roasted salmon. It's delicious on every manner of grilled fish and also poultry, ranging from chicken to squab. Because it's sweet, you should brush it on toward the end of grilling or right before serving, so it doesn't burn. Needless to say it also makes a great table sauce.

2⅓ cups honey
1 cup rice vinegar
1 cup ketchup
⅓ cup soy sauce
¼ cup fresh lime juice
3 tablespoons garlic chili paste
½ cup chopped fresh cilantro
1 tablespoon finely chopped fresh ginger

5 star anise
2 cinnamon sticks (3 inches each)
1 tablespoon black peppercorns
1 tablespoon coriander seeds
1 teaspoon whole cloves
1 teaspoon ground cardamom
1 teaspoon ground mace

Combine all the ingredients in a heavy nonreactive saucepan and bring to a boil over high heat. Reduce the heat to medium-low and simmer the sauce, uncovered, until thick, syrupy, and reduced to about 2 cups, 30 minutes. Strain through a fine-mesh strainer. Use right away or transfer to a large jar, cover, cool to room temperature, and refrigerate. The sauce will keep for several weeks.

Makes 2 cups

NORTH CAROLINA PULLED PORK

Pork shoulder cooked smoky as a fireplace, succulent as a biscuit dipped in bacon fat, and tender enough to pull apart with your fingers—such is North Carolina barbecue. As the name suggests, the traditional way to serve the pork is to pull it into shreds with your fingers. That's where a thin vinegar sauce comes in, because a Kansas City sauce would be too thick to be absorbed by the slender shreds of meat.

1 Boston butt (5 pounds; also known as bone-in pork shoulder roast)
1 tablespoon coarse salt (kosher or sea)
1 tablespoon freshly ground black pepper
1 tablespoon paprika
1 recipe Pig Picker Pucker Sauce (facing page)
6 cups shredded cabbage
10 to 12 hamburger buns, split

SPECIAL EQUIPMENT
4 cups hickory chips, soaked in cold water for 1 hour

1. Generously season the pork all over with salt, pepper, and paprika.

2. Set up the grill for indirect cooking, following the directions on page 5, and preheat to 325°F.

3. Place the pork shoulder, skin side up, on the grate over the drip pan. If using a charcoal grill, toss a quarter of the wood chips on the coals. If using a gas grill, place the chips in the smoker box. Don't grill until you see smoke. Cover the grill.

4. Smoke-cook the pork shoulder until fall-off-the-bone tender with an internal temperature of 195°F, 4 to 6 hours. If using charcoal, add 10 fresh coals and 1 cup wood chips per side every hour.

5. Transfer the cooked pork roast to a cutting board, tent with aluminum foil, and let rest for 15 minutes. Pull off and discard any skin. Pull the pork into pieces, discarding any bones or fat. You may wish to wear heavy-duty rubber gloves for pulling. Using your fingertips or a fork, pull each piece of pork into thin shreds. Or use a cleaver and cutting board to finely chop it. Transfer the pork to a large foil pan and stir in 1 to 1½ cups sauce, enough to keep the pork moist. Cover the pan with foil and place on the grill to keep warm.

6. Place the cabbage in a large bowl, add ½ to ¾ cup of the remaining sauce, and toss to mix.

7. To serve, pile the pork and cabbage on the hamburger buns, spooning on additional sauce if desired.

Serves 10 to 12

PIG PICKER PUCKER SAUCE

The Carolinas (particularly the northeastern part of North Carolina) occupy a unique position in the realm of American barbecue. Unlike the rest of the country, which enjoys ketchup-based sauces, the preferred condiment here is a piquant mixture of vinegar and red pepper flakes, sometimes with just a touch of sugar to cut the acidity. This makes sense, seeing as the favored meat for barbecue in these parts is pork—more precisely, a whole hog smoked in a pit until it's so tender you can pull the meat off the bones with your fingers.

Because you're eating whole hog or pork shoulder, you're dealing with fatty meat. The vinegar in the sauce offsets the pork's richness. There's another reason vinegar sauce is so well suited to a pig picking. Carolina-style pork is usually served chopped or shredded, so you need a thin sauce that can soak into the tiny pieces of meat. Put the pork and vinegar sauce together and you have some of the most damnably delectable barbecue ever to grace a bun.

TRY THIS!

Serve this sauce with pulled or chopped barbecue pork. Mix it in with the pork (this recipe makes enough for 4 to 5 pounds of meat) or spoon it on top. Save a little of the sauce to mix with chopped cabbage and pile the resulting coleslaw on top of the pork on a hamburger bun. Then imagine you're at a North Carolina pig picking, or a world-class barbecue joint, like Wilbur's or Lexington Barbecue.

1½ cups cider vinegar
¾ cup cold water
2 tablespoons sugar, or to taste
1 tablespoon hot pepper flakes

1 small onion, thinly sliced
1½ tablespoons coarse salt (kosher or sea), or to taste
½ teaspoon freshly ground black pepper

Combine all the ingredients in a bowl and stir until the sugar and salt are dissolved. Correct the seasoning, adding salt if needed. Serve this sauce on shredded barbecued pork. You could prepare this sauce ahead, but why bother? It's so quick and easy to prepare, you should make it from scratch as you need it.

Makes 2½ cups

CHARLIE TROTTER'S TRUFFLED PORCINI BBQ SAUCE

Ask and you shall receive. Charlie Trotter is one of the greatest chefs in North America. When I asked him to create a barbecue sauce for this book, I half expected to be told "We don't serve barbecue sauce at Charlie Trotter's." (Actually, Charlie's much too nice a guy to be supercilious.) Instead, he obliged with a perfectly Trotteresque recipe—a barbecue sauce flavored with truffles and porcini mushrooms. It is quite unlike any you've ever tasted. The fungi dance a minuet of flavor: The meaty flavor of the porcini is a luscious counterpoint to the woodsy aroma of the truffles.

Porcini mushrooms and truffles can be found at gourmet shops and specialty greengrocers or ordered from Marché aux Delices (see page 281). I have, on occasion, made the sauce with other mushrooms. Delicious!

2 cups beef stock, homemade, or canned salt-free beef broth

2 tablespoons vegetable oil (Charlie uses grapeseed oil)

1 large or 2 medium red onions, finely chopped

4 ounces fresh porcini mushrooms, trimmed, cleaned, and thinly sliced

1½ cups dry red wine

¼ cup sherry vinegar

¼ cup truffle oil

1 black truffle (½ to 1 ounce), scrubbed and finely chopped

2 tablespoons unsalted butter

Coarse salt (kosher or sea) and freshly ground black pepper, to taste

1. Place the stock in a heavy saucepan and bring to a boil over high heat. Continue boiling, uncovered, until reduced by half, about 10 minutes.

2. Heat the oil in a nonreactive saucepan over medium heat. Add the onions and cook until lightly browned, about 5 minutes, stirring with a wooden spoon. Add the porcini and sauté for 2 minutes. Add the red wine and simmer briskly (you may need to raise the heat) until reduced by two thirds, about 10 minutes. Add the reduced stock, vine-

gar, and truffle oil. Simmer the sauce until richly flavored, 3 minutes. Stir in the truffle and remove the pan from the heat. Stir in the butter and season the sauce with salt and plenty of pepper before serving. The sauce tastes best served within a few hours of making. Transfer any extra to a jar, cover, and refrigerate. The sauce will keep for up to 5 days.

Makes 2 cups

FIREHOUSE JACK'S MUSTARD SAUCE

TRY THIS!

This sauce goes great with just about anything. Serve it with your favorite barbecue, especially pork tenderloin and smoked pork shoulder and ribs.

In South Carolina and parts of Georgia, barbecue isn't complete without a sweet, tangy, yellow-brown sauce based on mustard. The basic ingredients are mustard (often the yellow ballpark variety) with vinegar and some sort of sweetener. The latter could be honey, molasses, brown sugar, or cane syrup—or a combination of two or more. By varying the type of vinegar, you can create an almost endless variety of sauces. Which is what Jack McDavid, owner of Jack's Firehouse in Philadelphia and consulting chef for Red's Backwoods BBQ, did to create this lip-smacking mustard sauce. Jack's sauce owes its kick to jalapeño chilies and its silken sweetness to a fillip of corn syrup. It's sweet, but not too sweet.

¾ cup distilled white vinegar
½ cup beef or chicken broth
½ cup finely chopped onion
¼ cup seeded minced
    jalapeño chilies
½ cup Dijon mustard
¼ cup honey mustard or
    brown deli-style mustard
¼ cup corn syrup, or to taste

2 tablespoons molasses
½ teaspoon freshly ground
    black pepper
½ teaspoon coarse salt
    (kosher or sea), or more
    to taste
¼ teaspoon cayenne
    pepper

Combine all the ingredients in a heavy nonreactive saucepan over high heat and bring to a boil. Reduce the heat and simmer, until thick and richly flavored, about 10 minutes, stirring occasionally. Taste the sauce for seasoning, adding salt or corn syrup as desired. Use right away or transfer to jars, cover, cool to room temperature, and refrigerate. The sauce will keep for several months.

Makes about 2 cups

HONEY-BALSAMIC-DIJON BARBECUE SAUCE

The Que Queens are a group of Kansas City food-industry people—all women—who gather to compete in barbecue competitions, write books, and manufacture barbecue products, with the proceeds going to charity. Several have become personal friends and they always go out of their way to rush me to the latest barbecue joints whenever I'm in town. (One night, we visited six!)

This recipe comes from the most seasoned pit master of the crew, Janeyce Michel-Cupito, founder of an award-winning team called Powderpuff BBQ (see page 25). Considering the abundance of vinegar, the sauce is remarkably mellow; it makes a wonderful slather on ribs, chicken, and pork chops. The edge of tartness keeps the sweetness of the honey and corn syrup in check.

⅔ cup cider vinegar
½ cup honey
½ cup Dijon mustard
¼ cup balsamic vinegar
¼ cup light corn syrup
2 tablespoons fresh lemon juice

2 tablespoons tomato paste
1 teaspoon coarse salt (kosher or sea)
1 teaspoon garlic powder
½ teaspoon freshly ground black pepper

Combine all the ingredients in a heavy nonreactive saucepan and bring to a boil over high heat. Reduce the heat to medium-low and gently simmer the sauce, uncovered, until thick and richly flavored, 30 minutes. Use right away or transfer to a large jar, cover, cool to room temperature, and refrigerate. The sauce will keep for several months. **Makes 2 cups**

VARIATION

To make a glaze, add ⅓ cup honey to 1 cup of finished sauce. Brush on ribs, chicken, and pork chops the last 5 minutes of grilling.

TRY THIS!

This sauce was created for barbecued ribs and chicken. It flatters game birds, such as pheasant and partridge, as well as duck, quail, and turkey.

CORROSION PROTECTION

In order to extend the shelf life of your barbecue sauce or relish, place a sheet of plastic wrap between the jar and the metal lid of a barbecue sauce or relish. The reason is simple: Eventually, the fumes from the vinegar or salt will corrode the inside of the lid, even a lid coated with rubber or plastic. The easiest way to prevent corrosion is to cover the mouth of the jar with plastic wrap before screwing on the lid. This may look funny, but it greatly increases the shelf life of the sauce.

BUBBA-LINA VINEGAR SAUCE

It takes a lot of gumption to serve a North Carolina–style vinegar sauce in Kansas City, home of America's favorite sweet sauce. But Jeff Stehney, head of the Slaughterhouse Five barbecue team and owner of the popular Oklahoma Joe's restaurant, has always marched to his own drummer, and his single-mindedness has paid off with numerous contest championships, including three Kansas City Royals.

A few years ago, Jeff teamed up with Joe Davidson to open a barbecue joint housed in a gas station. (Talk about one-stop shopping!) The bad news about Oklahoma Joe's is that it's always busy. The good news is that the line moves fairly quickly. Jeff wanted to serve a pulled pork sandwich in this city of ribs and briskets and he wanted to serve it with vinegar sauce, anathema in a place where the thick, sweet, red barbecue sauce that defines the Kansas City–style was invented. To make it more palatable—visually palatable at least—he added tomato paste, so that the sauce would at least look red. The result: a deliciously mouth-puckeringly tart vinegar sauce that goes great with pork and provides relief from the sugar fatigue you can experience when you eat too much Kansas City–style sauce. Here's how I imagine they make it.

2 cups cider vinegar
½ cup tomato paste
¼ cup dark corn syrup, or
    more to taste
¼ cup cold water
2 teaspoons coarse salt
    (kosher or sea), or more
    to taste

1 teaspoon freshly ground
    black pepper
1 to 2 cloves garlic, minced
½ teaspoon cayenne pepper
    or hot pepper flakes, or
    more to taste

Combine all ingredients in a nonreactive saucepan and bring to a boil over medium heat. Simmer for 3 minutes. Let cool and correct the seasoning, adding salt, cayenne, or corn syrup; the sauce should be very piquant. (The corn syrup should take the edge off the vinegar, not really make the sauce sweet.) Use right away or transfer to jars, cover, cool to room temperature, and refrigerate. The sauce will keep for several months. Shake well before using.

Makes 3 cups

TRY THIS!

This sauce was designed to be poured over or mixed into North Carolina–style chopped or pulled (shredded) pork. You can also serve it with barbecued chicken, lamb, or beef. The sauce works better mixed in with the chopped meat than spooned over it. You may screw your mouth in a pucker when you first taste it, but the sauce grows on you. A lot.

WORLD BARBECUE SAUCES

Americans aren't the only folks who love barbecue sauce. Argentinians could no more imagine grilled beef without their garlicky, tart, green parsley sauce called Chimichurri (page 172), than Thais could enjoy saté without a peanut sauce creamy with coconut milk and redolent with cilantro and chilies (page 208). In Spain, grilled meats are served with Romesco, a roasted vegetable and nut sauce (page 194), while in the Republic of Georgia, no barbecue would be complete without Tkemali (page 196), a mouth-puckering condiment made with sour plums or even rhubarb.

This chapter explores the lip-smacking world of barbecue sauces: from Monkey Gland Sauce (page 199) from South Africa (don't worry, it doesn't really contain primate parts) to Moroccan Charmoula (page 198) to Japanese Yakitori Sauce (page 204). If you're in the mood to torment your tongue, try fiery Peruvian Yellow Pepper Sauce (page 187) and extinguish chili fires with Raita (page 200), a cooling Indian yogurt sauce. Along the way, sample barbecue sauces made with miso, rhubarb, and even chocolate.

You may not come any closer to defining the perfect barbecue sauce, but you'll sure lick your fingers and have a lot of fun trying!

CARIBBEAN AND LATIN BARBECUE SAUCES

CHIMICHURRI
(Argentine Parsley Garlic Sauce)

Argentina is home of a pesto-like pugilist called *chimichurri*. The sauce owes its freshness and bright green color to flat-leaf parsley and its pungency to tongue-pounding doses of garlic. (Talk about ingenuity: Parsley is nature's mouthwash, so it helps counteract the breath-wilting fumes of the garlic.) Those are the basic ingredients, but there are as many variations as there are Argentinian grill jockeys. Some enliven their *chimichurri* with grated carrot or red bell pepper; others kick up the heat with hot pepper flakes or fresh chilies. Pebre (page 188) is a sort of Chilean *chimichurri* made with cilantro.

1 large bunch of fresh flat-leaf parsley, washed, stemmed, and dried
8 cloves garlic, peeled
3 tablespoons minced onion
5 tablespoons distilled white vinegar, or more to taste
5 tablespoons water

1 teaspoon coarse salt (kosher or sea)
½ teaspoon dried oregano
½ to 1 teaspoon hot pepper flakes, or to taste
½ teaspoon freshly ground black pepper
1 cup extra virgin olive oil

Finely chop the parsley and garlic in a food processor. Add the onion, vinegar, water, salt, oregano, pepper flakes, and black pepper and process in brief bursts until the salt crystals are dissolved. Add the oil in a thin stream. Don't overprocess; the *chimichurri* should be fairly coarse. Correct the seasoning, adding salt or vinegar if needed. Chimichurri is quick to make, so I usually prepare it as I need it. If you do choose to store it, transfer it to a jar, cover, and refrigerate. It will keep for several weeks, but it loses its bright green color in a day or two. Be sure to taste and reseason before serving.

Makes 2 cups; enough to serve 6 to 8

MOJO (Cuban Citrus Garlic Sauce)

TRY THIS!

Pour *mojo* over grilled fare, especially seafood, poultry, pork, and beef. *Mojo* is the traditional sauce for Cuban pit-roasted pork and *palomilla* (a thin steak cut from the round and grilled).

Here in my hometown, Miami, barbecue calls for a ketchup-free sauce called *mojo* (pronounced MO-ho, not mo-JOE). This edgy citrus sauce owes its intense flavor to the Holy Trinity of Cuban seasonings: oregano, cumin, and garlic. The garlic is fried to the color of amber to boost its flavor without making it bitter. The traditional souring agent is the juice of a tropical fruit called *naranja agria,* or sour orange, which in Miami is available at local supermarkets. If unavailable, you can approximate its flavor by combining fresh lime and orange juice. You'll be amazed by the electrifying effect *mojo* has on grilled fare of all ethnic persuasions. And it will certainly get your mojo rising!

½ cup olive oil

8 large cloves garlic, thinly sliced crosswise

⅔ cup fresh sour orange juice (see box, page 174) or ½ cup fresh lime juice and 3 tablespoons fresh orange juice

⅓ cup water

1 teaspoon ground cumin

½ teaspoon ground oregano

1½ teaspoons coarse salt (kosher or sea), or more to taste

½ teaspoon freshly ground black pepper, or more to taste

3 tablespoons chopped fresh cilantro or flat-leaf parsley

Heat the olive oil in a deep saucepan over medium heat. Add the garlic and cook until fragrant and pale golden brown, 2 to 3 minutes. Do not let the garlic brown too much, or it will become bitter. Stir in the sour orange juice, water, cumin, oregano, salt, and pepper. Stand back: The sauce may sputter. Bring the sauce to a rolling boil, correct the seasoning, adding salt and pepper if needed. Remove from the heat, cool to room temperature, then stir in the cilantro. To enjoy this distinctive Cuban barbecue sauce at its best, serve it within a few hours of making. Or transfer to a jar, cover, and refrigerate. The *mojo* will keep for several weeks. Shake well before serving.

Makes 1½ cups; enough to serve 6 to 8

VARIATION

Grapefruit-Mint Mojo: Substitute fresh grapefruit juice for the sour orange juice and chopped fresh mint for the cilantro.

SOUR ORANGE

Throughout much of the Caribbean, Central America, and the Yucatán, the preferred souring agent for marinades isn't lime juice or vinegar but the acidic juice of the sour orange. Known as *naranja agria* in Spanish, sour orange looks somewhat like a regular orange, but has a greenish tinge and bumpy rind. The size can range in diameter from 2 to 4 inches.

Sour orange juice has a highly distinctive flavor—imagine fresh lime juice with a hint of regular orange juice and grapefruit. If you're in a real hurry, you can use fresh lime juice in place of sour orange juice, but a closer substitute is probably 3 parts lime juice and 1 part fresh orange juice. Sour orange is available in Latino and West Indian markets and a growing number of supermarkets, especially in border towns, including Miami.

AJILIMOJILI
(Puerto Rican Pepper Sauce)

Mention *ajilimojili* to a Puerto Rican and his eyes will light with pleasure. For that matter, *your* eyes will light with pleasure simply saying this musical word, which is pronounced "a-HEE-lee-mo-HEE-lee" and means something like "little pepper sauce." The peppers in question are green bell and a distinctive Puerto Rican chili called rocotillo. Shaped like a Scotch bonnet, the rocotillo has something of that chili's floral aroma with considerably less heat. Put these chilies together with onion, celery, vampire-defying doses of garlic, olive oil, vinegar, cilantro, and *recao* (culantro, a thumb-shape leaf that tastes like a cross between cilantro and celery) and you've got an intensely aromatic sauce that rivals the Argentine Chimichurri (page 172).

Puerto Ricans tend to serve *ajilimojili* as a dip for fried vegetables, not as a steak sauce. But I think you'll find its flavors perfectly suited to grilled fish and meats. In the best of all possible worlds, use rocotillo chili and *recao*, but if you can't find them, red bell pepper will stand in just fine for the chili and flat-leaf parsley for the herb.

TRY THIS!

Ajilimojili goes great with grilled meats of all sorts, especially steak, pork, and chicken. You could also serve it with full-flavored fish, like grilled salmon or kingfish. You can even use it as a dip or sauce for grilled vegetables.

1 medium onion, cut into 1-inch pieces

6 cloves garlic, peeled

1 rib celery, thinly sliced

1 green bell pepper, stemmed, seeded, and cut into 1-inch pieces

8 rocotillo chilies, stemmed and seeded, or ¼ cup diced red bell pepper

1 bunch of fresh cilantro, washed and stemmed

6 recao (culantro) leaves or 6 sprigs of fresh flat-leaf parsley

½ teaspoon dried oregano

½ teaspoon ground cumin

½ teaspoon hot pepper flakes

1 cup extra virgin olive oil

⅓ cup red wine vinegar, or more to taste

1½ teaspoons coarse salt (kosher or sea), or more to taste

½ teaspoon freshly ground black pepper

Combine the onion, garlic, celery, bell pepper, chilies, cilantro, *recao* (if using), oregano, cumin, and pepper flakes in a food processor and process to a coarse purée. Add the oil, vinegar, salt, and pepper and process to mix. Correct the seasoning, adding vinegar or salt; the *ajilimojili* should be highly seasoned. *Ajilimojili* tastes best served within a few hours of making. Or transfer to jars, cover, and refrigerate. *Ajilimojili* will keep for several days. If you store it, be sure to taste and reseason it before serving.

Makes 3 cups; enough to serve 8 to 10

MOLE POBLANO
(Mexican Chocolate-Chili Sauce)

TRY THIS!

Serve *mole poblano* with any type of grilled poultry, especially chicken, Cornish game hen, and quail. It's also great with grilled vegetables. For Mexicans, the *mole* is the main attraction, so they spoon it over the grilled fare. But the final dish will look prettier if you spoon the *mole* on the plate, then arrange the grilled bird or vegetables on top.

Mole poblano is Mexico's most famous sauce—a dark, rich, rib-sticking gravy brewed from nuts, raisins, chilies, spices, and chocolate. When some Americans first hear about this chocolate-chili sauce, they envision a sort of hot fudge that would be more appropriate for dessert. Nothing could be further from the truth, for *mole poblano* is a serious food sauce that hits every note on the gustatory scale: sweet, sour, salty, bitter, spicy, earthy, fruity, pungent. Tradition calls for *mole poblano* to be served with boiled turkey. Over the years, I've taken to serving it with grilled chicken, Cornish game hen, squab, quail, and even grilled vegetables with spectacular results. The recipe may look complicated because it contains a lot of ingredients, but actually it's a series of simple steps.

Most of the ingredients in *mole poblano* can be found in your local supermarket. To be strictly authentic, you should use at least five types of dried chilies: anchos, mulatos, pasillas, guajillos, and chipotles. (For a full discussion of the chilies, see page 182.) I've called for all five, but you could replace some of the varieties with more ancho chilies. Just be sure to use eight to ten dried chilies in all. The next oddball ingredient is lard. This is the traditional fat for frying in Mexico, and it has a smoky meaty flavor that's unique. The real surprise is that lard is actually healthier for you than butter, containing half the cholesterol and a third of the saturated fat of an equal amount of butter. If you don't want to use lard, substitute olive oil; it will still give you a highly flavorful *mole poblano*.

2 ancho chilies
2 mulato chilies
2 pasilla chilies
2 guajillo chilies
1 to 2 dried chipotle chilies
4 ripe plum tomatoes
1 medium onion, quartered
3 cloves garlic, peeled
1 corn tortilla, torn into
    2-inch pieces
3 tablespoons slivered
    almonds
3 tablespoons sesame seeds
½ teaspoon black
    peppercorns
½ teaspoon coriander seeds
1 piece (1 inch) cinnamon
    stick

2 whole cloves
¼ teaspoon aniseed
Hot water, for soaking the
    chilies
¼ cup chopped fresh cilantro
3 tablespoons golden raisins
2 cups chicken broth, or
    more if needed, warm
¼ cup lard or olive oil
1 ounce unsweetened
    chocolate
2 teaspoons honey, or more
    to taste
1 tablespoon red wine
    vinegar, or more to taste
Coarse salt (kosher or sea),
    to taste

1. Heat a comal or dry cast-iron skillet over medium heat. Roast the chilies until fragrant, 1 to 2 minutes per side. Transfer to a platter to cool. Roast the tomatoes, onion, and garlic until browned on all sides. The garlic will take 4 to 6 minutes, the tomatoes and onion, 10 to 12 minutes. Set aside to cool. Toast the tortilla until crisp and brown, 3 minutes per side. Set aside to cool. Toast the almonds, shaking the pan to ensure even browning, until toasted and fragrant but not too brown, 2 to 3 minutes. Set aside to cool. Toast and cool the sesame seeds the same way. Add the peppercorns, coriander, cinnamon, and cloves to the pan and toast until fragrant and toasted, 2 minutes. Do not let the spices burn. Let cool.

2. Transfer the toasted peppercorns, coriander,

cinnamon, and cloves and the aniseed to a spice mill and grind to a fine powder. Breathe a sigh of relief: The hard part is over.

3. Tear the roasted chilies in half and remove the stems, veins, and seeds. Place the chilies in a bowl with hot water to cover. Soak until pliable, about 30 minutes, and drain well.

4. Place the tomatoes in a blender. Add the onion, garlic, chilies, almonds, sesame seeds, ground spices, cilantro, and raisins. Work in several batches if needed. Purée to a smooth paste, scraping down the sides of the blender bowl several times with a rubber spatula. If the mixture is too dry to purée, add a little chicken broth.

5. Heat the lard in a large, deep skillet or saucepan over medium heat. Add the chili mixture and cook, stirring constantly, until thick and fragrant, 5 minutes. Reduce the heat and stir in the broth, chocolate, honey, vinegar, and salt. Simmer the sauce, stirring occasionally with a wooden spoon, until thick and richly flavored, 10 minutes. The *mole* should be thick but pourable; add as needed. It should be very flavorful, with just the faintest hint of sweetness; add salt, vinegar, or just the least bit of honey. Use right away or transfer to jars, cover, cool to room temperature, and refrigerate. The *mole* will keep for several weeks.

Makes 4 cups; enough to serve 8 to 10

CHIRMOL
(Central American Tomato Sauce)

Order a steak in a Honduran or Salvadorian restaurant and you'll be offered a small bowl of a spicy tomato sauce called *chirmol*. At first glance, it looks like Mexican salsa, but the flavor profile is quite different—the result of adding oil and vinegar in addition to the lime juice. There are many types of *chirmol*, including a salsa-like uncooked version and a cooked one made rich with roasted vegetables.

FRESH CHIRMOL

This *chirmol* starts out like a Mexican salsa, but the radishes, vinegar, and olive oil give it a more complex flavor.

TRY THIS!

Use *chirmol* as you would any Mexican salsa. Spoon it over grilled seafood, poultry, and meats (especially steak). Serve it with *carnitas* (crusty bits of grilled beef or pork on tortillas). You could even serve it with the Fajitas on page 32.

2 medium ripe tomatoes, peeled, seeded, and finely diced (see box, page 246)

½ medium sweet onion, such as Vidalia or Walla Walla, finely chopped

2 radishes, finely chopped

2 scallions (white and green parts), trimmed and finely chopped

2 jalapeño chilies, seeded and finely chopped (for a spicier chirmol leave the seeds in)

1 clove garlic, minced

3 tablespoons chopped fresh cilantro

3 tablespoons olive oil

2 tablespoons distilled white vinegar

2 tablespoons cold water

1 tablespoon fresh lime juice, or more to taste

1 teaspoon coarse salt (kosher or sea), or more to taste

½ teaspoon freshly ground black pepper

Combine all the ingredients in an attractive serving bowl and stir to mix. Correct the seasoning, adding lime juice or salt; the *chirmol* should be highly seasoned. Serve within a few hours of making.

Makes about 2 cups; enough to serve 6 to 8

ROASTED CHIRMOL

The traditional way to make this sauce is to roast the vegetables in an ungreased cast-iron skillet for a concentrated, smoky flavor. That set me thinking about my favorite way to achieve a smoke flavor: grilling. Either method will produce a superlative *chirmol*.

TRY THIS!

Use as you would fresh *chirmol* on page 179. This variation has a more robust flavor than the preceding recipe, the result of roasting the vegetables. Thus, it's gutsy enough to stand up to lamb and beef.

4 plum tomatoes or 2 ripe tomatoes
1 small onion, quartered
2 cloves garlic
1 to 2 jalapeño chilies, seeded (for a spicier chirmol leave in the seeds)
3 tablespoons chopped fresh parsley
3 tablespoons olive oil
½ teaspoon dried oregano
2 tablespoons fresh lime juice
1 tablespoon distilled white vinegar
Coarse salt (kosher and sea) and freshly ground black pepper, to taste

Grill Method

1. Preheat the grill to high, placing a vegetable grate in the center. If you don't have a vegetable grate, thread the onion quarters, garlic, and chilies on skewers.

2. Place the tomatoes, onion, garlic, and chilies on the grate and grill until well browned on all sides, 4 to 6 minutes for the garlic and chilies, 10 to 12 minutes for the tomatoes and onions. Transfer the vegetables to a food processor or blender and purée. (Don't worry about a few charred pieces of skin; they'll add flavor.)

3. Heat the oil in a nonstick skillet. Add the vegetable purée, parsley, oregano, lime juice, and vinegar and cook, stirring often, until thick and flavorful, 5 minutes. Correct the seasoning, adding salt and pepper if needed. Use right away or transfer to a large jar, cover, cool to room temperature, and refrigerate. The *chirmol* will keep for up to 5 days.

Makes 1½ cups; enough to serve 6

Skillet Method

1. Heat a cast-iron skillet over medium heat. Add the tomatoes, onion, garlic, and chilies and cook until browned on all sides. This will take 4 to 6 minutes for the garlic and chili, 10 to 12 minutes for the tomatoes and onions. Transfer the vegetables to a food processor or blender and purée. (Don't worry about a few charred pieces of skin; they'll add flavor.)

2. Heat the oil in a nonstick skillet. Add the vegetable purée, parsley, oregano, lime juice, and vinegar and cook, stirring often, until thick and flavorful, 5 minutes. Correct the seasoning, adding salt and pepper if needed.

Makes 1½ cups; enough to serve 6

PANAMANIAN FISH SAUCE

TRY THIS!

This sauce was originally created for grilled fish and it remains an excellent enhancement to all sorts of seafood. But don't overlook it as a barbecue sauce for poultry, pork, steak, or even grilled vegetables.

Panama has some of the most soulful, flavorful cooking in Latin America. Yet most North Americans would be hard-pressed to name a single Panamanian dish. This was the case for me, until I met Rosario McNish, owner-chef of a boisterous Panamanian restaurant in Miami called Las Molas. Rosario is one of those natural-born cooks who instinctively knows which ingredients seem to go together best. She cooks with feeling not with measurements, and her food never fails to delight. The following sauce owes its zing to two ingredients not often used in Latino cooking— curry powder and mustard.

¼ cup olive oil
1 medium onion, thinly sliced
1 green bell pepper, stemmed, halved, seeded, and thinly sliced lengthwise
1 red bell pepper, stemmed, halved, seeded, and thinly sliced lengthwise
3 cloves garlic, thinly sliced
1 rib celery, thinly sliced
2 teaspoons mustard, or more to taste

1½ teaspoons curry powder, or more to taste
½ teaspoon dried oregano
½ teaspoon freshly ground black pepper
½ cup tomato purée
¼ cup dry white wine
½ cup cold water
Coarse salt (kosher or sea), to taste
1 tablespoon fresh lime juice, or more to taste

Heat the olive oil in a sauté pan over high heat. Add the onion, bell peppers, garlic, and celery and cook, stirring well, until crisp-tender and aromatic, 3 minutes. Stir in the mustard, curry powder, oregano, and pepper and cook for 1 minute. Stir in the tomato purée, wine, and water, bring to a boil, then reduce the heat and gently simmer the sauce until thick and richly flavored, about 5 to 10 minutes. Correct the seasoning, adding salt, curry, mustard, or lime juice; the sauce should be highly seasoned. Use right away or transfer to a large jar, cover, cool to room temperature, and refrigerate. The sauce will keep for up to 1 week. Bring back to room temperature before serving.

Makes about 2 cups; enough to serve 4

SOME LIKE IT HOT:
A GRILLER'S GUIDE TO CHILIES

As you travel the world's barbecue trail, heat is a constant. Not just the heat of the fire, but the gullet-blasting burn of chilies. Wherever people grill fish or meat over fire, the chances are you'll find some sort of chili pepper, from the chili-laced salsas of Mexico to the fiery sambals of Penang. Here's a guide to the chilies the world's grill jockeys use to set their food on fire.

Most of the heat in a chili resides in the seeds and veins. For a milder sauce, rub, or marinade, remove the seeds and veins before using by scraping them out with a paring knife. It's a good idea to wear rubber gloves when handling chilies, especially if you have sensitive skin.

To prepare dried chilies, remove the stems, tear open the chili, and discard the seeds. Soak the chilies in warm water to cover until soft and pliable, 30 to 60 minutes. Sometimes dried chilies are roasted on the grill or on a comal or griddle, or under the broiler before soaking. This roasting gives the chilies an added smoky dimension.

FRESH CHILIES

AJI DULCE: Sometimes called *aji cachucha,* this is a tiny pattypan squash–shape chili with the floral aroma of a Scotch bonnet, but no heat. Used extensively by Cuban grill meisters. Substitute red bell pepper.

HABANERO: The hottest chili in Mexico—a country that's no slouch when it comes to gustatory hellfire. Native to Cuba (a *habanero* is a resident of Havana) and to the Caribbean, the habanero is the preferred chili of the Yucatán, where it's used as an ingredient in marinades and the tongue-torturing salsas for which the region is

so famous (see pages 251 to 258). Its smoky, apricoty, floral aroma and excruciating heat are similar to that of the Jamaican Scotch bonnet.

HORN PEPPERS: Elongated, bright green chilies that are tapered and twisted like a steer's horn. The heat ranges from hot to lip-searing. Horn peppers are often grilled whole, especially in Turkey and Japan.

JALAPENO: The bullet-shaped jalapeño is our most readily available chili, sold at supermarkets everywhere. The flavor is grassy, rather like a green bell pepper. Jalapeños are relatively mild as chilies go, ringing in at around 5,000 Scovilles (the units used for measuring the heat of a chili). Compare that to the 200,000 Scovilles of the habanero or Scotch bonnet!

POBLANO: Could be described as a green bell pepper on uppers. Native to Mexico, this large (4 to 6 inches long, 2 to 3 inches wide), tapered, dark green chili is often grilled or roasted to make pepper strips *(rajas)*. It's also used for stuffing. The flavor is similar to that of green bell pepper, but hotter and more aromatic. If unavailable, use green bell peppers mixed with minced jalapeño.

ROCOTILLO: Similar to the aji dulce (see above) in its floral aroma, delicate bell pepper/Scotch bonnet flavor, but relative lack of heat (some rocotillos can be quite fiery, however). Orange, yellow, or pale green, the rocotillo can look like a miniature pattypan squash or smoother and more elongated, like a small habanero. This is a popular chili in Puerto Rico. Substitute aji dulce or red bell pepper.

SCOTCH BONNET: Red, orange, yellow, or green, the Scotch bonnet is 1 to 2 inches long and puffy and crinkled, like a Highlander's bonnet. Scotch bonnets and their Mexican cousins, habaneros, are the world's hottest chilies—50 times hotter than jalapeños. But behind the heat, there's a floral flavor that hints at apricots and smoke. Scotch bonnets are one of the defining flavors of Real Jamaican Jerk (page 85) and French West Indian marinade (page 61). Cousins of the Scotch bonnet include the goat pepper of the Bahamas and Haiti's *dame jeanne.* Scotch bonnets and habaneros can be used interchangeably; they are available at West Indian and Latino markets and many supermarkets.

SERRANO: A bright green or red bullet-shaped chili similar in flavor and heat to a jalapeño. The two are interchangeable. Serranos are available at most supermarkets, especially on the West Coast.

THAI CHILIES: There are two: the short (1 inch long), slender, bumpy *prik kee nu* (literally mouse dropping) and the longer (2 to 3 inches), slightly milder, horn-shape *prik chee far.* Both are members of the cayenne family and both are extremely hot. In other parts of the world, the prik kee nu is called *bird pepper.* Both types are available at Asian and Indian markets. In a pinch you can substitute jalapeños or serranos.

DRIED, CANNED, AND PRESERVED CHILIES

AJI AMARILLO: This long (3 to 4 inches), slender (½ to ¾ inch), fleshy, gold-yellow firebrand is Peru's preferred chili. It is used in marinades for *anticuchos* (Peruvian kebabs) as well as in a golden pepper sauce served with all kinds of grilled fare (see page 187). Fiery and fruity, the aji amarillo comes in many forms—fresh, dried, canned, pickled, powdered, and in paste. Aji amarillo remains fairly esoteric in North America. I believe that its distinctive flavor gives it the star potential of Mexico's chipotle. Unless you live near a market that caters to a Peruvian clientele, however, you'll probably need to substitute roasted yellow bell pepper with cayenne for heat and a pinch of turmeric for color.

ANCHO: A dried poblano chili. Large (3 to 4 inches long and 2 to 3 inches wide), reddish-black in color, and wrinkled like a prune, the ancho has a complex earthy-fruity flavor with hints of dried fruits, tobacco, and coffee. Relatively mild in terms of heat but very flavorful. Essential for Mexican *moles,* like Mole Poblano (page 176).

CASCABEL: A small, brown, cherry-shape chili with loose seeds that rattle when shaken. (The name literally means sleigh bell.) Hot and slightly sweet and woodsy. Used in salsas and marinades.

CAYENNE: An elongated, small (1 inch long) red chili enjoyed from Louisiana and Central America to India. Very hot but with a fairly monodimensional flavor.

CHINESE DRIED CHILIES: Small dried red chilies in the cayenne family. Sold at Asian markets, they're used extensively in Sichuan cooking and for making Chinese Fire Oil (page 123).

CHIPOTLE: This smoked jalapeño is my favorite dried chili. It's a perfect symbol for barbecue—all smoke and fire. There are two varieties of chipotles: *grandes* and *moritas*. Grandes are tan-brown, striped, 3 to 5 inches in length, very smoky and fiery, but quite expensive. Moritas are smaller (about 2 inches long), sweeter, milder, and more economical. Both are sold dried and canned. I don't usually prefer a canned food over a dried or fresh one, but in this instance I do, because canned chipotles come in a flavorful tomato sauce called adobo. Available at Mexican markets, gourmet shops, and at an increasing number of supermarkets.

DE ARBOL: This bright red, slender chili in the cayenne family is the preferred chili of northern Mexico and the main ingredient in a fiery salsa served with grilled beef and other meats in Sonora and Chihuahua.

GUAJILLO: A long (4 to 6 inches), slender, smooth-skinned, reddish-brown chili with a sweet mild flavor. The guajillo is one of the most common chilies in Mexico, a veritable workhorse used in numerous marinades, salsas, and *moles*. Fairly mild by Mexican heat standards and earthy and sweet tasting, like paprika.

MALAGUETA: Brazil's preferred chili, a tiny, ridged, red or green chili usually sold dried but sometimes pickled. The defining ingredient in Brazilian hot sauce (page 244).

MULATO: Related to the ancho chili (both are dried poblanos), the elongated, triangle-shaped "half breed" has a wrinkled, shiny, dark-brown to jet-black skin. The flavor is earthy, rich, and smoky, with hints of brandy, tobacco, and chocolate. The heat is gentle, especially if the seeds are removed. The mulato is an important ingredient in Mexican Mole Poblano (page 176).

PASILLA: This long slender chili takes its name from its wrinkled black skin (*pasa* means raisin in Spanish). The taste is both sweet and bitter, with hints of licorice and raisins. The heat is moderate to quite fiery. If unavailable, substitute ancho or mulatto chilies.

PEQUIN: A tiny, reddish-orange Mexican chili with a fiery bite. Substitute ground cayenne.

SALSA CRIOLLA
(Colombian Creole Sauce)

Order steak *a la criolla* (Creole-style) at a Colombian restaurant and you are likely to be offered a gutsy tomato sauce to go with it. Like good Creole sauces everywhere, this *salsa criolla* is built on tomatoes, ideally, the sort that are so juicy and ripe, they go splat if they fall off the table. Don't buy refrigerated tomatoes, and don't refrigerate your tomatoes once you get them home. Refrigeration destroys a tomato's succulence and flavor.

¼ cup extra virgin olive oil

1 medium onion, finely chopped

4 scallions (white and green parts), trimmed and finely chopped

1 piece (2 x 3 inches) of green bell pepper, finely chopped

2 cloves garlic, finely chopped

½ teaspoon dried oregano

½ teaspoon ground cumin

½ teaspoon hot pepper flakes, or to taste

3 medium ripe tomatoes, peeled, seeded, and chopped (see box, page 246)

1½ tablespoons red wine vinegar, or to taste

3 tablespoons chopped fresh parsley

Coarse salt (kosher or sea) and freshly ground black pepper, to taste

TRY THIS!

Steak is the traditional meat for this gutsy sauce, but it also goes well with grilled chicken, pork, and seafood.

Heat the oil in a nonstick skillet over medium heat. Add the onion, scallions, bell pepper, garlic, oregano, cumin, and pepper flakes and cook until soft and translucent but not brown, 4 minutes. Increase the heat to high. Add the tomatoes and vinegar and cook until the tomato pieces are soft and most of the tomato liquid has evaporated, 5 minutes. Reduce the heat to medium and stir in the parsley. Cook for 1 minute and add salt and pepper. The virtue of this sauce is its spontaneity. It's best to serve it right away.

Makes 1½ cups; enough to serve 4

PERUVIAN YELLOW PEPPER SAUCE

*A*nticuchos, spicy little kebabs, particularly those made from beef hearts, are enjoyed day and night in Peruvian restaurants and at the pushcarts of street vendors. Vinegar makes them tart and Peruvian chilies make them fiery, but what really sets them apart, aside from the beef hearts, is a sauce made from Peru's distinctive aji amarillo, a golden yellow chili. It tastes a bit like yellow bell pepper with a jolt of cayenne pepper, both of which are easy to find. So, I've retooled the recipe using them.

TRY THIS!

Serve the sauce with Peruvian- or Latin American–style kebabs. It goes great with any sort of grilled meat, poultry, or seafood.

1 large yellow bell pepper
2 scallions (white and green parts), trimmed and finely chopped
2 cloves garlic, minced
1 jalapeño chili, seeded and minced
3 tablespoons olive oil
2 tablespoons distilled white vinegar, or more to taste

1 tablespoon fresh lime juice, or more vinegar
½ teaspoon ground cumin
½ teaspoon ground turmeric
¼ teaspoon cayenne pepper, or to taste
Coarse salt (kosher or sea) and freshly ground black pepper, to taste
Cold water, if needed

1. Preheat the grill to high.

2. Place the yellow pepper on the grate and grill until black on all sides, 4 to 6 minutes per side. Transfer to a plate to cool. When the pepper is cool, scrape off the burnt skin (don't worry about removing every last bit). Stem and seed the pepper, and cut into 1-inch pieces.

3. Place the pepper in a blender or food processor, add the remaining ingredients, and purée to a smooth paste. The sauce should be thick but pourable; if too thick, add a little water. Correct the seasoning, adding salt and vinegar; the sauce should be piquant and highly seasoned. Serve at room temperature. The sauce can be stored in a jar, covered, in the refrigerator for up to 1 week; let it come to room temperature before serving.

Makes 1 cup; enough to serve 4

PEBRE
(Chilean Cilantro Sauce)

I first tasted this invigorating sauce at a cookout given by some Chilean friends in Miami, and although it was served with simple grilled steaks, the aromatic blast of cilantro and garlic made the beef taste truly exotic. The emerald-colored mixture may remind you of Argentinian Chimichurri (page 172), but there are several key differences. One is the use of cilantro in place of parsley. Another is the presence of the fiery green pebre chili, which tastes a little like a Scotch bonnet. (Some Chileans use hot pepper flakes instead.) The fact is you can make the *pebre* sauce as mild or as spicy as you desire.

TRY THIS!

Spoon the sauce over grilled meats, especially steaks. It's also good on poultry and seafood.

2 bunches of fresh cilantro, washed, stemmed, and dried
6 cloves garlic, finely chopped
½ to 1 Scotch bonnet chili or jalapeño, seeded and chopped (for a hotter sauce leave the seeds in)

1 teaspoon coarse salt (kosher or sea), or more to taste
½ teaspoon freshly ground black pepper
1 cup olive oil
⅓ cup distilled white vinegar, or more to taste
⅓ cup cold water

Place the cilantro, garlic, chili, salt, and pepper in a food processor and process until finely chopped. Add the remaining ingredients and process to mix. Or the ingredients can be chopped and mixed by hand. Correct the seasoning, adding salt or vinegar; *pebre* should be highly seasoned. Like most sauces that contain fresh herbs, *pebre* tastes best served within a few hours of making. Or transfer to a large jar, cover, and refrigerate. *Pebre* will keep for several days; shake before using.

Makes 2 cups; enough to serve 8 to 10

ST. BARTS BARBECUE SAUCE

This sauce dates from the days of Cooking in Paradise, my cooking school in St. Barts. This tiny island, with its sugar-white beaches and precipitous cliffs, truly is paradise, and since it is a French island, you can pig out on imported Camembert and foie gras, just as you would in Paris. Great restaurants notwithstanding, my favorite places to eat here are the casual seaside grills, where the spiny lobster and local fish are charred to smoky perfection and served with a Creole barbecue sauce. If you like a sauce that's loaded with fresh herb flavors, this red stuff is for you.

TRY THIS!

This sauce goes great with grilled lobster, shrimp, fish, and other seafood. You can slather it on burgers or grilled chicken. Or even use it with steak.

2 tablespoons unsalted butter
1 small onion, finely chopped
4 scallions (white and green parts), trimmed and finely chopped
2 cloves garlic, minced
½ to 1 Scotch bonnet chili, minced
3 tablespoons chopped fresh flat-leaf parsley
1 teaspoon fresh thyme leaves or ½ teaspoon dried thyme

1 cup ketchup
¾ cup water
2 tablespoons fresh lime juice, or more to taste
1 tablespoon red wine vinegar
½ teaspoon coarse salt (kosher or sea), or more to taste
½ teaspoon freshly ground black pepper

Melt the butter in a heavy saucepan over medium heat. Add the onion, scallions, garlic, chili, parsley, and thyme and cook until soft but not brown, 3 minutes. Stir in the remaining ingredients and bring the sauce to a boil. Reduce the heat to medium-low and gently simmer the sauce, stirring often, until thick and flavorful, 10 to 15 minutes. Correct the seasoning, adding salt or lime juice; the sauce should be highly seasoned. Use right away or transfer to a large jar, cover, cool to room temperature, and refrigerate. The sauce will keep for several weeks.

Makes 2 cups; enough to serve 6 to 8

EUROPEAN AND AFRICAN BARBECUE SAUCES

SALSA VERDE (Italian Green Sauce)

I talians serve this fragrant green sauce with some of their most cherished dishes: for example, *bollito misto* (boiled dinner), grilled fish fresh from the sea, or seafood roasted in a salt crust. Some people prize the salty tang of diced anchovy; others, the fiery bite of hot pepper flakes. I've made both optional, so feel free to customize the recipe to suit your taste.

TRY THIS!

L ike most vinaigrette-style sauces, *salsa verde* can be used as a marinade, baste, and sauce. It goes great with light meats, like grilled seafood, chicken, and veal, but it's rich enough to stand up to lamb or beef.

2 cloves garlic, minced
½ teaspoon coarse salt
    (kosher or sea), or more
    to taste
½ teaspoon freshly ground
    black pepper
¼ cup fresh lemon juice, or
    more to taste
½ cup finely chopped fresh
    flat-leaf parsley

2 teaspoon drained capers,
    chopped
½ teaspoon grated lemon
    zest
2 anchovies, drained and
    finely chopped (optional)
½ teaspoon hot pepper
    flakes (optional)
¾ cup extra virgin olive oil

Place the garlic, salt, and pepper in a bowl and mash to a paste with the back of a spoon. Stir or whisk in the lemon juice, followed by the remaining ingredients. Correct the seasoning, adding salt or lemon juice. The ingredients also can be combined in a jar and shaken or they can be blended in a food processor or blender. If you use the blender, you'll wind up with a smooth, bright green *salsa verde,* which isn't strictly traditional but which is very, very good. Like most fresh herb sauces, *salsa verde* tastes best served within a few hours of making. Or transfer it to a large jar, cover, and refrigerate. You can keep *salsa verde* for several days, but the bright green color will start to fade. If you do store it, be sure to taste and reason before serving.

Makes 1½ cups; enough to serve 4 to 6

SUN-DRIED TOMATO SAUCE

TRY THIS!

Serve the sauce warm or at room temperature. Drizzle it over grilled bread slices or spoon it over grilled fish or chicken. You can even drizzle it over a grilled porterhouse steak to make a sun-dried tomato *bistecca alla fiorentina* (Florentine steak).

Whenever I go to the restaurant of my friend Pino Saverino, I succumb to this fiendishly tasty, garlicky sun-dried tomato sauce. Pino serves it as a dip for crostini and no matter how many times I tell myself not to fill up on it, I always do. The tomato, garlic, and olive oil flavors transport you instantly to the sunny Mediterranean. I also love the way this crimson sauce dresses up a simple piece of grilled fish or chicken.

6 sun-dried tomatoes
1 cup boiling water
¾ cup olive oil
1 clove garlic, coarsely chopped
2 tablespoons balsamic vinegar, or more to taste
1 tablespoon fresh lemon juice

2 fresh basil leaves
½ teaspoon coarse salt (kosher or sea)
½ teaspoon freshly ground black pepper, or more to taste
Tiny pinch of sugar

1. Combine the tomatoes and boiling water in a bowl and let soak for 30 minutes.

2. Drain the tomatoes, reserving the soaking liquid. Place the tomatoes and 3 tablespoons of the soaking liquid in a blender. Add the oil, garlic, vinegar, salt, lemon juice, basil leaves, pepper, and sugar. Purée to a smooth sauce. Correct the seasoning, adding vinegar or salt; the sauce should be highly seasoned and the consistency of heavy cream. If the sauce is too thick, add a little more of the soaking liquid to thin it to a pourable consistency. Use right away or transfer to a jar, cover, and refrigerate. The sauce will keep for several weeks, but bring it to room temperature and stir well before serving.

Makes 1 cup; enough to serve 4

ROUILLE
(Saffron–Roasted Pepper Sauce)

This sauce, called *rouille* in French, is a pungent roasted red pepper and saffron sauce that's traditionally served with bouillabaisse and other fish soups. It's not a huge leap from fish soup to grilled fish and you'll be glad you made it, for this sauce fairly explodes with the Mediterranean flavors of saffron, cayenne, and roasted peppers. It also makes a pretty topping for bruschetta. Tradition calls for the peppers to be roasted in the oven, but I like the smoky sweetness they acquire over a high flame on the grill. (Both methods can be used for this sauce.) So how did the sauce acquire its hard-to-pronounce name? *Rouille* is the French word for rust—a fitting description of its orange-red hue.

2 large red bell peppers
2 slices white bread, crusts
    removed
½ teaspoon saffron threads
1 cup hot water
3 cloves garlic, coarsely
    chopped
1 cup extra virgin olive oil

1 tablespoon fresh lemon
    juice, or more to taste
¼ teaspoon cayenne pepper,
    to taste
Coarse salt (kosher or sea)
    and freshly ground black
    pepper, to taste

1. Preheat the grill to high.

2. Place the peppers on the grate and grill until the skins are charred on all sides, 4 to 6 minutes per side (16 to 24 minutes total). Grill the bread slices until nicely toasted, 2 minutes per side. Or broil the peppers and bread or char the peppers over a burner on the stove and toast the bread in the toaster. Set aside the toast. Transfer the peppers to a plate to cool. When the peppers are cool, scrape off the burnt skins (don't worry about removing every last bit—a few black specs will add character). Stem and seed the peppers and cut into 1-inch pieces.

3. Crumble the saffron threads between your thumb and forefinger and place in a small bowl with 1 tablespoon of the hot water. Let the saffron infuse for 10 minutes. Place the toasted bread in a bowl with the remaining hot water. Let soak for 5 minutes.

4. Wring the water out of the bread slices by squeezing them between your fingers. Place the bread in a food processor with the grilled peppers, saffron, and garlic. Purée to a thick paste. Add the olive oil in a thin stream with the machine running to obtain a thick creamy sauce. Add the lemon juice, cayenne, salt, and pepper. Correct the seasoning, adding salt, cayenne, or lemon juice; the sauce should be spicy and piquant. Use right away or transfer to a large jar, cover, and refrigerate. The sauce will keep for several weeks.

Makes about 2 cups; enough to serve 6 to 8

TRY THIS!

This sauce goes especially well with grilled seafood. (After all, it was originally created to accompany bouillabaisse.) You could certainly serve it with chicken or even over a grilled veal chop or steak. Spread it on grilled bread slices to make an off-beat bruschetta or even dish it up as a dip for grilled vegetables.

ROMESCO SAUCE

TRY THIS!

In Barcelona, this sauce is served with any type of grilled meat, seafood, poultry, or vegetables. Make Catalan-style bruschetta by spooning the sauce on grilled bread slices. And by all means, try it the traditional way, as a dip for grilled scallions and leeks.

Romesco is one of the traditional sauces served with grilled fare in Barcelona and on the Costa Brava. Few barbecue sauces anywhere can rival its earthy robustness—the result of charring the vegetables, chilies, and nuts before reducing them to a thick purée in the food processor. Romesco isn't pretty to look at (like most Catalan dishes, it's brown), but few sauces pack more punch with grilled seafood, meat, or vegetables. Romesco is the traditional accompaniment to *calçots* (grilled jumbo Spanish green onions). I like to serve it with grilled green Vidalias or scallions. In Spain, the sauce would be spiced up with a dried chili called *nyora*. The recipe below calls for ancho chilies, which taste similar and are more readily available.

1 ancho chili or 3 dried nyora chilies, stemmed

Hot water, to soak the chili

3 tablespoons slivered almonds

3 tablespoons hazelnuts

3 medium ripe tomatoes, cut in half

1 small onion, quartered

½ red bell pepper, stemmed and seeded

1 jalapeño chili, halved and seeded

5 cloves garlic, peeled

1 slice white bread

¼ cup finely chopped fresh flat-leaf parsley

½ cup extra virgin olive oil, preferably Spanish

2 tablespoons red wine vinegar, or more to taste

½ teaspoon sugar, or more to taste

Coarse salt (kosher or sea) and freshly ground black pepper, to taste

1. Soak the dried chili in hot water until soft and pliable, 30 minutes. Drain, reserving the soaking liquid, and blot dry.

2. Meanwhile, preheat the broiler. Line a baking sheet with aluminum foil.

3. Arrange the nuts on the prepared baking sheet and broil until toasted and fragrant, 4 to 6 minutes, shaking the pan 2 or 3 times to ensure even browning. Transfer the nuts to a plate to cool. Rub the hazelnuts between the palms of your hands to remove the skins (don't worry about removing every last bit).

4. Arrange the tomatoes, onion, bell pepper, jalapeño, and garlic on the baking sheet and broil until darkly browned, turning to ensure even browning, 4 to 8 minutes per side, depending on the vegetable. Transfer the vegetables to a plate and let cool.

5. Place the bread slice on the baking sheet and darkly toast under the broiler, 2 minutes per side. Break the toast into several pieces, transfer to a food processor, add the nuts, and process to a fine powder. Add the vegetables and parsley and process to a coarse paste. Add the oil, vinegar, sugar, salt, and pepper and process to mix. The romesco should be thick but pourable; if too thick, add a little chili soaking liquid. Correct the seasoning, adding salt, sugar, or vinegar; the romesco should be highly seasoned. Use right away or transfer to a jar, cover, and refrigerate. The sauce will keep for several weeks.

Makes 2 cups; enough to serve 4 to 6

RED CURRANT PORT SAUCE

TRY THIS!

If ever there were a sauce to go with spit-roasted partridge, pheasant, venison, or grilled elk, this is it. It's also great with turkey, duck, and quail.

If you like the robust flavor of game, this spice-scented, sweet-sour Central European–style sauce is just the ticket. The inviting flavors of red currant jelly and Port wine also make a great accompaniment to grilled chicken, spit-roasted duck, smoked turkey, and even barbecued pork. Game calls for a touch of sweet and sour: That's why I've included lemon juice and orange marmalade.

1 orange, scrubbed
1 lemon, scrubbed
4 whole cloves
1 cinnamon stick (3 inches)
⅓ cup red currant jelly
1 cup chicken broth
½ cup plus 1 tablespoon
    Port

⅓ cup orange marmalade
2 teaspoons cornstarch
⅛ teaspoon cayenne pepper
Coarse salt (kosher or sea)
    and freshly ground black
    pepper, to taste

1. Using a vegetable peeler, remove 2 strips of zest from the orange and 2 strips from the lemon. Stick 1 clove in each piece of zest.

2. Squeeze the orange and lemon and strain the juice into a medium-size nonreactive saucepan. Add the zests, cinnamon stick, red currant jelly, and stock and gradually bring to a boil over high heat. Reduce the heat to medium and simmer the mixture until the jelly is dissolved and the mixture is reduced by one quarter, about 10 minutes. Remove and discard the orange and lemon zest and cinnamon stick.

3. Add the ½ cup Port and orange marmalade and simmer until the marmalade is dissolved and the sauce is richly flavored, 5 minutes. Dissolve the cornstarch in the remaining 1 tablespoon Port. Stir or whisk this mixture into the sauce and simmer for 15 seconds; the sauce will thicken. Correct the seasoning, adding salt and pepper. Serve the sauce warm or transfer to a large jar, cover, and refrigerate. The sauce will keep for 5 days. Warm it before serving.

Makes 2 cups; enough to serve 4 to 6

TKEMALI (Georgian Rhubarb Sauce)

The Republic of Georgia is a hotbed not only of politics but of grilling. According to Greek mythology, it was here, in the Caucasus Mountains, that Prometheus gave man the gift of fire. Barbecue sauce in this region means *tkemali,* a mouth-puckering purée of sour plums or other sour fruit, garlic, and dill. This isn't quite as strange as it sounds: After all, many Americans add lemons or pineapple to their barbecue sauce. Here's a *tkemali* made with fresh rhubarb, which comes in season just in time for the start of barbecue season. The sauce is very intense: A little dab spread on meat or used as a dipping sauce will do.

1 pound rhubarb, cut into
   ½-inch slices
1 cup cold water
2 tablespoons fresh lemon
   juice, or to taste
2 tablespoons olive oil
3 cloves garlic, minced
1 teaspoon ground coriander
½ teaspoon coarse salt
   (kosher or sea), or more
   to taste

½ teaspoon hot pepper
   flakes, or to taste
2 tablespoons finely chopped
   fresh cilantro
2 tablespoons finely chopped
   fresh dill
½ teaspoon sugar, or more to
   taste

TRY THIS!

Serve *tkemali* at room temperature in tiny bowls or ramekins, providing one for each guest. It goes great with grilled chicken, pork, lamb, salmon, or vegetables.

1. Combine the rhubarb and water in a heavy nonreactive saucepan and cook over medium heat until the rhubarb is soft and mushy, 8 minutes.

2. Stir in the lemon juice, oil, garlic, coriander, salt, and pepper flakes and simmer for 3 minutes. Transfer the mixture to a food processor and process to a smooth purée. Return the purée to the saucepan and stir in the cilantro and dill.

3. Continue simmering the sauce until thick and flavorful, about 5 minutes. Correct the seasoning, adding salt or sugar; *tkemali* should be highly seasoned and quite tart but not unpalatably sour. Use right away or transfer to a large jar, cover, and refrigerate. The sauce will keep for up to 2 weeks.

Makes 2 cups; enough to serve 8

CHARMOULA
(Spicy Moroccan Herb Sauce)

Imagine the spices of Morocco, the freshness of Italian pesto, and the acidic tang of French vinaigrette. Put them together and what you get is *charmoula*. This bold Moroccan table sauce traditionally accompanies seafood, but it's equally tasty with grilled chicken, lamb, beef, even vegetables. Best of all, you can use it simultaneously as a marinade, baste, and table sauce, enjoying a triple blast of its evocative North African flavors.

½ cup chopped fresh parsley
½ cup chopped fresh cilantro
3 cloves garlic, minced
1 teaspoon coarse salt
    (kosher or sea), or more
    to taste
1 teaspoon paprika
½ teaspoon freshly ground
    black pepper

½ teaspoon ground cumin
½ teaspoon hot pepper
    flakes, or to taste
¼ cup fresh lemon juice, or
    more to taste
¾ cup extra virgin olive oil
3 tablespoons water

Combine the parsley, cilantro, and garlic in a food processor and finely chop. Add the salt, spices, lemon juice, oil, and water and process to a coarse purée, running the machine in short bursts. Correct the seasoning, adding salt and/or lemon juice; the *charmoula* should be highly seasoned. Like most sauces made with fresh herbs, *charmoula* tastes best served within a few hours of making.

Makes 1 cup; enough to serve 4

MONKEY GLAND SAUCE

TRY THIS!

This sauce is customarily served hot, with grilled meats, such as steak and lamb chops. You can also serve it cold. It can also be used for basting.

Spend enough time with a South African *brai* (barbecue) master and the talk will turn to one of the most curiously named condiments in the world of live-fire cooking: monkey gland sauce. The very notion would fill a North American with apprehension, but for a South African, nothing tastes better at a barbecue than this sweet-spicy blend of chutney, wine, and hot sauce. This version comes from Garth Stoebel, executive chef of the posh Mount Nelson Hotel in Capetown and grill jockey extraordinaire. For chutney, you could also use one of the recipes in this book (see pages 271 to 278) or a good commercial brand, like Major Grey's.

Note that the butter and liquid smoke aren't strictly traditional, but I love the way they round out the flavor of the sauce.

1 cup fruit chutney

3 tablespoons dry red wine

3 tablespoons Port

2 tablespoons salted butter

1 teaspoon Tabasco sauce,
   or your favorite hot sauce

½ teaspoon freshly ground
   black pepper

½ teaspoon liquid smoke

Coarse salt (kosher or sea)

Combine all the ingredients in a heavy nonreactive saucepan over medium-high heat and bring to a boil. Reduce the heat to medium and simmer the sauce until the chutney dissolves and the sauce is richly flavored, stirring often, 5 to 10 minutes. For a chunky sauce, serve as is. For a smooth sauce, purée in a food processor or blender. Use right away or transfer to a jar, cover, and refrigerate. The sauce will keep for several weeks; bring to room temperature before serving.

Makes 1¼ cups; enough to serve 4 to 6

VARIATION

Tomato Monkey Gland Sauce: Replace half the chutney with ketchup.

ASIAN BARBECUE SAUCES

RAITA (Indian Yogurt Sauce)

TRY THIS!

Serve this sauce with tandoori and other Indian-style dishes. In fact, you can serve it with any type of assertively seasoned grilled meat or seafood.

The brewheads have it all wrong. Beer *isn't* the best cure for a mouth ravaged by chili hellfire. When your taste buds burn, the best way to put out the flames is with a dairy product like yogurt. Which brings us to a classic accompaniment to Indian barbecue: raita. This cooling dip, confected from yogurt and cucumbers, was put on earth expressly to soothe taste buds inflamed by chilies and spices. The mint reinforces the message: Keep cool.

Traditionally the yogurt would be drained to make it extra rich and creamy. I achieve the same effect by adding sour cream. Many Indian cooks add a little fresh chili to the raita. This partially defeats the cooling action of the raita, but it tastes great. It's up to you.

½ teaspoon cumin seeds
1 pint plain whole milk yogurt
½ cup sour cream
1 cucumber, peeled, seeded, and cut into ¼-inch dice
1 ripe tomato, seeded and cut into ¼-inch dice (see page 246)

3 tablespoons chopped fresh mint
1 jalapeño chili, seeded and minced (optional)
1 clove garlic, minced
½ teaspoon coarse salt (kosher or sea)
¼ teaspoon freshly ground black pepper

1. Heat a dry skillet over medium heat. Add the cumin seeds and toast until fragrant, 2 minutes. Let cool.
2. Grind the cumin in a spice mill, then transfer it to a

bowl. Add the yogurt and sour cream and stir to mix. Stir in the cucumber, tomato, mint, jalapeño, if using, garlic, salt, and pepper. You can serve the raita right away, but it will taste better if you let it ripen in the refrigerator for 10 to 15 minutes. Serve it the same day you make it.

Makes 3½ cups; enough to serve 6 to 8

VARIATIONS

Banana Raita: Substitute ground cardamom for the cumin (there's no need to toast it) and replace the tomato with a diced ripe banana. Add 1 to 2 teaspoons brown sugar for sweetness. Banana raita goes especially well with grilled seafood.

Pineapple Raita: Substitute 1 cup diced fresh pineapple for the tomato. Add 1 teaspoon minced fresh ginger, ½ teaspoon ground coriander, and ¼ teaspoon crumbled saffron threads. Pineapple raita goes well with grilled poultry and seafood.

Carrot Raita from Goa: Substitute 1 cup finely diced cooked carrots for the cucumber and tomato. Add ½ teaspoon black mustard seeds and toast them with the cumin. Add 1 seeded and minced jalapeño chili. Carrot raita goes especially well with lamb.

CHINESE BARBECUE SAUCE

TRY THIS!

Serve with barbecued chicken and ribs. To heighten the Asian effect, rub the chicken or ribs with Sweet and Licoricey Duck Rub (page 50) before cooking.

North Americans aren't the only people to serve a sweet, sticky sauce with barbecue. Consider this Chinese barbecue sauce, a specialty of my friend Nina Simonds, author of more than a half dozen terrific books on Chinese cooking. In the West, we use ketchup or tomato sauce and brown sugar to obtain that satisfying contrast of sweet and sour. The Chinese achieve a similar effect with hoisin sauce, a thick purplish-brown condiment made from soybean paste, garlic, sugar, and spices. Hoisin sauce varies widely in quality: Recommended brands include Pearl River Bridge, Ma Ling, Amoy, and Koon Chun.

½ cup hoisin sauce

3 tablespoons Chinese rice
   wine, sake, or dry sherry

2 tablespoons soy sauce

2 tablespoons sugar

2 tablespoons ketchup

1 tablespoon rice vinegar or
   distilled white vinegar

2 tablespoons minced garlic

Combine all the ingredients in a nonreactive saucepan over medium heat and slowly bring to a boil. Reduce the heat slightly and simmer the sauce for 5 minutes. Use right away or transfer to a jar; cool to room temperature, cover, and refrigerate until using. The sauce will keep for several weeks.

Makes 1 cup; enough to serve 4

CHINESE BARBECUED CHICKEN

Nina Simonds cooks this incredibly tasty bird in the oven. I've added an element of smoke and fire by barbecuing it on the grill. If you like garlic and spice, you'll lick your fingers after this one.

1 frying chicken (3½ pounds), lumps
   of fat removed, cut in half

1 tablespoon Sweet and Licoricey
   Duck Rub (page 50)

1 cup Chinese Barbecue Sauce
   (page 201)

¼ cup chopped fresh cilantro

SPECIAL EQUIPMENT

1 cup wood chips, soaked in 1 cup
   cold water for 1 hour, then
   drained

3 strips of tangerine or orange peel

1. At least 6 hours before, place the chicken in a baking dish. Rub all over with the rub. Spread the sauce all over the chicken, using a spatula. Let marinate, covered, in the refrigerator.

2. Set up the grill for indirect grilling, following the directions on page 5, and preheat to 350°F. If using a charcoal grill, toss the wood chips and tangerine peel on the coals. If using a gas grill, place them in the smoker box. Don't grill until you see smoke. Arrange the chicken halves in the center of the grate, away from the fire.

3. Roast the chicken until tender and cooked, 40 to 60 minutes, to an internal temperature of 165°F, taken at the thigh. Transfer the chicken to a platter, sprinkle with cilantro, and serve at once.

Serves 2 to 4

GREAT WALL BARBECUE SAUCE

TRY THIS!

Serve this sauce with barbecued or grilled ribs, chicken, or duck. To complete the Chinese theme, season the meat with the Chinese rub on page 46 before grilling.

This recipe comes from one of the legends of barbecue— Dr. Rich Davis, inventor of K.C. Masterpiece barbecue sauce. Davis got the idea for the sauce on a trip to China, where he made it a point to enjoy the local barbecue (smoked beef, pork, and duck). This is what you might call a "doctor sauce"—it starts with a commercial sauce that you doctor to suit your taste. In this case, the doctoring includes ginger, rice vinegar, and soy sauce—ingredients that give the sauce a Chinese accent.

½ teaspoon anise seed
¾ cup K.C. Masterpiece
   Original Barbecue Sauce
2 tablespoons soy sauce

1 tablespoon peanut oil
1 tablespoon rice vinegar
1 clove garlic, minced
½ teaspoon ground ginger

Grind the anise seed in a spice mill or pulverize in a mortar with a pestle. Place it in a heavy saucepan. Add all the remaining ingredients and bring to a gentle simmer over medium heat. Simmer for 5 minutes. Transfer the sauce to a serving bowl and let cool to room temperature. Use right away or transfer to a jar, cover, and refrigerate. The sauce will keep for several weeks.

Makes 1 cup; enough to serve 4

KOREAN BARBECUE SAUCE

Korea's barbecue sauce is not so much a slather as a dip—a delicate blend of sake (rice wine) and soy sauce, with a dollop of honey for sweetness and a sprinkle of toasted sesame seeds for crunch. To my knowledge, this is the world's only barbecue sauce that contains pear (although surely someone in Kansas City has tried it). Asian pear is remarkable for its crispness and succulence; it's sweet, but not quite as sweet as an American pear, which makes it perfect for serving with beef. Look for this singular fruit at your supermarket and buy the firmest one you can find. (Asian pears lose their goodness when they go soft.) If unavailable, use a firm bosc or anjou pear.

TRY THIS!

Ladle the sauce into small bowls, providing one for each person. The traditional way to eat Korean barbecue is to wrap the grilled beef in a lettuce leaf, then dip it in the sauce with your chopsticks.

2 tablespoons sugar
1 scallion, white part only, trimmed and minced
1 clove garlic, minced
½ teaspoon freshly ground black pepper
½ cup soy sauce
½ cup sake
2 tablespoons honey

4 scallions (green parts only)
2 tablespoons toasted sesame seeds (see box, page 105)
1 small or ½ large Asian pear, peeled, cored, and cut into the finest possible dice

Combine the sugar, scallion whites, garlic, and pepper in a bowl and mash to a smooth paste with the back of a spoon. Add the soy sauce, sake, and honey and stir until the sugar and honey are dissolved. Stir in the scallion greens, sesame seeds, and pear. Correct the seasoning, adding honey for sweetness or soy sauce for salt. Serve within a few hours of making.

Makes 2½ cups; enough to serve 6 to 8

YAKITORI SAUCE

TRY THIS!

Brush the sauce as a glaze on grilled chicken. Or to be even more authentic, follow the instructions in the recipe for Yakitori (facing page). The sauce was created for grilled chicken, but it's also good on tiny kebabs of grilled beef and pork.

In the Middle East it's shish kebab, in Japan it's *yakitori*. These tiny skewers of chicken and various chicken parts, such as skin, liver, and embryonic eggs, are enjoyed at innumerable *yakitori* parlors around Japan, for lunch or as a snack when workers gather for drinks and camaraderie after work. Sweet and salty, shiny and dark, *yakitori* sauce resembles teriyaki sauce, but contains more soy sauce. Many *yakitori* masters simmer the sauce with a roasted chicken leg bone for extra flavor. Tradition holds for the partially cooked *yakitori* to be dipped in the sauce, then returned to the grill for glazing and final cooking. If you wish to try this, please follow the food safety notes on page 13.

1 cup soy sauce
1 cup turbinado sugar (Sugar
    in the Raw brand)
¼ cup mirin
1 scallion (white part only),

flattened with a cleaver
1 strip lemon zest, about
    2 × ½ inch
1 roasted or grilled chicken
    leg bone (optional)

Combine all the ingredients in a nonreactive saucepan over medium heat and slowly bring to a gentle simmer, uncovered, stirring with a wooden spoon to prevent scorching. Reduce the heat slightly and simmer for 5 minutes. Discard the scallion, lemon zest, and chicken bone, if using. Use right away or transfer to a large jar, cover, cool to room temperature, and refrigerate. The sauce will keep for 5 days.

Makes 2 cups; enough for 2 pounds of chicken

YAKITORI

Yakitori are tiny chicken kebabs, served in dazzling variety in Japan and enjoyed as a snack.

The Japanese prefer chicken thighs to breasts because they're more moist and flavorful. You could substitute 1 pound boneless skinless chicken breasts.

2 pounds chicken thighs
2 bunches of scallions, trimmed
1 recipe Yakitori Sauce (facing page)

SPECIAL EQUIPMENT
Small bamboo skewers, soaked in
    cold water for 1 hour, and drained

1. Skin and bone the chicken thighs and cut each into pieces of meat about 1½ inches long and ½ inch wide. Cut the scallions into pieces the same length. Skewer the pieces onto small bamboo skewers crosswise, alternating chicken and scallion. Pour the sauce into a deep bowl.

2. Preheat the hibachi or grill to high.

3. Place the *yakitori* on the grate and grill until almost cooked, about 3 minutes per side.

4. Dip the skewers in the sauce to coat the chicken and scallions, then return them to the grill. Grill for 1 minute per side, dip again, and continue grilling until the *yakitori* are golden brown and cooked, 1 to 2 minutes per side. Or brush the sauce on the chicken as it grills, using a basting brush. If you use the dip method and want to store any remaining sauce to use again, boil it before storing, covered, in the refrigerator.

Serves 6 to 8

SOY SAUCE

As you might expect, soy sauce is a prime barbecue seasoning in Korea, Japan, and China. It's also widely used by American grill jockeys to add a salty tang to marinades, bastes, and barbecue sauce. But which soy sauce? There are dozens of different styles and grades to choose from.

Japanese soy sauce, known as *shoyu*, is a salty, tangy condiment made from fermented soy beans, wheat, salt, and water. The resulting brew is aged for a period of several months to years to give it a rich, mellow, complex taste. *Tamari* refers to a soy sauce traditionally brewed only with soybeans, which was supposed to give it a more elegant flavor. Tamari is considered something of a health food in the United States. (Look for it at your local natural foods store.) But read the label to determine whether the tamari is really made solely from soy beans or with wheat. Relatively new to the American market is light soy sauce, which contains about 30 percent less sodium than regular soy sauce. One good brand of Japanese soy sauce is Kikkoman, which is manufactured in Wisconsin.

The Chinese manufacture both light and dark soy sauce—both heavier than Japanese soy sauce. Dark soy sauce is enriched with molasses to make it sweeter and thicker. Mushroom soy sauce is a thick, pungent condiment made from soy sauce, sweeteners, and straw mushrooms.

In Indonesia, the preferred soy sauce is *kejap manis*, a very thick, sweet, sticky soy sauce flavored with coriander, galangal, and other spices. Kejap is used in Indonesia much the way its western namesake—ketchup—is used in the West: for drizzling over cooked satés and other types of grilled meats.

Soy sauces vary widely in price, but it's worth spending the extra dollar. Good soy sauce is a naturally fermented product with complex layers of flavor. Cheap soy sauce contains caramel food coloring and hydrolyzed vegetable proteins for flavor. Read the label and look for the words "natural cultures" or "naturally fermented." As in so much else in life, you get what you pay for.

MISO BARBECUE SAUCE

This creamy golden sauce turns up wherever the Japanese grill tofu or eggplant. Which is to say pretty much everywhere, for these grilled foods are as popular in Japan as hot dogs and hamburgers are in the United States.

Like great barbecue sauces everywhere, it's sweet, salty, and tangy. The sweetness comes from sugar and mirin (sweet rice wine), while saltiness is one of the defining characteristics of the main ingredient, miso. This is a thick, tangy paste of pickled soybeans and grains, and it tastes a lot better than it sounds. If you've ever had miso soup at a Japanese restaurant, you know how exquisite this healthful food can be. Further excitement is provided by the sake and grated lemon zest.

Miso and mirin are both available at natural foods stores and many supermarkets. Dashi is a broth made with dried bonita flakes and kelp. For ease in preparation, I call for instant dashi, but chicken broth will give you a perfectly tasty miso barbecue sauce.

TRY THIS!

Miso sauce is the traditional topping for Japanese grilled tofu and eggplant. It's delicious spooned over grilled salmon and grilled chicken.

¾ cup boiling water	3 tablespoons sugar
1 teaspoon instant dashi	3 tablespoons sake
1 cup white miso, at room temperature	3 tablespoons mirin
	½ teaspoon grated lemon zest
3 egg yolks	

1. Combine the boiling water and instant dashi in a bowl and mix. Set aside.

2. Bring 2 inches of water to a simmer in the bottom of a double boiler or saucepan. Place the miso, egg yolks, sugar, sake, and mirin in the top of a double boiler or in a heatproof bowl and whisk to mix. Set the pan or bowl with the miso mixture over the simmering water. Whisk in the dashi in a thin stream.

3. Cook the miso sauce over the simmering water until thick and creamy, 6 to 10 minutes, whisking steadily. Remove the pan from the heat and whisk in the lemon zest. Cool to room temperature. Transfer the miso sauce to serving bowls if serving immediately. Or transfer to a large jar, cover, and refrigerate. The miso sauce will keep for up to 5 days.

Makes 2 cups; enough to serve 6 to 8

VARIATION

Substitute ¾ cup chicken or vegetable broth for the brewed dashi.

RICH PEANUT DIPPING SAUCE

Peanut sauce is the requisite accompaniment to saté in most of Southeast Asia. Here's a rich, more complex sauce made in the style of Penang in northern Malaysia. Penang enjoys the sort of mythical status in Malaysian cuisine that New Orleans does in America. The aromatics—garlic, shallots, lemongrass—are stir-fried, which produces a rich caramelized flavor and earthy sweetness. If you're in a hurry, try the Quick Peanut Dipping Sauce on the facing page.

TRY THIS!

Divide the sauce among small bowls and serve with satés (tiny kebabs) and other Asian-style barbecue.

2 tablespoons peanut oil
2 to 3 shallots, minced
    (about ½ cup)
3 cloves garlic,
    minced
3 Thai chilies or jalapeños,
    seeded and minced (for a
    spicier sauce leave the
    seeds in)
1 tablespoon minced fresh
    ginger
1 stalk lemongrass, trimmed
    and minced
½ cup peanut butter

1½ cups unsweetened
    coconut milk
¼ cup finely chopped fresh
    cilantro leaves
3 tablespoons fish sauce or
    soy sauce, or more to
    taste
2 tablespoons fresh lime
    juice, or more to taste
1½ tablespoons dark brown
    sugar
1 teaspoon ground coriander
½ teaspoon freshly ground
    black pepper

1. Heat the oil in a wok or nonreactive saucepan over medium heat. Add the shallots, garlic, chilies, ginger, and lemongrass and stir-fry to a rich golden brown. Reduce the heat to obtain maximum caramelization without burning. When cooked to the proper degree, the oil will start to separate out. The whole process will take 8 to 10 minutes.

2. Add the peanut butter and stir-fry for 1 minute. Add the remaining ingredients and simmer the sauce until thick and richly flavored, stirring or whisking to blend, 6 to 8 minutes. Correct the seasoning, adding fish sauce or lime juice. Cool to room temperature and serve. Or transfer to a large jar, cover, and refrigerate. The sauce will keep for up to a week.

Makes 2½ cups; enough to serve 8 to 10

QUICK PEANUT DIPPING SAUCE

The sweet nutty flavor of peanut sauce goes great with smokily charred chicken, pork, or beef. There are probably as many different recipes as there are individual saté vendors. Here's a quick peanut sauce that can be made in a food processor in a couple of minutes. For a richer, more complex sauce, see the facing page.

TRY THIS!

Place the sauce in bowls or ramekins and serve as a dip for satés.

1 tomato, peeled, seeded, and diced

2 cloves garlic, minced

2 scallions, trimmed and minced

1 to 3 Thai chilies or jalapeños, seeded and minced (for a spicier sauce leave the seeds in)

¼ cup chopped fresh cilantro leaves

½ cup chunky peanut butter

½ cup chicken or vegetable broth, or more as needed

3 tablespoons fish sauce or soy sauce, or more to taste

3 tablespoons fresh lime juice, or more to taste

1 tablespoon light brown sugar, or more to taste

½ teaspoon freshly ground black pepper

Sprigs of fresh cilantro, for garnish

Place the tomato, garlic, scallions, chilies, and cilantro in a food processor and process to a fine paste. Add the remaining ingredients, except the cilantro sprigs, and process to obtain a smooth sauce. Correct the seasoning, adding fish sauce, lime juice, or brown sugar. The sauce should be salty, tart, and sweet. It should also be thick but pourable; if too thick, add a little more broth. Transfer the sauce to a bowl or ramekins and use right away garnished with sprigs of cilantro. Cover and refrigerate any leftover sauce. It will keep for 3 to 4 days.

Makes about 2 cups; enough to serve 6 to 8

CAMBODIAN BARBECUE DIPPING SAUCE

Rhode Island is renowned for its grilled pizza, red chowder, and "stuffies" (stuffed clams). Providence is also home to a large Cambodian community. It's a great place to try this terrific dipping sauce for Asian barbecue. Like most Southeast Asian condiments, it offers a broad spectrum of flavors: the salty tang of fish sauce and soy sauce, the pique of vinegar, the pungency of garlic, and the explosive freshness of cilantro and mint. I often make a double batch of the sauce, using half as a marinade.

Fish sauce is a malodorous but tasty condiment made from pickled anchovies. Look for it in Asian markets and gourmet shops.

3 cloves garlic, minced
⅓ cup sugar, or to taste
½ cup fish sauce
½ cup distilled white vinegar
¼ cup soy sauce
1 to 3 teaspoons Vietnamese chili paste, sambal oelek, or your favorite hot sauce

3 tablespoons chopped scallion greens
3 tablespoons chopped fresh cilantro leaves
3 tablespoons chopped fresh mint leaves
¼ cup finely chopped dry-roasted peanuts
¾ cup water, or to taste

Combine the garlic and 2 tablespoons of the sugar in a bowl and mash to a paste with the back of a spoon. Add the remaining sugar, fish sauce, vinegar, soy sauce, and chili paste and stir or whisk until the sugar is completely dissolved. Stir in the scallion greens, cilantro, mint, peanuts, and enough water to make a mellow sauce. Serve this sauce within a few hours of making.

Makes about 2 cups; enough to serve 6 to 8

FISH SAUCE

A malodorous condiment made from fermented anchovies may not be your idea of a winning barbecue sauce ingredient. But for legions of grill jockeys in Thailand, Cambodia, Laos, and Vietnam, satés and other grilled foods just wouldn't taste right without it. Made from pickled anchovies, the salty brown condiment is used throughout Southeast Asia the way soy sauce is in China and Japan.

Known as *nam pla* in Thai and *nuoc mam* in Vietnamese, fish sauce serves both as a marinade ingredient, as in the Basic Thai Saté Marinade (page 77), and as a table sauce (see the Cambodian Barbecue Dipping Sauce on the facing page). The strong, cheesy aroma can be off-putting, but the flavor quickly becomes addictive.

Fish sauce is available at Asian markets and in the Asian food section in most supermarkets. The best grades come in glass bottles; good brands include Flying Lion, Three Crabs, and Squid Brand. Avoid the cheap fish sauce sold in plastic bottles or Filipino fish sauce, which most Americans will find unpalatably fishy.

MAM NEM (Vietnamese Pineapple-Shrimp Dipping Sauce)

The global barbecue trail abounds with fruit-based barbecue sauces. But none is quite as distinctive as *mam nem,* the Vietnamese pineapple shrimp sauce. Pineapple, shrimp, and fish sauce (sometimes anchovies are used) may sound like odd flavorings to pair with grilled beef—until you stop to think that American steak sauces often contain tamarind and anchovies. The sweet and salty flavors go great with grilled foods of all sorts, be they Asian or Western.

2 tablespoons peanut oil

3 cloves garlic, minced

1 shallot, minced

3 Thai chilies or 1 to 2 jalapeños, seeded and minced

8 ounces fresh shrimp, peeled, deveined, and minced

1 cup finely chopped fresh pineapple with juices

3 tablespoons fish sauce, or more to taste

1 tablespoon Vietnamese chili paste, or more to taste

½ teaspoon freshly ground black pepper

TRY THIS!

Serve this thick sauce as a dipping sauce for grilled fish, shrimp, chicken, pork, or beef.

Heat the oil in a nonreactive wok or sauté pan over medium heat. Add the garlic, shallot, and chilies and stir-fry until just beginning to brown, about 1 minute. Add the shrimp and stir-fry until opaque, 1 to 2 minutes. Stir in the pineapple with the juices and bring to a boil. Stir in the fish sauce, chili paste, and pepper and bring back to a boil.

Reduce the heat and simmer the sauce until thick and richly flavored, 3 minutes. Correct the seasoning, adding fish sauce or chili paste. Let the sauce cool to room temperature before serving. Cover and refrigerate any leftovers. The sauce will keep for up to 4 days.

Makes 2 cups; enough to serve 6 to 8

SLATHER SAUCES
KETCHUPS
MUSTARDS
STEAK SAUCES
VINAIGRETTES
AND
HOT SAUCES

Slather sauces is a catch-all term for the ketchups, mustards, steak sauces, egg sauces, and vinaigrettes we love to smear on burgers, chops, and steaks. You may learn some surprising things about these seemingly commonplace condiments.

That ketchup, for example, derives from a Chinese pickled fish sauce called *ket-tsiap*. That mustard was so important in the Middle Ages, Pope John XXII had his own private mustard maker. That Worcestershire sauce came from India and was a big flop before it became a commercial success. That A.1. Steak Sauce got its name from King George IV. That aïoli (garlic mayonnaise) is the focal point of a community feast in Provence.

In this chapter are recipes for making ketchup and mustard from scratch, and not just the likely suspects, but exotic banana ketchup, mango-mint ketchup, and even a purple mustard from a superstar chef

from Sweden. Soothe your guests' tongues with silky French béarnaise sauce and blast them with Hell's Fury hot sauce. Make a simple but satisfying steak sauce from one of the most celebrated chefs in New York. And don't forget main-course vinaigrettes, which were pioneered by health-conscious chefs.

So grab on to your spoon and get ready for some righteous feasting. Hot dogs and hamburgers will never seem quite the same.

KETCHUPS, MUSTARDS, AND STEAK SAUCES

TODD'S KETCHUP

Todd English is an old friend and the founder of the popular Olives and Figs restaurants in Boston (and now in Las Vegas and Washington, D.C.). When he cooks, people take notice, because Todd loves to load up his plates with bold in-your-face flavors—even when he tackles something as seemingly plebeian as ketchup. Blurring the boundary between traditional ketchup and chutney, Todd has taken

TRY THIS!

Finally, here's a ketchup you won't be embarrassed to ask for to put on steak. You can pretty much use it as you would any commercial ketchup—only it's better.

this commonplace condiment to another level. Orange and lemon add an unexpected tropical touch that's reinforced by the ginger and allspice.

2 tablespoons olive oil

1 small onion, finely chopped

2 cloves garlic, minced

½ cup red wine vinegar

½ cup (packed) dark brown sugar

½ cup honey

½ cup fresh orange juice

1 lemon, peeled (remove both zest and rind), seeded, and diced

2 teaspoons coarse salt (kosher or sea)

2 teaspoons ground allspice

1 teaspoon ground ginger

½ teaspoon mustard powder

½ teaspoon freshly cracked black pepper

½ teaspoon ground cloves

1 can (28 ounces) whole plum tomatoes, juices strained and reserved, tomatoes coarsely chopped by hand or in a food processor

1. Heat the olive oil in a medium-size nonreactive saucepan over medium heat. Add the onion and garlic and cook until soft but not brown, stirring with a wooden spoon, 3 minutes. Increase the heat to high, stir in the vinegar and brown sugar, and boil until the mixture is reduced by half. Add the honey, orange juice, lemon, salt, spices, and reserved tomato juices. Simmer until thick and syrupy, 5 minutes. Stir in the chopped tomatoes and simmer the ketchup until thick and flavorful, 10 minutes.

2. Transfer the mixture to a food processor and process to a coarse purée. Correct the seasoning, adding salt, vinegar, or any other ingredient; the ketchup should be highly seasoned. Transfer the purée to jars, cover, cool to room temperature. Refrigerate until serving. The ketchup will keep for several weeks.

Makes 4 cups

KETCHUP

Ketchup could be called the lifeblood of American barbecue. Not only would hamburgers look positively anemic without it, ketchup is the main ingredient in hundreds, if not thousands, of American barbecue sauces, as well as cocktail sauce and its variations, which go so well with grilled seafood. It's pretty hard to imagine a cookout without at least one squeeze bottle of a condiment that feels as American as apple pie.

Ketchup, in fact, originated in China and was introduced to the West more than three centuries ago. Our term ketchup (also spelled catsup and catchup) comes from a Chinese pickled fish sauce known as *kĕchap.* British seafarers acquired a taste for it in Malaysia in the eighteenth century. They described the condiment to cooks back home, who tried to recreate *kĕchap,* using more familiar English ingredients, like mushrooms and walnuts. By 1748, ketchup was so popular that the author of a book called *The Housekeeper's Pocketbook* cautioned the homemaker "never to be without [it]."

The ketchups of the eighteenth and nineteenth centuries were very different from those of today. A recipe in a 1778 cookbook, *The Experienced English House-Keeper,* called for red

FIVE SEASONS KETCHUP

Ketchup may not seem like the sort of condiment you'd expect to find at a macrobiotic restaurant. But when I lived in Boston, I'd make special trips to the Five Seasons just to enjoy the made-from-scratch french fries served with a natural ketchup concocted by the brother chefs, Jon and Rob Pell. If you find commercial ketchup overly sugary, you'll love the subtle, gentle sweetness of this one—sweetened with barley malt syrup (or rice syrup). Both sweeteners are available at natural foods stores.

wine, anchovies, shallots, ginger, and "two quarts of old strong beer." The resulting ketchup could be kept for seven years, the author boasted. *The Cook's Oracle,* published in 1823, proposed a mushroom ketchup, which, when boiled down to double strength, became a "dog-sup."

Tomatoes didn't enter ketchup until 1792. Most Americans considered the tomato to be poisonous well into the nineteenth century. In 1830, a daredevil named Robert Johnson ate a raw tomato on the steps of the Salem, New Jersey, courthouse. According to food historian James Trager, the horrified spectators predicted he would be dead before morning. He survived. It was believed that prolonged cooking was required to rid the tomato of its toxins. And ketchup was an excellent use for lengthily cooked tomatoes.

Thus reasoned an enterprising young man from Sharpsburg, Pennsylvania, who at the age of 25 began bottling and selling homemade condiments. He designed a special wide-based, slender-necked bottle for ketchup. His name was Henry Heinz. In 1876, armed with $3,000, he founded the H. J. Heinz Company, and the modern age of ketchup was born.

We've come full circle. Visit cutting-edge grill restaurants, and you'll find ketchups made from banana, pineapple, and even guava. Fruit ketchups capture the flavor dynamics of traditional tomato ketchups—the yin-yang of sweet and sour (sugar and vinegar), the spicy sweetness of allspice and ground cloves.

In this chapter, you'll find recipes for several homemade ketchups, both traditional and esoteric. It's a whole new ball game.

TRY THIS!

Use any way that you'd use commercial ketchup. This one isn't too sweet, so you could even serve it with seafood.

1 can (28 ounces) tomato purée (one good brand is the organic Muir Glen)

¾ cup barley malt syrup or rice syrup, or to taste

½ cup tarragon vinegar, or more to taste

2 tablespoons pure chili powder (not a blend)

1 tablespoon Tabasco sauce

1 tablespoon prepared mustard

1 teaspoon coarse salt (kosher or sea), or more to taste

1 teaspoon garlic powder

1 teaspoon onion powder

1 teaspoon ground coriander

½ teaspoon freshly ground black pepper

½ teaspoon cayenne pepper

½ teaspoon celery seeds

¼ teaspoon ground allspice

¼ teaspoon ground cloves

¼ teaspoon ground mace or allspice

½ cup cold water, or as needed

Place all the ingredients in a large, heavy nonreactive saucepan over medium heat and bring to a simmer. Reduce the heat to medium-low and continue simmering until the ketchup is thick and richly flavored, whisking often to keep it from scorching, 15 minutes. The ketchup should be thick but pourable; if too thick, add a little more water. Correct the seasoning, adding more of any ingredient to taste. The ketchup should be highly seasoned. Transfer the ketchup to jars or squirt bottles, cover, cool to room temperature. Refrigerate until serving. The ketchup will keep for several weeks. Note: For a sharper tomato flavor, replace up to half the tomato purée with tomato paste.

Makes 3 cups

MANGO-MINT KETCHUP

Mango has been described as a peach that grew up in the tropics. We grow a lot of them in my hometown, Miami, and after we've all gorged ourselves on fresh mango and mango salsa for a few weeks, we try to find ways to preserve this fragrant fruit for the months when it's not in season. A few years ago, eager to jazz up a grilled fish sandwich, I came up with this mango ketchup. It fits perfectly with the light tropical fare we enjoy in South Florida (the mint has a cooling effect) and my northern friends find it pretty tasty, too.

When a mango is ripe, it smells very fragrant and feels soft, or at least yielding, to the touch. You can't go by the color, as some mangos remain green even when ripe. Note that if you have sensitive skin, wear gloves when peeling the mangos. The oils in the mango skin can cause a poison ivy–like rash.

3 to 4 ripe mangos
(about 2 pounds)
2 tablespoons unsalted
butter
¼ cup minced shallots
½ to 1 Scotch bonnet or
habanero chili, seeded and
minced (for a hotter
ketchup leave the seeds in)
1 tablespoon minced fresh
ginger
½ teaspoon ground cinnamon
¼ teaspoon ground allspice
⅛ teaspoon ground cloves
3 tablespoons dark brown
sugar, or more to taste

3 tablespoons cider vinegar
2 tablespoons fresh lime
juice, or more to taste
1 to 2 teaspoons Caribbean-
style hot sauce such as
Matouk's or Busha
Browne's
½ teaspoon coarse salt
(kosher ar sea), or more
to taste
½ teaspoon freshly ground
black pepper, or more to
taste
¼ cup chopped fresh mint
leaves
Water, if needed

1. Peel the mangos, cut the flesh off the seeds, and dice. Melt the butter in a heavy nonreactive saucepan over medium heat. Add the shallots and cook until soft and translucent but not brown, 4 minutes. Stir in the remaining ingredients, except for the mint leaves, and cover the pan. Cook the ketchup over medium heat, stirring often, until the mango is soft and the flavors are well blended, 10 to 15 minutes.

2. Transfer the ingredients to a blender or food processor and purée until smooth. Return the ketchup to the saucepan and stir in the mint. Simmer until the mint has lost its rawness, 2 minutes. Correct the seasoning, adding brown sugar, lime juice, salt, or pepper; the ketchup should be sweet, sour, and highly seasoned. If too thick, add a little water. Transfer the ketchup to jars, cover, cool to room temperature, and refrigerate until serving. Mango ketchup will keep for several weeks in the refrigerator.

Makes 4 cups

BANANA KETCHUP

When fruit ketchups began appearing on American restaurant menus in the 1990s, they seemed the epitome of cutting-edge. As it turns out, they belong to a centuries-old tradition that dates back to the very birth of this popular condiment. Thumb through an eighteenth-century English cookbook and you'll find recipes for ketchups made with gooseberries, walnuts, and even mushrooms. This banana ketchup explodes with the Caribbean flavors of all-spice, lime, and rum. It's hard to beat it at a summer cookout.

TRY THIS!

The sweetness of the bananas makes this a perfect accompaniment to grilled chicken, pork, and seafood. Banana ketchup also goes great on snapper and tuna burgers. Or use it as a dip for grilled vegetables.

3 ripe bananas, peeled and diced
1 small onion, finely chopped
2 cloves garlic, minced
½ to 1 Scotch bonnet or habanero chili, minced (for a spicier ketchup leave the seeds in)
1 cup cold water
¼ cup fresh lime juice
¼ cup cider vinegar, or more to taste
¼ cup molasses
¼ cup golden raisins
¼ cup honey, or more to taste
¼ cup tomato paste
¼ cup dark rum, or more to taste
½ teaspoon ground cinnamon
¼ teaspoon ground allspice
¼ teaspoon ground nutmeg
¼ teaspoon ground cloves
¼ teaspoon freshly ground black pepper
¼ teaspoon cayenne pepper
Water, if needed

1. Place all the ingredients in a heavy nonreactive saucepan and bring to a boil over high heat. Reduce the heat to medium and simmer, partly covered, until the mixture is thick and richly flavored, 15 minutes.

2. Transfer the ketchup to a blender or food processor and blend until smooth. Return it to the saucepan and simmer for 3 minutes. Correct the seasoning, adding honey, rum, or vinegar; the ketchup should be highly seasoned. If too thick, add a little water. Transfer to jars, cover, cool to room temperature, and refrigerate. The ketchup will keep for several weeks.

SWEET AND SPICY MUSTARD

This sweet-spicy mustard is the forerunner of an American deli classic. The brown sugar and corn syrup soften the bite of the mustard and vinegar, while the cinnamon, allspice, and cloves add a spicy sweetness. The mustard seeds are only partially ground, giving the mustard its signature speckled appearance and pleasing semisoft crunch.

The actual preparation time of this mustard is brief, but because of the various infusions and soakings, you'll need a couple of hours from start to finish.

2 tablespoons yellow mustard seeds	1 small onion, minced
2 tablespoons brown mustard seeds	1 clove garlic, minced
5 tablespoons mustard powder	3 tablespoons dark brown sugar
1 cup cider vinegar	2 teaspoons coarse salt (kosher or sea)
¼ cup hot water	½ teaspoon ground cinnamon
3 tablespoons dark corn syrup	¼ teaspoon ground allspice
	⅛ teaspoon ground cloves

TRY THIS!

Use as you would any mustard. It goes especially well with grilled hot dogs, sausages, and pork.

1. Combine the yellow and brown mustard seeds, mustard powder, ½ cup of the vinegar, and the water in a small bowl and stir to mix. Let stand for 1 hour at room temperature.

2. Combine the remaining ½ cup vinegar, ¼ cup water, the corn syrup, onion, garlic, brown sugar, salt, cinnamon, allspice, and cloves in a saucepan. Bring to a boil over high heat and boil, uncovered, for 1 minute. Remove the pan from the heat, cover, and let stand for 1 hour.

3. Combine the soaked mustard mixture and the spice mixture in a food processor and purée to a coarse paste. Transfer the purée to the top of a nonreactive double boiler or to a nonreactive saucepan sitting in a sauté pan of simmering water and cook, stirring often, until thick and creamy, 15 to 20 minutes. Don't worry if the mixture isn't quite as thick as commercial mustard; it will thicken on cooling. Transfer the mustard to a large jar, cover, cool to room temperature, and refrigerate. The mustard will keep for several months.

Makes 2 cups

CUTTING THE
MUSTARD

Wherever there's a grill, there are hot dogs. (Not to mention bratwurst, chorizo, linguiça, kielbasa, and merguez.) And wherever you find grilled sausages, you'll also find a condiment that's practically as old as live-fire cooking itself: mustard.

Mustard seeds have been found at Stone Age archaeological sites across Europe. According to food historian Waverley Root, the ancient Egyptians chewed mustard grains when they ate meat and the Greeks used mustard to cure scorpion bites. Others have suggested it was the Romans who made the first spreadable mustard by mashing mustard seeds with must (unfermented grape juice). They called the preparation *mustum ardens,* literally burning must—the origin of our word mustard.

Mustard is well connected to the idea of potency. It underlies the expression "to cut the mustard," or to succeed in performing or accomplishing something. When the French are exasperated, they say *la moutarde me monte au nez,* literally, "the mustard's up to my nose," or figuratively, "I'm about to lose my temper." A person with a particularly overinflated sense of self-importance thinks himself *le premier moutardier du pape,* or the Pope's mustard maker, a colorful expression dating to the papacy of Pope John XXII, who created the office of Papal Mustard Maker in the fourteenth century to keep a foolish nephew out of trouble.

Prepared mustard begins with mustard seeds, which are ground and mixed with some sort of liquid (water, wine, and/or vinegar) and seasonings (which may include salt, pepper, sugar, honey, or turmeric). White (yellow) mustard seeds produce the mildest mustard, followed by brown mustard seeds, a key ingredient in deli-style mustards. Black mustard seeds—a staple in Indian cooking—are the hottest of all. Mustard seeds can be ground to make a smooth mustard (Dijon-style), or left whole to make a grainy mustard (Meaux-style).

French mustards are tart and salty; German mustards, hot and sweet. American mustards owe their sharp tang to vinegar and their lurid yellow color to turmeric. The English and Chinese favor mustard powder mixed with water just before serving to form a sinus-blasting paste. New Englanders have a long-standing tradition of sweet mustards, flavored with maple syrup or honey.

If you want to be a master griller, you have to cut the mustard.

PURPLE MUSTARD

This snappy purple mustard is what Marcus Samuelsson, chef of Aquavit in New York, likes to serve with grilled fish and cured salmon. (Mustard with fish is a Swedish thing—Marcus was born in Sweden.) The wine reduction gives it a shocking purple hue and a winy tartness that plays a great supporting role to the mustard. Purple and black mustard seeds are available at Indian markets.

3 cups dry red wine
1 cup Port
2 shallots, finely chopped
4 white peppercorns
2 sprigs of fresh tarragon
1 tablespoon purple or black
   mustard seeds

1 teaspoon mustard powder
3 tablespoons Dijon mustard
Coarse salt (kosher or sea)
Freshly ground black pepper,
   to taste

Combine all the ingredients in a heavy nonreactive saucepan and bring to a boil over high heat. Reduce the heat to medium and briskly simmer the mixture until only ¾ cup remains. Let cool to room temperature. Correct the seasoning, adding salt and pepper. Transfer to a jar, cover, and refrigerate. The mustard will keep for several months.

Makes ¾ cup

GREEN PEPPERCORN MUSTARD

Green peppercorns are the firm green berries that give us black and white pepper. They possess some of the aromatic heat of their progeny, but they also have an exotic herbal quality that endears them to chefs from Penang to Paris. Green peppercorns are available water-packed or brined (in cans or jars) and freeze dried, from specialty markets and by mail order (page 281).

3 tablespoons yellow
mustard seeds
⅓ cup mustard powder
½ cup white wine
vinegar
½ cup dry white
wine

3 tablespoons green
peppercorns, drained if
water-packed, or freeze
dried
2 teaspoons coarse salt
(kosher or sea)
2 teaspoons honey

TRY THIS!

Use as you would any mustard, keeping in mind the special affinity green peppercorns have for grilled tuna, chicken, and beef.

1. Combine the mustard seeds, mustard powder, and vinegar in a bowl and stir until the power is dissolved. Let stand for 30 minutes at room temperature.

2. Meanwhile, combine the wine, peppercorns, salt, and honey in a small saucepan and simmer over medium heat, until the peppercorns are soft, 5 minutes. Transfer to a food processor, add the mustard mixture, and purée to a coarse paste.

3. Transfer the purée to the top of a nonreactive double boiler or to a nonreactive saucepan sitting in a sauté pan of simmering water and cook, stirring often, until thick and creamy, 15 to 20 minutes. Don't worry if the mixture isn't quite as thick as commercial mustard; it will thicken on cooling. Transfer the mustard to a large jar, cool to room temperature, cover, and refrigerate. The mustard will keep for several months.

Makes 1¼ cups

HORSERADISH MUSTARD

First, the good news about this mustard. If you have a cold, it will blast you back to health, and if you have stuffed-up sinuses, it will clear them. The bad news is that if you've got a delicate palate, you're toast. The tang of mustard seed and withering heat of fresh horseradish give new life to grilled hamburgers and hot dogs. It can even stand up to steak.

The actual preparation takes only 15 minutes, but

you'll need to allow a couple of hours from start to finish for soaking the mustard seeds and cooling the mustard. I call for fresh horseradish here, but 2 to 3 tablespoons of prepared horseradish will work out just fine, too.

¼ cup yellow mustard seeds

¼ cup brown mustard seeds
   (or more yellow)

½ cup white wine vinegar

½ cup dry white wine

3 tablespoons hot water

2 teaspoons coarse salt
   (kosher or sea)

2 teaspoons light brown
   sugar

1 teaspoon freshly ground
   black pepper

2 ounces (about 2 inches)
   fresh horseradish root,
   peeled and cut into
   ½-inch pieces

TRY THIS!

Sparingly! There isn't a sausage, burger, or steak in existence that would not benefit from a dab of this fiery condiment. But use it sparingly!

1. Combine the yellow and brown mustard seeds, vinegar, wine, and hot water in a nonreactive saucepan and bring to a boil, over high heat. Remove the pan from the heat and cool to room temperature. Soak the mustard seeds at room temperature until soft, 1 hour.

2. Transfer the mustard seed mixture to a blender or food processor and process to a coarse purée. Transfer the purée to the top of a nonreactive double boiler or to a nonreactive saucepan sitting in a sauté pan of simmering water. Add the salt, pepper, and brown sugar and cook, stirring often, until thick and creamy, 15 to 20 minutes. Don't worry if the mixture isn't quite as thick as commercial mustard; it will thicken on cooling. Remove the pan from the heat and let the mustard cool to room temperature.

3. Place the horseradish in a food processor fitted with a chopping blade and finely chop. (Take care not to inhale the volatile fumes.) Add the mustard and process to mix. Transfer the mustard to a large jar, cover, and refrigerate. The mustard will keep for several months.

   Makes 1½ cups

VARIATION

Sun-Dried Tomato Mustard: Prepare as for Horseradish Mustard, substituting 4 sun-dried tomatoes for the horseradish. Soak the tomatoes in hot water until soft, 1 hour. Chop and add them to the mustard mixture when you purée it in step 2.

OLD-FASHIONED BEARNAISE SAUCE

TRY THIS!

In France, this silky sauce is the classic accompaniment to filet mignon and grilled salmon. It's delectable on lamb and even grilled asparagus. Which just goes to show that the classics never go out of fashion.

This wantonly rich sauce is the closest the French get to barbecue sauce. A dollop spooned over a grilled tenderloin or smokily charred salmon steak makes you feel a little less sorry for the French than you normally would for a people deprived of true barbecue. Yes, it's rich. How could it not be? The main ingredients are egg yolks and butter. But offsetting the richness are an acidic reduction of white wine and vinegar, a blast of black pepper, and a licoricey hit of fresh tarragon. I learned to make béarnaise at the La Varenne cooking school in Paris in the 1970s, but in the wake of the low-fat cooking revolution in America, I hadn't made it for twenty years. I recently whipped up a batch and I was amazed at how thoroughly satisfying this French sauce could be with American grilled steak.

I won't say that béarnaise is easy to make. Indeed, without the right mastery of heat control and whiskmanship, it's easy to wind up with tarragon-flavored scrambled eggs. But there are three tricks that will help ensure success. First, use a heavy non-aluminum saucepan. (This keeps the eggs from scorching or discoloring.) Second, have handy a bowl of ice water to shock-cool the pan if the yolks start to scramble. Finally, add the melted butter when hot but not scalding and add it in a very thin stream, whisking for all your worth. Traditionally, the sauce would be strained for extra suaveness, but I like the crunchy texture of the shallots.

⅔ cup dry white wine

⅓ cup tarragon vinegar, or more to taste

½ cup minced shallots

3 tablespoons chopped fresh tarragon leaves

Freshly ground black pepper

1 tablespoon cold water

4 egg yolks

12 tablespoons (1½ sticks) unsalted butter, melted and cooled slightly

⅛ teaspoon cayenne pepper

Coarse salt (kosher or sea), to taste

1.   Combine the wine, vinegar, shallots, 1½ tablespoons of the chopped tarragon, and 10 grinds of pepper in a non-reactive saucepan. Bring to a boil over high heat and boil, uncovered, until only 3 tablespoons liquid remain, 5 to 8 minutes. Add the cold water and let the mixture cool to room temperature. Have ready a large bowl of ice water.

2. Add the egg yolks to the vinegar mixture and cook over medium-low heat, whisking for all you're worth, until the mixture thickens to the consistency of mayonnaise and you can see traces of the whisk on the bottom of the pan, 1 to 2 minutes. Do not overcook, or the yolks will scramble. (If the yolks start to scramble, set the pan in the bowl of ice water. A little scrambling won't harm the final sauce.)

3. Remove the pan from the heat and add the melted butter in a thin stream, whisking steadily; the sauce will thicken. Whisk in the cayenne, the remaining tarragon, and salt; the sauce should be highly seasoned. If additional tartness is desired, add a few more drops of tarragon vinegar. Keep the sauce warm on a shelf over the stove or in a pan of hot tap water. Do not attempt to warm the sauce over direct heat or in a double boiler, or it will curdle. Use within 2 hours of making.

Makes about 1¼ cups; enough to serve 4 to 6

VERY FRENCH STEAK SAUCE

This is a highly unusual recipe on two accounts: first because the French simply don't use steak sauce. (At least not often.) Second, because this simple recipe was inspired by one of the most celebrated practitioners of French haute cuisine: Daniel Boulud of the restaurants Daniel and the Café Boulud in New York. I find it reassuring that a guy who usually deals in foie gras and truffles is democratic enough to concoct a sauce from mustard, ketchup, Worcestershire sauce, and Tabasco sauce. The fact is that Daniel created this sauce for a traditional French bistro dish, chicken

STEAK SAUCE

Rummage around a sauce master's kitchen and you're sure to find a distinctive tall, slender, square-sided bottle of A.1. Steak Sauce. Steak lovers have reached for this thick, pungent, sweet-sour sauce for more than 150 years.

The original A.1. Steak Sauce was invented by Henderson William Brand, chef to King George IV of England from 1824 to 1831. The king liked the sauce so much, he proclaimed it "A.1." Armed with this endorsement, Brand went into the condiment business, but he turned out to be a better sauce maker than businessman. His sauce venture ended in bankruptcy. (Luckily, he also found the time to write several cookbooks, including *The Complete Modern Cook*.)

In 1906, the liquor distributors G.F. Heublein & Brother acquired the exclusive right to manufacture and distribute A.1. sauce in the United States. It proved to be a lifesaver for the company, for the sauce kept Heublein afloat during Prohibition. The sauce's fortunes have risen and fallen with general meat consumption trends in the United States. With the current enthusiasm for steak, martinis, and cigars, A.1. is enjoying a comeback.

A.1. Steak Sauce is a popular ingredient among barbecue sauce makers, who prize it for its thick consistency and complex sweet-sour flavor. A.1. owes its sweetness to corn syrup, its pucker to distilled vinegar, and its richness to puréed raisins, oranges, and tomato paste. As befits any good meat sauce, it also contains onion and garlic.

A.1. possesses a distinctive sharpness and flavor. A little goes a long way in adding depth and richness to barbecue sauce. But too much—even a little too much—can quickly overpower a sauce.   Use it sparingly.

à la diable (grilled or broiled with a mustard crust). You'll also love the way it peps up steak. Just so you know: I like the way the sour cream and corn syrup round out the flavor of the sauce, but they're not part of Daniel's original recipe. I've made them optional.

½ **cup Dijon mustard**
¼ **cup ketchup**
¼ **cup sour cream (optional)**
3 **tablespoons A.1. Steak Sauce**
4 **teaspoons Worcestershire sauce**

1 **tablespoon cane syrup or corn syrup (optional)**
1 **teaspoon Tabasco sauce**
½ **teaspoon freshly ground black pepper**

TRY THIS!

Grilled chicken and steak are obvious targets for this tangy sauce, but don't overlook grilled pork, fish, or even vegetables.

Combine all the ingredients in a bowl and whisk to mix. Cover and refrigerate. In the unlikely event that you have any left after the first day, transfer to a jar, cover, and refrigerate. The sauce will keep for up to 1 week.

Makes 1 cup; enough to serve 4 to 6

CAJUN SWAMP SAUCE

TRY THIS!

Cajun swamp sauce goes well with grilled seafood, especially catfish, snapper, and shrimp.

If you like the bold flavors of Cajun cooking, you'll love this creamy sauce, which is assertively seasoned with mustard, horseradish, and Tabasco sauce and audibly crunchy with finely chopped celery and shallots. Louisianans aren't particularly famous for barbecue, but this singular sauce will spice up anything from barnyard, bayou, or ocean you may choose to throw on the grill.

Try to use Creole mustard, which is sharper than your average American mustard. One good brand is Zatarain's.

1 cup mayonnaise

¼ cup Creole mustard

2 tablespoons prepared
horseradish

2 tablespoons
Worcestershire sauce

2 tablespoons fresh lemon
juice

1 tablespoon ketchup

1 to 2 teaspoons Tabasco
sauce, or more to taste

1 tablespoon sweet paprika

½ teaspoon freshly ground
black pepper

¼ teaspoon sugar

1 large shallot, minced

1 rib celery, minced

3 tablespoons finely chopped
fresh flat-leaf parsley

1 scallion (white and green
parts), trimmed
and finely chopped

Coarse salt (kosher
or sea), to taste

Combine all the ingredients in a mixing bowl and stir or whisk to mix. Correct the seasoning, adding salt or hot sauce to taste. Transfer to a large jar, cover, and refrigerate. The sauce will keep for several weeks.

Makes 2 cups; enough to serve 8

VOLCANIC HORSERADISH SAUCE

When it comes to finding the perfect foil for the rich flavor of roast beef or steak, few condiments can beat horseradish sauce. So where's the volcano come in? You make the sauce with freshly grated horseradish, which is volcanic enough for anyone.

TRY THIS!

Serve volcanic horseradish sauce in a bowl on the side with steaks, chops, and roast beef. Spoon cool dollops on the hot meat and watch it dissolve into a flavorful puddle. Yum.

1 piece (about 3 inches)
fresh horseradish root

½ cup sour cream

1 tablespoon fresh lemon
juice, or more to taste

½ teaspoon grated lemon
zest

½ teaspoon coarse salt
(kosher or sea), or more
to taste

½ teaspoon coarsely ground
black pepper

1 cup heavy (or whipping)
cream, chilled

1. Peel the horseradish and finely grate by hand or in a food processor fitted with a chopping blade. If using the latter, cut the horseradish into ¼-inch-thick slices before pro-

cessing. Whichever method you use, take care not to breathe in the pungent horseradish fumes. Transfer the horseradish to a bowl and stir or whisk in the sour cream, lemon juice, lemon zest, salt, and pepper.

2. Pour the heavy cream into a chilled bowl and beat with chilled beaters to soft peaks. Gently fold the whipped cream into the sour cream mixture. Correct the seasoning, adding salt or lemon juice to taste. Cover and refrigerate until using. The horseradish sauce tastes best served within a couple of hours of making; restir before serving.

Makes 2 cups; enough to serve 6 to 8

JALAPENO TARTAR SAUCE

Tartar sauce was once a glory of American gastronomy, but the sugary versions dispensed in packets have reduced it to a culinary cliché. I say it's time to rehabilitate a sauce that goes so well with grilled seafood and that, when properly prepared, fairly explodes with flavor.

TRY THIS!

Serve with any sort of grilled seafood, chicken, or vegetables.

1 cup mayonnaise

1 hard-cooked egg, finely chopped

1 tablespoon finely chopped pickled or fresh jalapeño pepper

1 tablespoon finely chopped shallots

1 tablespoon finely chopped cornichons

1 tablespoon chopped drained capers

2 tablespoons mixed chopped fresh herbs, such as parsley, tarragon, basil, and/or cilantro

Freshly ground black pepper, to taste

Lemon juice, to taste

Place the mayonnaise in a bowl and stir or whisk in the remaining ingredients, adding pepper and lemon juice as desired. The tartar sauce should be highly seasoned. Transfer to a jar, cover, and refrigerate. The tartar sauce will keep for up to 5 days.

Makes 1½ cups; enough to serve 6

VINAIGRETTES

BASIC HERB VINAIGRETTE

Here's the grand-daddy of vinaigrettes—a simple emulsification of oil and vinegar, with mustard for stability and fresh herbs for excitement. The recipe takes me back to my first restaurant job at a Michelin-starred restaurant in Brittany called the Auberge de la Porte de France. As lowest man on the kitchen totem pole, it was my duty to whisk the oil and vinegar together to make vinaigrette, and I prayed it wouldn't break. If it did, a spoonful of ice water often brought it back to life. You may be surprised by the use of canola oil instead of olive oil, but bland oil is what makes a true French vinaigrette taste French.

This vinaigrette is best served the day it's made.

2 tablespoons Dijon mustard
½ teaspoon coarse salt
 (kosher or sea), or more
 to taste
½ teaspoon freshly ground
 black pepper
2 tablespoons white wine
 vinegar, tarragon vinegar,
 or champagne vinegar, or
 more to taste

1 cup canola oil
2 tablespoons fresh lemon
 juice
3 tablespoons mixed
 chopped fresh herbs,
 including chives, chervil,
 tarragon, and/or flat-leaf
 parsley

Whisk method: Combine the mustard, salt, pepper, and vinegar in a heavy bowl and whisk to mix. Gradually whisk in the oil in a very thin stream; the sauce should thicken. Whisk in the lemon juice and herbs. Correct the seasoning, adding more salt or vinegar.

Blender method: Combine the mustard, salt, pepper, vinegar, and lemon juice in a blender and blend to mix. Add the oil through the hole in the blender lid, running the

blender on low, then medium speed. Stop the blender and stir in the herbs by hand.

Jar method: Combine all the ingredients in a jar with a tight-fitting lid. Shake vigorously until blended.

Makes 1⅓ cups; enough to serve 6 to 8

HOMEMADE ITALIAN DRESSING MARINADE

TRY THIS!

Italian dressing works wonders with chicken, pork, or beef, whether the meat is grilled over a hot fire or slowly smoked in a pit. It also makes a great dressing for the iceberg lettuce salads that seem to go so well with steak—of course.

Italian salad dressing is a popular sauce and marinade base on the competition barbecue circuit. The purist in me rebels at using a bottled salad dressing, but people win big with it. Here's an Italian dressing you can make from scratch. It tastes almost like factory made!

2 teaspoons cornstarch
½ cup cold water
¾ cup distilled white vinegar
2 teaspoons sugar
1 teaspoon coarse salt (kosher or sea)
2 teaspoons dried red bell pepper flakes (optional)
2 teaspoons dried garlic flakes
2 teaspoons dried oregano

2 teaspoons dried parsley
2 teaspoons freeze-dried chives
1 teaspoon dried onion flakes
1 teaspoon mustard powder
½ teaspoon hot pepper flakes
½ teaspoon freshly ground black pepper
1 cup canola oil

1. Combine the cornstarch and 1 tablespoon of the water in a small bowl and stir to form a thick paste. Place the remaining water, the vinegar, sugar, and salt in a nonreactive saucepan and bring to a boil over medium heat. Stir the cornstarch mixture again and whisk it into the boiling vinegar mixture. Bring to a boil, whisking steadily; the mixture should thicken. Remove the pan from the heat and let cool to room temperature.

2. Transfer the vinegar mixture to a bowl and whisk in the remaining ingredients. Transfer to a jar, cover, and refrigerate. The dressing will keep for several weeks.

Makes 2¼ cups

JUMPIN' JIM'S BARBECUED CHICKEN

Jumpin' Jim Woodsmall won the 1999 prize for the best barbecued chicken at the Kansas City Royal. His secret? An overnight bath—for the chicken, not for Jim—in bottled Italian dressing. That, and using flavorful chicken thighs, and cooking them both by smoking and grilling.

2 pounds chicken thighs

1 recipe Homemade Italian Dressing Marinade (page 233) or 2¼ cups your favorite bottled brand

¼ cup barbecue rub, preferably homemade (Jim uses a sweet Kansas City–style rub like Kansas City Sweet and Smoky Rub, page 134)

SPECIAL EQUIPMENT

2 cups mixed wood chips (hickory and cherry work well), soaked in 2 cups water for 1 hour, then drained

1. Place the chicken thighs in a glass baking dish and pour the dressing over them. Cover with plastic wrap and marinate overnight in the refrigerator, turning several times to ensure even seasoning.

2. Set up the grill for indirect grilling, following the directions on page 5, and preheat to 225°F. If using charcoal, toss half the soaked wood chips on the coals. If using a gas grill, place the wood chips in the smoker box. Don't grill until you see the smoke.

3. Remove the chicken from the marinade and arrange skin side up in the center of the grate away from the heat. Sprinkle with half the barbecue rub. Smoke-cook until cooked through, 2 to 3 hours. (If working over charcoal, replenish the coals and wood chips after 1 hour.)

4. Sprinkle the chicken pieces on both sides with the remaining rub. Move them directly over the coals (if using charcoal) or over the lit burners on a gas grill. Grill the chicken to brown and crisp the skin, about 5 minutes per side. Serve at once.

Serves 4

CATALAN VINAIGRETTE

Order grilled fare in Barcelona and you'll receive a trio of sauces: Romesco (page 194), Alli-oli (garlic mayonnaise), and this tongue-tingling vinaigrette. What makes it more than mere salad dressing is the addition of capers, shallots, tomato, and tiny tart cornichon pickles. This recipe comes from the homey Barcelona chop house, La Tomaquera, and I defy you to find a grilled meat, poultry, seafood, or vegetable that isn't improved by a spoonful.

1 clove garlic, minced
½ teaspoon coarse salt (kosher or sea), or more to taste
1 tablespoon Dijon mustard
¼ cup red wine vinegar or sherry vinegar
1 cup extra virgin olive oil
1 large to 2 medium shallots, minced (about ¼ cup)

2 tablespoons capers with juices
6 cornichons, finely chopped
1 ripe tomato, peeled, seeded, and finely chopped (see box, page 246)
Freshly ground black pepper, to taste

Place the garlic and salt in a large bowl and mash to a paste with the back of a spoon. Add the mustard and vinegar and whisk until the salt crystals are completely dissolved. Gradually whisk in the oil in a thin stream; the sauce should emulsify. Whisk in the shallots, capers, cornichons, and tomato. Correct the seasoning, adding salt and pepper. Cover and refrigerate. The vinaigrette will keep for several days, but it tastes best served within a few hours of making. Bring to room temperature and whisk well before serving.

Makes 2 cups; enough to serve 6 to 8

VARIATION

Some Spanish cooks enrich their vinaigrette with flat-leaf parsley and finely chopped hard-cooked eggs.

THE NEW
VINAIGRETTES

It seems like an obvious idea looking back on it. But when chefs first began spooning vinaigrette sauce over grilled seafood and chicken breasts in the 1970s, the gesture was downright revolutionary. Gone were the artery-clogging egg-and-butter sauces of yesteryear and those laboriously reduced demi-glaces that made life miserable for kitchen apprentices. In their place came light, healthy, explosively flavorful vinaigrettes. It was a blast of fresh air for grill jockeys everywhere, and we're still feeling the effects of the vinaigrette revolution.

Infinitely varied, quick and easy to prepare, vinaigrettes go great with a wide variety of grilled fare. Cholesterol free, they are the perfect sauce for a nation obsessed with flavor but with little tolerance for fat.

Not that vinaigrettes are particularly new. In the Middle Ages, vinaigrette-like sauces were made with verjuice (unripe grape juice). The legendary nineteenth-century French chef, Auguste Escoffier, included dozens of vinaigrette recipes in his seminal *Guide Culinaire*. Jean-Georges Vongerichten, the cutting-edge owner-chef of Jean Georges, Jo Jo, Vong, Mercer Kitchen, and other restaurants in New York, recalls enjoying vinaigrette not only on salads but with sausage

BARBECUE VINAIGRETTE

Kansas meets Paris in this recipe—a vinaigrette flavored with barbecue sauce. Use it when conventional barbecue sauce would be too heavy, on a grilled veal chop, for example, or over grilled fish. You can vary the final effect with your choice of barbecue sauce: For a sweeter vinaigrette, use a commercial Kansas City–style sauce, like the Sweet-and-Smoky Barbecue Sauce (page 134) or K.C. Masterpiece; for a hotter vinaigrette, use Lean-and-Mean Texas

and *pot au feu* as a child in Alsace. "With rich food, you need something acidic to cut the fat," say Vongerichten. "Vinaigrette is the perfect sauce."

Nor are vinaigrettes exclusively French. Morocco's Charmoula (page 198), a vivid sauce made with lemon juice, olive oil, cilantro, parsley, and garlic might be called a North African vinaigrette. *Bollito misto* (Italian boiled dinner) would seem naked without Salsa Verde (page 190), a piquant sauce flavored with capers, anchovies, and parsley. Cuban Mojo (page 173) gives vinaigrette a Latin accent; so does Mexican salsa.

Vinaigrette literally means "little vinegar" in French. Traditionally, the sauce was just that: a little wine vinegar mixed with olive oil or vegetable oil, salt, and pepper. The classic proportion is one part vinegar to three to four parts oil. A spoonful of mustard is often added to help emulsify the ingredients. Today's vinaigrettes are as likely to be made with walnut or hazelnut oil as olive oil and with balsamic or rice vinegar—or even lemon or lime juice—as with traditional wine vinegar. But the basic principle remains the same.

Because oil is lighter than water (and by extension vinegar and fruit juice), vinaigrettes have a natural tendency to separate. In classic French cuisine, an egg yolk or a spoonful of mustard is added to help bind the ingredients together. Other emulsifiers include honey and maple syrup.

During my apprenticeship years in France, we combined the oil and vinegar with up to 10 minutes of laborious whisking. The same effect can be achieved by using a blender, or even by shaking the ingredients together in a jar.

So the next time you're casting about for a sauce for grilled seafood or chicken, whip up a batch of vinaigrette.

TRY THIS!

This may be the only vinaigrette ever designed to be served with hamburgers. You can also spoon it over grilled pork, salmon, or snapper or even over chicken or beef.

Barbecue Sauce (page 138); or even a mustard barbecue sauce, like Firehouse Jack's (page 167).

⅔ cup vegetable oil
3 tablespoons red wine
   vinegar
2 tablespoons barbecue
   sauce
½ teaspoon Tabasco sauce,
   or your favorite hot sauce

½ teaspoon coarse salt
   (kosher or sea)
½ teaspoon freshly
   ground
   black
   pepper

Combine all the ingredients in a blender and blend to mix. Or combine in a jar with a tight-fitting lid and shake to mix. Refrigerate, covered, until ready to use. The vinaigrette will keep for up to 1 week. Shake well before using.

Makes 1 cup

SESAME-GINGER-SOY VINAIGRETTE

The Asian origins of this fragrant vinaigrette are obvious—first in the spicing (garlic and ginger), then in the nutty flavor of the roasted sesame oil and the delicate piquancy of the rice vinegar. It's a great example of the good things that can happen when East meets West—in other words, fusion food at its best. Besides, who can resist the speckled look of the black and white sesame seeds?

The easiest way to make ginger juice is to press fresh ginger in a garlic press. Or you can grate the ginger on a Japanese ginger grater or the fine side of a box grater.

TRY THIS!

This flavorful vinaigrette is delicate enough to go with grilled lobster or chicken breasts and robust enough to stand up to steak. It's fantastic on grilled fish and vegetables of all sorts.

1 clove garlic, minced
1 scallion (white part only), trimmed and minced
1 teaspoon ginger juice
2 teaspoons sugar
¼ cup soy sauce
¼ cup rice vinegar

5 tablespoons canola oil
3 tablespoons Asian (dark) sesame oil
¼ cup boiling water
1 tablespoon toasted sesame seeds (see box, page 105)

Combine the garlic, scallion, ginger juice, sugar, soy sauce, vinegar, and canola and sesame oils in a blender and blend at high speed until mixed. Add the water and blend for 10 seconds. Add the sesame seeds and run the blender in short bursts just to mix. Or place all the ingredients in a jar, tightly cover, and shake to mix. Store in a jar, covered, in the refrigerator for up to 1 week. Bring to room temperature and shake well before using.

Makes 1 cup

SAFFRON-LEMON-HONEY VINAIGRETTE

Saffron and turmeric give this vinaigrette a chic golden sheen, while the honey and walnut oil create the sort of sweet-nutty richness that goes so well with grilled salmon and pork. This recipe was inspired by one from chef Tony Ambrose, owner of the hip Boston restaurant called Ambrosia.

Walnut oil is available at gourmet shops.

½ cup champagne vinegar
¼ cup honey
¼ cup water
2 tablespoons fresh lemon juice, or more to taste
½ teaspoon coarse salt (kosher or sea), or to taste

¼ teaspoon turmeric
¼ teaspoon saffron threads
¼ teaspoon freshly ground white pepper
¾ cup walnut oil

TRY THIS!

This golden vinaigrette looks and tastes great on white grilled foods, like chicken and cod or halibut. It's also terrific on pork and over rich, oily fish, like salmon and bluefish.

1. Combine the vinegar, honey, water, and lemon juice in a saucepan and slowly bring to a boil over medium heat. Stir in the salt, turmeric, saffron (crumbling it between your thumb and forefinger as you add it), and pepper, then cool to room temperature. Transfer the mixture to a blender or jar with a tight-fitting lid.

2. If using a blender, with the machine running, add the oil in a thin stream through the hole in the lid. If using a jar, add the oil all at once and shake to mix. Or place the vinegar mixture in a bowl and whisk in the oil. Correct the seasoning, adding more salt or lemon juice. Transfer to a large jar, cover, and refrigerate. This vinaigrette will keep for several weeks. Bring to room temperature and shake well before using.

Makes 2 cups

BALSAMIC DRIZZLE

Balsamic vinegar burst upon the American food scene in the early 1980s, and this rich, sweet-sour vinegar from Emilia-Romagna in Italy was an instant sensation. We loved its fruity aroma, the result of making the vinegar from must (unfermented grape juice) rather than wine. We loved its complex flavor, achieved by lengthy aging in wood. True balsamic vinegar owes its extraordinary richness and concentration to a minimum of twelve years' aging in a series of barrels, each made of a different wood. The result is *tradizionale*—aged balsamic vinegar, which can cost as much as $40 an ounce!

There's a way to simulate the concentrated flavor of a *tradizionale* without having to mortgage your home, and it turns up on some of the best-dressed plates from Malibu to Manhattan. It's made by boiling inexpensive commercial balsamic vinegar into a thick, fragrant syrup. Balsamic syrup is sublime drizzled over a grilled veal chop or salmon fillet. It raises a platter of grilled vegetables to the level of art.

TRY THIS!

Drizzle this over grilled veal chops, salmon steaks (or other fish), or grilled vegetables. Or, for dessert, drizzle it over grilled fresh fruit— superb! Use sparingly —the flavor is very intense.

1 cup good commercial balsamic vinegar
⅓ cup honey

⅓ cup sugar
3 tablespoons soy sauce

Place all the ingredients in a large, heavy, nonreactive saucepan over medium heat and bring to a boil. Simmer the mixture until reduced to 1 cup, about 15 minutes. Skim off and discard any foam that may rise to the surface. Strain the mixture into a bottle and cool to room temperature. Cork or cap the bottle. The drizzle will keep for several months at room temperature.

Makes 1 cup

HOT SAUCES

OUCH SAUCE

My two-year-old goddaughter, Myana Millison, calls things that hurt her "ouch." Thus, a cactus is an ouch and so is a bee sting. Myana has never tasted this fiery salsa from the Yucatán, but it would definitely qualify as an ouch. After all, it's made with the world's hottest chili, the habanero. Hot? Well, a habanero is 50 times hotter than a jalapeño. In the Yucatán this sauce goes by an equally curious name, *xni pec,* literally dog's nose, although whether because it bites you or because it makes your nose cold and runny like a dog's, I'm not sure.

1 small red onion, cut into small dice (about ¾ cup)

Ice water

3 tablespoons fresh sour orange juice (see box, page 174) or 2 tablespoons fresh lime juice and 1 tablespoon fresh orange juice, or more to taste

2 medium ripe tomatoes, peeled, seeded, and cut into small dice (see box, page 246) (about 2 cups)

1 habanero or Scotch bonnet chili, seeded and minced, or more if you dare

¼ cup finely chopped green cabbage or 3 to 4 radishes, cut into small dice

2 tablespoons chopped fresh cilantro

½ teaspoon coarse salt (kosher or sea), or more to taste

1. Place the onion in a bowl with ice water to cover and let soak for 10 minutes. Drain well in a strainer and gently blot the onion dry with paper towels. Transfer the onion to a bowl and stir in the sour orange juice. Let stand for 5 minutes.

2. Gently stir in the remaining ingredients. Correct the

seasoning, adding salt or sour orange. The salsa tastes best served within a few hours of making.

Makes about 2 cups

VARIATION

Grill jockeys in the Yucatán also make a grilled version of this salsa. Char the onion, tomato, and chili on the grill, then make the salsa.

JALAPENO SAUCE

This simple salsa turns up on the tables of Central American restaurants around Miami. A Honduran or Salvadoran steak just wouldn't taste right without it. The salsa can be made in not much more time than it takes to pull out your food processor—always a cardinal virtue in my house. Don't be scared off by the seemingly large quantity of jalapeños: You can manage the heat by seeding the chilies.

TRY THIS!

Serve this salsa with any type of grilled meat or seafood. It goes especially well with grilled beef.

1 medium sweet onion, such as Vidalia or Walla Walla, finely chopped

8 jalapeño chilies, seeded and diced (for a hotter salsa leave some of the seeds in)

3 tablespoons chopped fresh cilantro

¾ cup distilled white vinegar

2 teaspoons coarse salt (kosher or sea), or more to taste

½ teaspoon freshly ground black pepper, or more to taste

Place the onion and chilies in a food processor and process to a coarse purée. Add the cilantro, vinegar, salt, and pepper and pulse to blend. Correct the seasoning, adding salt or pepper; the salsa should be highly seasoned. The salsa tastes best served the day it's made. Transfer any leftovers to a jar, cover, and refrigerate. The salsa will keep for several days.

Makes 1½ cups

HELL'S FURY

TRY THIS!

Use as you would any hot sauce. I like to slather it on grilled chicken and fish sandwiches.

There are hot sauces and then there are hot sauces. This one separates the men from the boys, the diehards from the wannabes. Hell's Fury derives its heat from Scotch bonnet chilies and mustard, with a hint of mango thrown in for sweetness. The overall effect is rather like eating a peach, taking a whiff of turpentine (mango has a turpentiny aroma), then biting a high voltage cable. Exercise extreme caution when serving.

I've given a range of chilies: Two will give you a very hot sauce; six will make your tongue blister.

1 cup diced ripe mango or frozen mango purée
2 to 6 Scotch bonnet chilies, seeded and chopped
½ small onion, chopped
3 cloves garlic, minced
⅔ cup fresh orange juice
¼ cup Dijon mustard
¼ cup distilled white vinegar
3 tablespoons vegetable oil

3 tablespoons chopped fresh cilantro
2 tablespoons light brown sugar, or more to taste
1 tablespoon fresh lime juice
2 teaspoons coarse salt (kosher or sea), or more to taste
½ teaspoon freshly ground black pepper

Combine all the ingredients in a nonreactive saucepan and cook over medium heat until the mango and onion are soft, 10 minutes. Transfer the mixture to a blender or food processor and process to a coarse or smooth purée. Correct the seasoning, adding salt or brown sugar. Transfer the sauce to a jar. You can use it right away, but the flavor will improve if you let it age for a few days. Cover and refrigerate. The sauce will keep for several months. Shake well before serving.

Makes about 2 cups

SIMPLE BRAZILIAN HOT SAUCE

TRY THIS!

Brazilians would serve this fiery sauce over simply grilled chicken, pork, or beef. I'd expand the list to include seafood, especially grilled tuna and shrimp.

No Brazilian barbecue would be complete without some sort of hot sauce. The firepower in this one comes from a tiny chili called *malagueta*. Tiny, but ferocious. The malagueta starts a slow burn in the front of your mouth that won't quit until it's in your belly. You can find malagueta chilies dried or in vinegar at Brazilian markets. If unavailable, use dried Chinese chilies or hot pepper flakes. I give a range of chilies, leaving it up to you to decide how much pain you want to inflict.

1 clove garlic, minced

1 teaspoon coarse salt (kosher or sea)

1 to 4 tablespoons dried malagueta chilies or other dried chilies or 1 to 3 teaspoons hot pepper flakes

⅓ cup fresh lime juice

½ medium onion, finely chopped

⅔ cup olive oil, preferably Portuguese

½ teaspoon freshly ground black pepper

Combine the garlic and salt in a bowl and mash to a paste with the back of a spoon. If using whole dried chilies, crumble them into the bowl with your fingers. If using pepper flakes, there's no need to crumble them. Add the lime juice and stir until the salt is dissolved. Stir in the onion, olive oil, and pepper. You can serve the sauce right away, but it will be even more flavorful if you let it sit for 30 minutes. Stir again with a fork before serving. This sauce tastes best served the day it's made.

Makes 1¼ cup

VARIATION

Country-Style Hot Sauce: For a more elaborate country-style hot sauce, stir in 1 finely diced seeded tomato, ¼ cup finely diced green bell pepper, and 3 tablespoons finely chopped flat-leaf parsley.

PIRI-PIRI SAUCE

West Africa's contribution to the world of hot barbecue sauces is *piri-piri*—a sort of fiery vinaigrette ignited with a tiny African chili. Don't let its size fool you, because the piri-piri pepper is a real scorcher. Piri-piri chilies may be hard to come by in the United States, unless you live near an African Iberian market. (This sauce is very popular in Portugal, too.) Fortunately, you can substitute fresh Thai chilies, Mexican pequin chilies, or even red Scotch bonnets, serranos, or jalapeños. To keep the proper heat level, I use whole chilies, but you could remove the veins and seeds if a milder sauce is desired.

The mustard and garlic aren't strictly traditional, but I like the way they round out the flavor. Purists can leave them out.

1 clove garlic, finely chopped
½ teaspoon coarse salt
   (kosher or sea)
1 to 3 tablespoons finely
   chopped fresh red chili
   peppers

1 tablespoon Dijon mustard
¼ cup white wine vinegar
¾ cup extra virgin olive oil,
   preferably Portuguese

Place the garlic and salt in a bowl and mash to a paste with the back of a spoon. Add the chilies and continue to mash. Add the mustard. Whisk in the vinegar in a thin stream. Whisk in the oil; the sauce should thicken slightly. Or combine the ingredients in a jar and shake to mix. Transfer to a jar, placing a sheet of plastic wrap between the top of the jar and the lid, cover, and refrigerate. The piri-piri sauce will keep for several days at room temperature. Stir before serving.

Makes 1 cup

TRY THIS!

This fiery sauce is popular on three continents, so you could serve it with Portuguese, Brazilian, or African-style barbecue. Spoon it sparingly over your favorite grilled seafood, chicken, pork, or beef.

HOLY TOMATO

Tomatoes are an indispensable ingredient in the world of barbecue—a major player in sauces, salsas, and relishes and great served in the accompanying salads. Most grill jockeys are pretty informal when it comes to using tomatoes, but occasionally a recipe asks you to peel and seed them. Here's how to do it.

To peel a tomato (grill method): Preheat the grill to high. Grill the tomatoes until the skins are blackened on all sides, 8 to 12 minutes total. Transfer the tomatoes to a plate to cool, then pull off the burnt skins with your fingers. Don't worry about removing every last bit of black. A little burnt skin adds character. I prefer the grill method because it gives the tomato a smoky flavor.

To peel a tomato (water method): Bring a saucepan of water to a boil. Cut a small shallow X on the rounded end of the tomato. Using the tip of a paring knife, cut out the stem. Plunge the tomato into rapidly boiling water for 15 to 60 seconds. (The riper the tomato, the shorter the cooking time you'll need.) Transfer the tomato to a plate and let cool. Pull off the skin with your fingers.

To seed a tomato: Cut the tomato in half crosswise and gently squeeze each half, cut side down, to wring out the seeds and liquid. If necessary, help the seeds out with your fingers. If you like, work over a bowl and strainer, so you can reserve the tomato water, which is pleasant in drinks and soups.

One final word of advice: Never refrigerate tomatoes. If they're not completely ripe when you buy them, they will continue to ripen at room temperature. Refrigeration stops the ripening process dead in its tracks. If the tomatoes are ripe, refrigerating will make them mealy.

ZEHUG (Yemenite Pepper Sauce)

TRY THIS!

The obvious destination for *zehug* is any Middle East–style shish kebab, grilled fish, or vegetables. It also makes an electrifying dip for grilled pita bread.

Fire is a good thing at a barbecue and I don't just mean in your grill. A properly hellish, homemade hot sauce can do much to enhance a griller's reputation. Israeli grill jockeys bolster their status with a fiery pepper sauce called *zehug*. Brought to Israel by Yemenite Jews, *zehug* starts with puréed chilies and garlic and can be embellished with cumin, cilantro, lemon, tomatoes, or a combination of all these ingredients. To make a red *zehug*, use red chili peppers; a green *zehug*, use green. Watch out: This is a hot one! Add as many peppers as you think you can handle.

2 ripe tomatoes, peeled and seeded (see box, facing page)

3 to 6 red or green jalapeño peppers, seeded and coarsely chopped (for a hotter zehug leave the seeds in)

6 cloves garlic, coarsely chopped

1 teaspoon coarse salt (kosher or sea)

1 teaspoon ground cumin

1 teaspoon ground coriander

½ teaspoon freshly ground black pepper

3 tablespoons fresh lemon juice

¼ cup extra virgin olive oil

¼ cup chopped fresh cilantro

Combine all the ingredients in a blender and blend until smooth. Correct the seasoning, adding any of the ingredients as desired. Use right away or transfer to a large jar, cover, and refrigerate. The sauce will keep for several weeks.

Makes 2 cups

SCOTCH BONNET JAM

I first tasted this electrifying jam at my stepson Jake's restaurant. Electrifying is the word for it, from the jolt of the Scotch bonnet chili to the sweetness of candied bell

TRY THIS!

Serve with any grilled food that can benefit from heat and sweetness. Grilled shrimp, fish, and lobster are a few appropriate matches, also chicken, pork, or Asian kebabs, like satés.

pepper. The recipe is easy to make and even easier to customize: You could add yellow or green bell peppers for color, for example, or a different type of chili, like a chipotle. As for serving suggestions, well, this jam never met a piece of grilled fish or chicken it couldn't improve.

1 large red bell pepper, stemmed, seeded, and cut into ½-inch dice
½ to 1 Scotch bonnet chili, seeded and minced (for a really spicy jam leave the seeds in)

1 cup sugar
1 tablespoon fresh lemon juice
1 teaspoon coarse salt (kosher or sea)
1 strip (2 x ½ inch) of lemon zest

Combine all the ingredients in a nonreactive saucepan and cook over medium-low heat until the pepper pieces have released their juices and are translucent and the cooking liquid is thick and syrupy, about 15 minutes. (If the syrup gets too thick, add a few drops of water.) Transfer the mixture to a food processor and coarsely purée. Transfer to a large jar, cover, and refrigerate. The jam will keep for several months.

Makes 1¼ cups

SALSAS RELISHES SAMBALS AND CHUTNEYS

These may not have the sex appeal of barbecue sauces or spice rubs, but a cookout wouldn't be quite complete without the explosively flavorful condiments known variously as salsas, relishes, sambals, and chutneys.

Well, actually salsas do have sex appeal and they aren't just limited to Mexican cooking anymore. Salsas add a lively south-of-the-border flavor to grilled fare from anywhere on the planet.

And speaking of anywhere on the planet, relishes range from the cucumber salads served with saté in Southeast Asia, to the *encurtidos* (chopped pickled vegetables) dished up with Central American steaks, to the sweet and spicy pickle relishes that proudly adorn hot dogs. Our word relish seems to come from the French *relever,* to heighten or sharpen (as in a flavor). Relish gives you a blast of flavor that increases the thrill quotient of simply grilled meats and seafood.

Malaysia and Indonesia are home to another great family of barbecue condiments: sambals (sometimes called *sambars*). Sambal is a catch-all term broad enough to include fiery chili pastes, mild sweet peanut sauces, fragrant relishes of lemongrass and coconut milk, and even seafood dishes. Sambals are an integral part of the barbecue scene in Southeast Asia. Tiny bowls or dollops of these seasonings accompany satés in Indonesia, Malaysia, and Singapore.

Chutneys are jamlike concoctions of fruits, spices, vinegar, and sugar. As the name suggests (*chatni* is a Hindi word), chutneys come from India. Actually, the spicy fruit mixtures that most Westerners think of as chutney are an English invention (or at least an English adaptation of an Indian dish). Like sambals, chutneys are made with everything from coconut to cilantro to onion. In fact, the latter are two of the most popular chutneys, served with kebabs and tandoori. Thick or thin, mild or spicy, savory or sweet, chutneys make a great accompaniment to barbecue. I always keep several jars on hand in my refrigerator.

SALSAS AND RELISHES

BASIC MEXICAN SALSA

This fresh, lively salsa is Mexican cuisine at its best. Make it with the sort of produce a Mexican would use—shockingly red, ripe tomatoes that have never seen the inside of a refrigerator, crisp sweet white onion, fresh cilantro, and fresh lime juice—and you'll understand why it turns up at every self-respecting Mexican cookout. So popular is this salsa, it goes by several names besides *salsa fresca,* including *salsa mexicana* and *pico de gallo.*

3 medium ripe tomatoes, seeded (see box, page 246)
½ medium onion
2 to 4 serrano or jalapeño chilies, seeded and minced (for a spicier salsa leave the seeds in)

1 clove garlic, minced
¼ cup finely chopped fresh cilantro
3 tablespoons fresh lime juice, or more to taste
½ teaspoon coarse salt (kosher or sea), or more to taste

Cut the tomatoes and onion into the finest dice you have patience for. Transfer the tomatoes and onion to a bowl. Add the chilies, garlic, cilantro, lime juice, and salt to the tomato mixture and gently stir to mix. Correct the seasoning, adding salt or lime juice; the salsa should be highly seasoned. The virtue of this salsa lies in its freshness. Serve it within 1 to 2 hours of making.

Makes 2¾ cups; enough to serve 6 to 8

SALSA
LESSONS

I hate to date myself, but when I was growing up, no one knew from salsa. Once the province of humble Tex-Mex eateries, salsa has become a mainstay of contemporary American cuisine. (Mainstay? In 1991, salsa sales actually outstripped those of ketchup.) Originally made with tomatoes, salsa now comes in a myriad of exotic flavors, from mango to papaya.

Salsa is a quick, fresh table sauce that originated in Mexico. You really only need five ingredients to make salsa—tomatoes, onions, chilies, lime juice, and cilantro, but there are hundreds of different types in Mexico, varying from cook to cook and region to region. Traditionally, these ingredients were blended in a rough stone mortar called a *molacajete* with a pestle.

Some salsas are simple, spur-of-the-moment affairs that can be assembled in the time it takes to chop tomatoes, onions, and jalapeños. Such is *pico de gallo* (literally, rooster's beak salsa), the traditional accompaniment to fajitas (see page 32). Others involve roasting the vegetables in a cast-iron griddle called a comal to concentrate their flavor (try the Smoky Two-Chili Salsa on page 256). Others include vegetables that have been charred on the grill (see Flame-Charred Salsa Verde, below).

Often, tomatillos (a green tomato-like fruit in the gooseberry family) will

FLAME-CHARRED SALSA VERDE

This tart green salsa—a mainstay of Mexican cooking—owes its piquancy to one of the most distinctive ingredients in the Mexican larder: the tomatillo, a hard, round, tart, green fruit that tastes and looks like a green tomato with a papery husk. Really it's a fruit, and there's something fruity about its acidity. Salsa verde contains virtually the same ingredients in roughly the same proportions

stand in for the tomatoes and fried or toasted dried chilies for the fresh. Central Mexico's *Salsa Borracha* (drunken salsa), the traditional accompaniment to barbecued goat, contains a vivifying shot of tequila. Other salsas skip the tomatoes and onions, concentrating solely on the flavor of the chilies.

Whatever the ingredients, a good salsa will offer an orchestral range of flavors: the fruitiness of the tomatoes or tomatillos, the acidity of fresh lime or vinegar, the heat of the chilies, and the nose-tweaking pungency of the cilantro. A good salsa will also give you a gamut of tactile sensations, from the cool, moist kiss of a fresh tomato to the crunch of fresh onion or jicama.

Salsas make a great accompaniment to grilled seafood, a fact appreciated by anyone who's enjoyed grilled fish on Mexico's coast. *Carne asado* and other Mexican grilled meats would seem downright naked without it. Salsas are quick to make—a boon to time-harried cooks in the summer. And health-conscious grillers love them, because most salsas contain no fat.

Given these virtues, it's not surprising that North American chefs should have become hooked on salsa. Recently I've eaten contemporary American salsas made with apples, pears, bananas, pineapples, and exotic vegetables. I've even had main-course salsas made with black beans, conch, and lobster.

So the next time you're looking for a quick, colorful, explosively flavorful accompaniment to your favorite food on the grill, you only have to think salsa.

wherever you go in Mexico, but how you cook them gives you radically different salsas. For the mildest salsa verde, you would boil the tomatillos and vegetables. For a richer flavor, roast them on a comal or griddle. For even more flavor, fry the resulting purée in lard. But the most dynamic flavor of all is obtained by a nontraditional method: charring the tomatillos and vegetables on the grill. Grilling adds a smoky dimension you won't soon forget.

Lard may be an unfashionable ingredient these days, and you can certainly substitute olive or canola oil, but

TRY THIS!

Most restaurants, whether homey *fondas* (snack bars) or fancy dining establishments, include salsa verde in the assortment of salsas placed on each table. It's meant to be consumed with all kinds of grilled fare, hooved, finned, or feathered. Nonetheless, I've always felt that salsa verde goes especially well with seafood and light meats, such as poultry and pork.

lard is what a Mexican would use, and the salsa won't taste authentic without it. Fresh tomatillos used to be hard to find in the United States; now they're available at most supermarkets.

1 pound fresh tomatillos, husked

½ medium onion, cut in half

3 cloves garlic, peeled

4 serrano or 2 jalapeño chilies, stemmed

¼ cup chopped fresh cilantro

¼ cup chopped fresh flat-leaf parsley

½ teaspoon sugar, or more to taste

½ teaspoon coarse salt (kosher or sea), or more to taste

1½ tablespoons lard or olive oil

1 cup chicken broth or water

1. Preheat the grill to high and set a vegetable grate on top. If you don't have a vegetable grate, thread the tomatillos, onion, garlic, and chilies on skewers.

2. Place the tomatillos on the grate and grill until soft and lightly browned, 4 to 6 minutes, turning with tongs. Remove to a cutting board. Grill the onion, garlic, and chilies. The garlic and chilies will take 4 to 6 minutes, the onions 10 to 12 minutes. Transfer to a cutting board and let cool. For a milder salsa, cut the chilies in half and scrape out the seeds. For a hotter salsa, leave them in.

3. Place the grilled vegetables, cilantro, parsley, sugar, and salt in a food processor or blender and process to a coarse paste.

4. Heat the lard in a deep saucepan over medium-high heat. Add the vegetable mixture and fry until thick, aromatic, and slightly darkened, 3 to 5 minutes. Stir the mixture with a long-handled wooden spoon as it fries and watch out for spatters. Stir in the broth and simmer the salsa until thick but pourable and richly flavored, 6 to 8 minutes. If too thick, add more stock. Correct the seasoning, adding salt or sugar. Serve at room temperature. Transfer leftover salsa to a jar, cover, and refrigerate. It will keep for up to 1 week, but may thicken. Let the salsa come to room temperature before serving and thin with a little water if needed.

Makes 3 cups; enough to serve 6 to 8

HOW TO PEEL, PIT, AND DICE AN AVOCADO

There are at least two ways to peel, seed, and dice an avocado. Use the first when you want large pieces of avocado. Use the second when you need smaller dice. Whichever method you use, squeeze fresh lime juice over the cut avocado to keep it from browning.

To cut large pieces: Using the tip of your knife, make four shallow lengthwise slits evenly spaced around the avocado from end to end. Pinching one corner of one section of the peel between the knife blade and your thumb, gently pull it away from the avocado—almost like peeling a banana. Repeat to remove all four sections of the skin. Cut the flesh off the pit in lengthwise strips.

To cut small pieces: Cut the avocado in half lengthwise with a single cut to the seed, rotating the avocado 360° while cutting. Twist the halves in opposite directions: The pit will pop out of one half. Sink the blade into the pit with a flick of the knife. Gently rotate the knife: The pit will pop out completely. Carefully remove the pit from the tip of your knife. Using the tip of the knife, make a series of cuts through the avocado flesh to, but not through, the skin. The cuts should be parallel and spaced ½ inch apart. Make another series of cuts at a 90-degree angle to the first. Use a spoon to scrape the avocado out of the skin: The flesh will come out in neat dice.

AVOCADO SALSA

It's a short jump from everyday guacamole to this unusual avocado salsa, but the leap is definitely worth taking. This creamy salsa—piqued with jalapeño peppers and pungent with cilantro—makes a stimulating accompaniment to grilled seafood, poultry, or pork. It's delectable on *tacos al pastor* (grilled pork and pineapple tacos), which is how I first tasted it at the famous taqueria El Lago de los Cisnos (Swan Lake) in Mexico City. Avocado salsa is easy to make, but unless you start with ripe, squeezably soft Hass avocados, you won't get the right effect.

Tomatillos look like green tomatoes with a papery cap or husk. Look for them in the produce section of the supermarket. If you don't have time to grill the tomatillos, boil them.

5 medium tomatillos, husked
2 to 4 jalapeño chilies,
    seeded and minced (for a
    hotter salsa leave the
    seeds in)
½ cup chopped fresh cilantro
¼ cup minced onion
1 clove garlic, minced
1 tablespoon fresh lime
    juice, or more to taste

½ teaspoon sugar
½ teaspoon coarse salt
    (kosher or sea), or more
    to taste
½ teaspoon freshly ground
    black pepper
1 ripe Hass avocado, peeled,
    seeded, and diced

TRY THIS!

I first tasted this salsa with grilled pork, but I kept thinking how delicious it would be with grilled seafood. And it is!

1. Preheat the grill to high.

2. Place the tomatillos on the grate and grill, until lightly browned on all sides and soft, 6 to 8 minutes. Transfer to a plate and let cool. Or bring 2 cups water to a boil in a saucepan. Add the tomatillos and simmer, covered, until soft, about 4 minutes. Stir occasionally to ensure even cooking. Drain the tomatillos, reserving the cooking liquid.

3. Transfer the tomatillos to a food processor and process to a coarse purée. Add the chilies, cilantro, onion, garlic, lime juice, sugar, salt, and pepper and process just to mix. The mixture should be soupy; if too thick, add a few tablespoons of water or tomatillo cooking liquid. Add the avocado and process just to mix. Don't overprocess; the avocado should remain in small pieces. Correct the seasoning, adding salt or lime juice; the salsa should be highly seasoned. Serve within 1 to 2 hours of making.

Makes 2 cups; enough to serve 4 to 6

SMOKY TWO-CHILI SALSA

To most Americans, salsa means tomatoes, but many salsas in Mexico are made mainly from puréed dried chilies. The lack of tomatoes gives the salsa a thicker, more paintlike consistency. It's a very ancient taste, almost as ancient as Mexico itself. The chili changes as you move through Mexico—fiery de árbol in the north, mild guajillo

TRY THIS!

Serve the salsa with Mexican-style grilled meats, including steaks, pork, chicken, *carne asado*, fajitas, and *taquitos*. It's also great with flame-charred chilies and grilled *chiles rellenos*.

in central and southern Mexico—but the procedure remains the same. This version calls for two chilies, guajillo for its mild earthy flavor and chipotles (smoked jalapeños) for their heat. When possible, use canned chipotles, so you can add a spoonful of the flavorful juices.

8 guajillo chilies or dried New Mexican red chilies (2½ to 3 ounces), stemmed

2 cups hot water

½ medium onion, cut in half

3 cloves garlic, peeled

1 to 2 canned chipotle chilies

1 to 2 teaspoons chipotle can juices

¼ cup chopped fresh cilantro

1 teaspoon fresh lime juice, or more to taste

½ teaspoon coarse salt (kosher or sea), or more to taste

1. Place the guajillos in a bowl, add the hot water, and soak until soft and pliable, 30 minutes. Drain the chilies, reserving the soaking liquid, tear them open, and discard all of the seeds.

2. Heat a comal or cast-iron skillet over medium heat. Add the onion and garlic and roast, turning with tongs, until the vegetables are darkly browned. The garlic will take 4 to 6 minutes, the onion 10 to 12 minutes.

3. Combine the guajillos, 1 cup of the soaking liquid, the onion, garlic, chipotles, chipotle juice, cilantro, lime juice, and salt in a blender and purée until smooth. Add soaking liquid as needed to obtain a thick but pourable salsa; it should be the consistency of heavy cream. Correct the seasoning, adding lime juice or salt to taste. Use right away or transfer to a large jar, cover, placing a sheet of plastic wrap under the lid, and refrigerate. The salsa will keep for several weeks.

Makes 2 cups; enough to serve 6 to 8

SALSA BORRACHA (Drunken Salsa)

This is one of Mexico's most unusual salsas. Bitter and piquant, it's not the sort you'd serve with chips, but *barbacoa* (pit-roasted lamb or goat) just wouldn't taste right without it. The salsa owes its handsome mahogany color, smoky flavor, and gentle heat to the pasilla chili, a wrinkled dried pepper. (Look for it in Mexican markets or gourmet shops, or see mail-order sources on page 281.) The traditional liquid in the salsa is a cactus wine called *pulque*. Pulque is hard to find in the United States, but a highly satisfactory *salsa borracha* can be made with beer and tequila.

TRY THIS!

This salsa is traditionally served with pit-roasted lamb or goat. I like it with just about any sort of Mexican-style grilled meat or poultry.

¼ **cup vegetable oil**	1 **teaspoon honey**
8 **pasilla chilies**	1 **teaspoon coarse salt**
1 **large onion, finely chopped**	**(kosher or sea), or more**
(2 cups)	**to taste**
⅔ **cup beer**	½ **teaspoon freshly ground**
½ **cup distilled white vinegar**	**black pepper**
½ **cup cold water**	½ **cup grated salty cheese,**
2 **tablespoons tequila**	**like Mexican queso**
¼ **cup chopped fresh cilantro**	**fresco or feta**

1. Heat the oil in a skillet over medium heat to 350°F on a deep-fry thermometer. Add the chilies a few at a time and fry until puffed and crisp, 10 to 20 seconds per side. Do not let the chilies burn. Transfer the chilies to a paper towel–lined plate and let cool. Stem the chilies and break into 1-inch pieces.

2. Add the onion to the pan and fry until golden brown, 4 to 6 minutes. Let cool slightly, then transfer the onion to a blender or food processor. Add the chilies, beer, vinegar, water, tequila, cilantro, honey, salt, and pepper and blend to a coarse purée. Correct the seasoning, adding salt. Transfer to a jar, cover, and refrigerate. The salsa will keep for several days. Just before serving, transfer the salsa to bowls and sprinkle with grated cheese.

Makes 2 cups; enough to serve 8 to 10

SPICY CORN RELISH

I've always associated fresh corn with barbecue. Grilling, for example, is my favorite way to cook fresh corn on the cob. (Nothing accentuates the sweetness of fresh corn like the smoky char of the fire.) I love corn chutneys and relishes, which I often serve with simply grilled poultry or seafood. This relish offers a Southeast Asian touch in the form of cilantro, chopped peanuts, and Thai hot sauce. If fresh corn is unavailable or you're in a hurry, you could use canned or frozen kernels.

TRY THIS!

Corn relish is traditionally associated with North American barbecue—and this one would be at home at a cookout anywhere in the U.S. The ginger and peppers give it a Caribbean accent, while the peanuts, cilantro, and chili sauce suggest Southeast Asia. Which is to say that this tangy relish goes well—hot or cold—with almost any sort of grilled seafood, poultry, or meat.

2 ears of fresh corn
(1½ cups kernels)
2 tablespoons olive oil
2 shallots, finely chopped
1 clove garlic, minced
2 teaspoons minced or
grated fresh ginger
1 to 2 jalapeño chilies,
seeded and finely
chopped (for a spicier
relish leave the seeds in)
½ red bell pepper, stemmed,
seeded, and cut into
¼-inch dice
½ green bell pepper,
stemmed, seeded, and
cut into ¼-inch dice
1 ripe tomato, peeled,
seeded, and diced
(see box, page 246)

2 tablespoons dark brown
sugar, or more to taste
2 tablespoons rice vinegar or
cider vinegar, or more to
taste
1 to 3 teaspoons Thai chili
sauce
½ teaspoon coarse salt
(kosher or sea), or more
to taste
½ teaspoon freshly ground
black pepper
3 tablespoons coarsely
chopped dry-roasted
peanuts
3 tablespoons chopped fresh
cilantro

1. Husk the corn and cut off the kernels. The easiest way to do this is to lay the ears flat on the cutting board and slice off the kernels with broad lengthwise strokes of a chef's knife.

2. Heat the oil in a skillet, preferably nonstick, over medium heat. Add the shallots, garlic, ginger, and chilies and cook over medium heat until soft but not brown, 3 min-

utes. Increase the heat to high and add the corn, red and green bell peppers, and tomato. Cook until the vegetables render their juices and most of those juices evaporate, 3 to 5 minutes.

3. Add the brown sugar, vinegar, chili sauce, salt, and pepper and cook until the vegetables are tender and the relish is richly flavored, 5 minutes. Stir in the peanuts and cilantro and cook for 1 minute. Correct the seasoning, adding salt, sugar, or vinegar; the relish should be highly seasoned. The relish can be served hot or at room temperature. Transfer to jars, cover, cool to room temperature, and refrigerate. The relish will keep for 5 days.

Makes 2¼ cups; enough to serve 6 to 8

CHILI PASTE AND CHILI SAUCE

These fiery sauces and pastes are found in every corner of Asia. The basic ingredients, chilies, garlic, and salt, are often placed in giant jars to pickle. The flavor of each chili paste and sauce is quite different, so you should try to use the one called for in a particular recipe. But in the end, it's better to substitute one Asian chili paste or sauce for another than do without it entirely.

Here are some of the regional variations:

■ Chinese hot bean paste offers the added richness of fermented soybeans to the basic ingredients.

■ Thai chili pastes often contain fresh basil. There's also a sweet, red, mildly hot chili sauce for table use called Sriracha. Thais use it like ketchup.

■ Indonesian *sambal ulek* (sometimes spelled *oelek*) is the ultimate chili paste, a bright red fiery purée of chilies, garlic, and salt.

■ Vietnamese chili paste is an incendiary mixture of red chilies, vinegar and salt sold in clear plastic jars.

THAI CUCUMBER RELISH

This colorful side dish—part salad, part relish—is the traditional accompaniment to Thai satés. The cool wet crunch of cucumber makes a perfect foil for these tiny spicy kebabs. Like many great barbecue accompaniments, cucumber relish requires only 10 minutes of preparation time, but it tastes like a million bucks. For the best results, choose smallish cucumbers with a minimum of seeds.

TRY THIS!

Serve cucumber relish with Thai, or Malaysian, or Indonesian style satés.

FOR THE DRESSING
⅓ cup distilled white vinegar
⅓ cup sugar
⅓ cup cold water
Generous ½ teaspoon coarse
    salt (kosher or sea)
1 clove garlic, lightly
    flattened with the side of
    a cleaver

TO FINISH THE RELISH
1 large or 2 small cucumbers
1 shallot, thinly sliced
1 hot red chili pepper,
    seeded and minced
2 tablespoons chopped fresh
    cilantro
2 tablespoons chopped dry-
    roasted peanuts

1. Prepare the dressing. Combine the vinegar, sugar, water, salt, and garlic in a saucepan over high heat and bring to a boil. Reduce the heat and simmer until the sugar and salt are completely dissolved, 3 minutes. Transfer the mixture to a bowl and let cool to room temperature. Discard the garlic.

2. Peel the cucumber with a vegetable peeler, removing the skin in lengthwise strips about ⅛ inch apart. This will give you pretty green stripes when you slice the cucumber. Cut the cucumber lengthwise in quarters, then crosswise into ¼-inch slices. Add the cucumber to the cooled dressing. Add the shallots, chili, and cilantro and toss to mix. Just before serving, sprinkle the relish with peanuts. You can serve the relish right away, but it will taste better if you let it stand for 1 hour. Serve it the same day you make it.

Makes 2 cups; enough to serve 4

HOW TO SEED CUCUMBERS

In many parts of the world, barbecue is served with diced cucumbers, cucumber salads, or cucumber relishes. With good reason! The cool, moist crunch of fresh cucumber is great for extinguishing the chili fires associated with much of the world's grilling. Recipes usually call for the cucumbers to be peeled and from time to time seeded. Here's how to do it.

Scrub the skin of the cucumber well. Peel it by removing the skin in lengthwise strips. Leave a little space between each strip—this will give you thin, dark green stripes running the length of the cucumber. When you cut the cucumber crosswise, you'll get decorative stripes on the slices.

And now on to seeding. Cut the cucumber in half lengthwise. Use a melon baller or spoon to scrape out the seeds. For half moon–shaped slices, slice each cucumber half crosswise. For cucumber chunks, slice each half in half again lengthwise and then crosswise.

MELON-MINT RELISH

You can work up a pretty good sweat at a barbecue—first, tending the grill under a blazing sun, then licking a hellfire hot sauce off your fingers. The following relish is designed to keep you cool under fire. It's made with that most refreshing of all fruits, melon, or, even better, with an assortment of melons, such as watermelon, cantaloupe, and honeydew. Vary the melon according to what's in season and what looks best at the market.

You can cut the melons into as large or as small dice as you want or have patience to. You can even form balls with a melon baller. I generally go for a ½-inch dice, which is large enough to let you appreciate the taste of the individual melons, but small enough to blend into a tasty relish.

¼ cup fresh lime juice

2 tablespoons light brown sugar

4 cups diced mixed ripe melons

1 cucumber, peeled, seeded, and cut into ½-inch dice (see box, facing page)

⅓ cup finely diced red onion

2 to 4 jalapeño chilies, seeded and finely chopped (for a spicier relish leave the seeds in)

2 tablespoons finely chopped candied ginger

¼ cup chopped fresh mint

Combine the lime juice and sugar in a bowl and stir or whisk until the sugar is dissolved. Add the remaining ingredients and gently toss to mix. Serve within a few hours of making.

Makes 4 cups; enough to serve 4 to 6

MEDITERRANEAN RELISH

You've probably enjoyed this colorful relish on crostini. But you may not have considered that it also makes a wonderful topping for grilled seafood, chicken, or veal chops. In the interest of speed, I call for bottled pimiento, but if you have a roasted bell pepper left over from an earlier cookout, the relish will be even better.

1 ripe red tomato, peeled, seeded, and diced (see box, page 246)

1 ripe yellow tomato (or use another red tomato), peeled, seeded, and diced

1 small jar (2 ounces) pimientos, diced

8 fresh basil leaves, thinly slivered

3 tablespoons finely chopped fresh flat-leaf parsley

3 tablespoons pitted black olives, preferably

Kalamata

3 tablespoons toasted pine nuts (optional, see box, page 105)

2 tablespoons drained capers

3 tablespoons extra virgin olive oil

1 tablespoon balsamic vinegar, or more to taste

¼ to ½ teaspoon hot pepper flakes (optional)

Coarse salt (kosher or sea) and freshly ground black pepper, to taste

Combine all the ingredients in a bowl and gently toss to mix. Correct the seasoning, adding salt or vinegar; the relish should be highly seasoned. You won't need much salt, as the olives and capers are quite salty. Serve within 1 hour of making; the virtue of this relish lies in its freshness. You can have the vegetables diced ahead of time, but mix at the last minute.

Makes 2 cups; enough to serve 4 to 6

HELLAS RELISH

TRY THIS!

Every which way you can. Spread it on grilled bread to make incredibly flavorful crostini or bruschetta. Spoon it over grilled fish or chicken. Pair it with grilled pork, veal, and chicken.

Greeks love barbecue—especially grilled lamb and seafood. They keep the accompaniments pretty simple. Cucumber, red onion, and tomatoes are the primary ingredients in a simple relish that invariably accompanies grilled meats and seafood in Greece, particularly souvlaki (lamb shish kebab) and spit-roasted lamb. There are two ways to serve the relish—plain or dressed with olive oil and vinegar.

1 cucumber, peeled, seeded, and cut into ¼-inch dice (see box, page 262)

1 large or 2 medium ripe tomatoes, peeled, seeded, and cut into ¼-inch dice (see box, page 246)

½ medium red onion, cut into ¼-inch dice

½ cup chopped fresh flat-leaf parsley

3 tablespoons extra virgin olive oil, preferably Greek

2 tablespoons fresh lemon juice, or more to taste

1 tablespoon red wine vinegar

½ teaspoon dried oregano

½ teaspoon coarse salt (kosher or sea), or more to taste

½ teaspoon cracked black pepper, or to taste

Combine the cucumber, tomatoes, onion, and parsley in a serving bowl. Add the oil, lemon juice, vinegar, oregano, salt, and pepper. Toss to mix. Correct the seasoning, adding salt or lemon juice. The virtue of this relish is its freshness. Don't make it more than 1 or 2 hours before you plan to serve it.

Makes 3 cups; enough to serve 4 to 6

HELLISH RELISH

I f you like heat, you'll love this relish, which is powered by the world's hottest chili: the habanero. Just how hellish a relish is it? Well, the heat of a chili is measured in units called Scovilles. A jalapeño chili rings in at 5,000 Scovilles. A habanero at 200,000 to 300,000! (You can also use the habanero's hot-headed cousin, the Scotch bonnet chili.) We put the heat to good use in this relish, a tangy hash of grilled peppers, onions, and garlic. Serve it to bold palates (it's not for the faint-hearted) and be sure there's plenty of yogurt or beer to extinguish the fires.

1 medium onion, quartered
3 cloves garlic, peeled
½ to 3 habanero chilies
1 green bell pepper or poblano chili
1 red bell pepper
1 yellow bell pepper
3 tablespoons finely chopped fresh cilantro
2 tablespoons extra virgin olive oil

2 tablespoons distilled white vinegar, or more to taste
2 tablespoons fresh orange juice
1 tablespoon fresh lime or lemon juice
2 teaspoons sugar
Coarse salt (kosher or sea) and freshly ground black pepper, to taste

1. Preheat the grill to high. Thread the onion quarters, garlic cloves, and habanero chilies onto separate skewers.

TRY THIS!

Serve this relish with any grilled fare you want to blast with flavor—chicken, pork, lamb, even seafood. Spoon it on top of grilled bread to make a fire-eater bruschetta. But watch out—it burns!

Grill the vegetables until charred on all sides. This will take 2 to 3 minutes per side for the garlic and habaneros, 4 minutes per side for the onions, and 4 to 6 minutes per side for the bell peppers. Transfer the vegetable skewers to a plate and let cool. When cool, remove the vegetables from the skewers.

2. Scrape the burnt skins off the vegetables. (Don't worry about removing every last bit; a few specks of black add character.) Finely chop the onions and garlic. For a milder relish, seed the habaneros and finely chop; for a truly hellish relish, chop the habaneros, seeds and all. Stem and seed the peppers and cut into thin strips or ½-inch dice.

3. Place the vegetables in a nonreactive saucepan with the remaining ingredients. Bring to a boil over high heat, reduce the heat to medium, and simmer the relish until thick and richly flavored, about 5 minutes. Most of the juices should be absorbed by the vegetables. Correct the seasoning, adding salt or vinegar to taste. Transfer the relish to clean jars, cover, cool to room temperature, and refrigerate. The relish will keep for several weeks.

Makes 2 cups; enough to serve 8 to 10

VARIATION

Tuscan Relish: Omit the habaneros. Substitute flat-leaf parsley for the cilantro and balsamic vinegar for the distilled. Add 1 tablespoon drained capers and 2 tablespoons chopped black olives.

CHILEAN ONION RELISH

Whenever I'm in New York and hungry for a simple, satisfying, affordable meal, I head for a cozy Chilean restaurant in the theater district called Pommaire. I suppose I could have something grilled there, but I always seem to order a corn casserole chock-full of chicken, beef, raisins, and olives, called *pastel de choclo*. Whatever you order at Pommaire, you'll get a tiny bowl of an onion relish that goes by the name of *pebre*. (It's different from the pebre sauce on page 188.) It seems to contain only two main ingredients—onion and tomato—but it's so extraordinarily flavorful, I wind up eating it straight out of the bowl with the serving spoon. You will too, so be sure to make some extra, so that you have some left to serve with steak.

TRY THIS!

This relish was expressly made for grilled beef, but I wouldn't overlook it as an accompaniment to grilled chicken, seafood, or vegetables. To make Chilean-style bruschetta, spoon it over grilled bread slices.

1 medium onion, cut into very fine dice
Ice water, for soaking the onions
¼ cup red wine vinegar or distilled vinegar, or more to taste
1 teaspoon coarse salt (kosher or sea), or more to taste
1 large ripe tomato (it doesn't need to be too ripe), seeded, and very finely diced (see box, page 246)
½ teaspoon freshly ground black pepper
¼ to ½ teaspoon cayenne pepper, or more to taste
2 tablespoons vegetable oil
¼ cup chopped fresh cilantro or flat-leaf parsley

1. Place the onion in a bowl with ice water to cover. Let stand for 30 minutes, then drain well in a colander and blot dry with a paper towel.

2. Combine the vinegar and salt in a bowl and stir or whisk until the salt crystals are dissolved. Add the onion, tomato, pepper, cayenne, oil, and cilantro and gently toss to mix. Correct the seasoning, adding salt, vinegar, or cayenne; the relish should be highly seasoned. The relish is good now; it will be amazing if you let it stand to ripen for a few hours before serving. Serve the relish the same day you make it.

Makes 2 cups; enough to serve 4 to 6

KENYAN TOMATO RELISH

TRY THIS!

Serve with simply grilled beef, lamb, or goat. Have plenty of beer on hand to put out the fires.

Her name was Angela and she grew up in Nairobi, Kenya. She followed a man to America (long since gone) and now drives a cab in Atlanta. And that is where I met her. As is my wont, I asked about the barbecue of her homeland. (I ask *every* cabdriver about the barbecue of his or her homeland.) According to Angela, Kenyans grill very simply—just meat and salt and fire. The creativity comes with the condiments. The most popular is a fresh tomato relish that will make your mouth pucker with lemon and make your brow sweat from the Kenyan version of a Scotch bonnet chili.

For the full effect, you must use juicy, ripe, red tomatoes.

2 ripe tomatoes
½ medium red onion, finely
    chopped
½ to 2 Scotch bonnet or
    habanero chilies, seeded
    and minced (for a hotter
    relish leave the seeds in)
3 tablespoons chopped fresh
    flat-leaf parsley

3 tablespoons fresh lemon
    juice, or more to taste
½ teaspoon coarse salt
    (kosher or sea), or more
    to taste
½ teaspoon freshly ground
    black pepper

Cut the tomatoes into ¼-inch dice, working on a grooved cutting board to catch the juices. Transfer the tomatoes and juices to a serving bowl and stir in the remaining ingredients. Correct the seasoning, adding salt or lemon juice; the relish should be tart and highly seasoned. Serve within a few hours of making.

Makes 2 cups; enough to serve 4 to 6

SAMBALS AND CHUTNEYS

SHALLOT SAMBAL

Sambal embraces a large family of relishes, sauces, and chili pastes that accompany saté and other grilled fare in Indonesia, Malaysia, and Singapore. A simple sambal might consist of nothing more than roasted shrimp paste and chilies. A more elaborate version could contain any of a dozen fruits or vegetables or even fried fish, squid, or shrimp.

Here's a simple shallot sambal I enjoyed at a restaurant in Jakarta.

TRY THIS!

Serve this shallot sambal at room temperature as you would Grilled Tomato Sambal on page 270. The briny tang of the shrimp paste makes it especially good for grilled seafood and shrimp.

4 teaspoons canola oil
1 teaspoon shrimp paste, or
    1 anchovy fillet, chopped
1 cup thinly sliced shallots
    (about 6)
4 to 8 hot chili peppers, such
    as Thai chilies or
    jalapeños, seeded and
    minced (for a hotter
    sambal leave in the
    seeds)

2 cloves garlic, minced
3 tablespoons fresh lime
    juice
Coarse salt (kosher or sea)
    and freshly ground black
    pepper to taste

Heat the oil in a nonreactive wok or small skillet over medium heat. Add the shrimp paste and fry until fragrant, 30 seconds to 1 minute. Add the shallots, chilies, and garlic and fry until golden brown, 6 to 8 minutes, reducing the heat if necessary to prevent the shallots from burning. Transfer the mixture to a blender or food processor and finely chop. Add the lime juice and salt and pepper. Transfer to a jar, cover, and refrigerate. The sambal will keep almost forever.

Makes 1 cup; enough to serve 4

VARIATION

For a bolder, more in-your-face sambal, cook half the chilies, leaving the other half raw. Add these raw chilies when you chop the sambal. Hold on to your tongue, for this one hurts!

GRILLED TOMATO SAMBAL

Grilling tomatoes and chilies adds a smoky dimension to this sambal, a condiment I discovered in Bali. Horn chilies, which are shaped like a ram's or a steer's horn, are available at most supermarkets and they're easier to grill than smaller chilies. Seeding the peppers reduces the heat to a level acceptable to most Americans. Masochists, of course, can leave the seeds in.

TRY THIS!

Serve this sambal at room temperature with satés and other Asian-style grilled fare. It's strong enough to stand up to grilled pork or beef, but not so aggressive that you couldn't serve it with a grilled chicken breast or fish fillet.

4 plum tomatoes
2 to 4 horn peppers
3 tablespoons vegetable oil
2 cloves garlic, minced
1 large shallot, minced
1 stalk lemongrass, trimmed
   and minced, or ½
   teaspoon grated lemon
   zest
2 teaspoons minced fresh
   ginger

½ teaspoon shrimp paste or
   fish sauce
2 tablespoons distilled white
   vinegar, or more to taste
½ teaspoon sugar
Coarse salt (kosher or sea)
   and freshly ground black
   pepper to taste

1. Preheat the grill to high.

2. Place the tomatoes and chilies on the grate and grill until nicely browned on all sides, 6 to 8 minutes for the peppers, 10 to 12 minutes for the tomatoes. Transfer the vegetables to a plate to cool.

3. Scrape any really burned skin off the vegetables, leaving a little on for color and flavor. Stem and seed the pep-

pers. Coarsely purée the vegetables in a food processor.

4. Heat the oil in a nonreactive wok or small skillet over medium heat. Add the garlic, shallot, lemongrass, ginger, and shrimp paste and fry until golden brown, 4 minutes. (If using fish sauce, add it with the vinegar.) Stir in the tomato-chili mixture and fry until thick and flavorful, 4 minutes. Add the vinegar, sugar, and fish sauce, if using, and bring to a boil. Correct the seasoning, adding salt, pepper, or vinegar. Cool to room temperature. Transfer the sambal to bowls if serving immediately or to a large jar, cover, and refrigerate. Bring to room temperature before serving. The sambal will keep for several months.

Makes a scant 2 cups; enough to serve 6 to 8

GINGER-PEAR CHUTNEY

This recipe takes me back to some of my earliest days as a foodie. The year was 1978, and I'd just signed on as the U.S. Program Coordinator for the La Varenne cooking school in Paris. My job was to accompany and translate for French chefs on tour in the United States. As we criss-crossed the country, bringing the gospel of haute cuisine to the hinterlands, we often met remarkable cooks who wowed the French masters with down-home American cooking. One such cook was a Floridian named Frances Cauthen, who served barbecued quail, which her husband had hunted. Accompanying the quail was an unforgettable ginger-pear chutney. Thanks to the chili powder and chopped lemon, this is one chutney you won't find too sweet.

3 pounds ripe pears
1 lemon, scrubbed, cut in half, and seeded
1½ cups (packed) dark brown sugar, or more to taste
1½ cups cider vinegar, or more to taste
6 ounces dark raisins
3 tablespoons thinly slivered candied ginger
⅓ cup toasted walnut pieces (see box, page 105)

2 cloves garlic, minced
1½ tablespoons pure chili powder (not a blend)
1 to 2 teaspoons hot pepper flakes
1 teaspoon coarse salt (kosher or sea), or more to taste
½ teaspoon ground cinnamon
¼ teaspoon ground allspice
¼ teaspoon ground cloves
¼ teaspoon freshly grated nutmeg

TRY THIS!

Serve this chutney with grilled or barbecued poultry, especially game birds, like quail, pheasant, or partridge. It also goes exceedingly well with smoked turkey or rotisseried duck. It's also good with grilled ham steaks and barbecued or grilled pork.

1. Peel, halve, and core the pears, rubbing each piece with cut lemon to prevent browning. Cut the pears into ½-inch dice; you should have about 4 cups. Cut the lemon, rind and all, into ¼-inch dice.

2. Combine the brown sugar and vinegar in a large, heavy nonreactive saucepan and bring to a boil over medium heat. Add the pears, lemon, and remaining ingredients and bring to a boil. Reduce the heat to medium-low, partially cover the pan, and gently simmer, stirring from time to time, for 20 minutes. Uncover the pan and continue simmering until the chutney is thick and flavorful, 10 minutes more.

3. Correct the seasoning, adding vinegar, sugar, or salt; the chutney should be highly seasoned. Transfer to jars, cover, cool to room temperature, and refrigerate. The chutney will keep for several weeks.

Makes about 3 cups; enough to serve 6 to 8

PEACH-PECAN CHUTNEY

Chutneys originated in India, where they're a traditional accompaniment to curry. American chefs have adopted them with gusto and serve them with grilled fare of all ethnic persuasions. This chutney plays the summery sweetness of fresh peach against the gentle piquancy of rice vinegar, with a generous dose of jalapeño chili for heat. Dried cranberries add color and tartness, pecans, a touch of crunch. (For a really sensational chutney, use spiced or smoked pecans.) Make this chutney when ripe peaches are in season and you'll want to eat it right out of the bottle.

TRY THIS!

Peach chutney goes great with such Southern fare as grilled chicken, turkey, and pork.

4 pounds ripe peaches
1 cinnamon stick (3 inches)
4 allspice berries
4 whole cloves
10 black peppercorns
½ small red onion, finely chopped (½ cup)
½ red bell pepper, stemmed, seeded, and cut into ½-inch dice
½ yellow bell pepper, stemmed, seeded, and cut into ½-inch dice
2 to 4 jalapeño chilies, seeded and diced (for a spicier chutney leave the seeds in)

2 slices candied ginger, finely chopped
½ cup dried cranberries
½ cup toasted pecan pieces (see box, page 105)
¼ cup rice wine vinegar or cider vinegar, or more to taste
¼ cup (packed) dark brown sugar, or more to taste
3 tablespoons chopped fresh cilantro or mint

1. Bring a deep pot of water to a boil over high heat. Plunge the peaches into the water for 30 seconds. Transfer them to a colander, rinse under cold water, and slip off the skins. Cut the peaches into 1-inch pieces, discarding the pits.

2. Tie the cinnamon, allspice, cloves, and peppercorns in a piece of cheesecloth or wrap in aluminum foil and perforate with a fork.

3. Place the peaches, spices, and remaining ingredients in a heavy nonreactive saucepan and bring to a simmer over medium heat. Reduce the heat and simmer until the peaches are soft, 10 minutes. Correct the seasoning, adding sugar or vinegar; the chutney should be a little sweet and a little sour. Transfer to jars, cover, cool to room temperature, and refrigerate. The chutney will keep for several months.

Makes 3 cups; enough to serve 6 to 8

APPLE-FIG CHUTNEY

This is one of the more unusual chutneys you'll find at a barbecue. I've always loved the flavor of dried figs and the gritty crunch of their seeds. To round out the flavor, I add fresh apples and apple cider, with plenty of spices for drama. If you don't have cheesecloth for tying up the spices, wrap them in foil and perforate the package with a fork.

TRY THIS!

This chutney has a natural affinity for all manner of grilled poultry and pork. It's not too sweet, so you could serve it with a rich fish, like salmon.

2 cups hot apple cider, or more if needed
2 cups dried figs
1 cup dark raisins
6 whole cloves
6 allspice berries
6 blades mace or ¼ teaspoon freshly grated nutmeg
1 cinnamon stick (3 inches)
2 apples, cored and coarsely chopped
½ teaspoon grated lemon zest

1 cup (packed) dark brown sugar, or more to taste
1 cup cider vinegar, or more to taste
2 tablespoons finely chopped candied ginger
1 clove garlic, minced
1 tablespoon pure chili powder (not a blend)
¼ teaspoon cayenne pepper, or more to taste
Coarse salt (kosher or sea) and freshly ground black pepper

1. Warm the cider in a large, heavy, nonreactive saucepan over medium heat. Remove the pan from the heat, add the figs and raisins, and let soften for 15 minutes.

2. Tie the cloves, allspice, mace, and cinnamon in a square of cheesecloth or wrap in aluminum foil and perforate with a fork. Add to the figs and raisins.

3. Add the remaining ingredients. Bring to a boil over medium heat, reduce the heat to medium-low, partially cover the pan, and gently simmer, 20 minutes. Uncover the pan and continue simmering until the chutney is thick and richly

flavored, 5 minutes more. If the chutney gets too thick, add a little more cider or water.

4. Correct the seasoning, adding sugar, vinegar, or cayenne; the chutney should be highly seasoned. Transfer to jars, cover, cool to room temperature, and refrigerate. The chutney will keep for several months.

Makes 4 cups; enough to serve 8 to 10

FRESH MANGO CHUTNEY

To most people, mango chutney calls forth visions of a jamlike mixture of candied green mangos and spices. Delectable, of course, but sometimes you hunger for a pourable chutney to spoon over grilled chicken or fish like a sauce. Barbecue condiments come thick and thin in India, and this one will make you rethink your notion of this chutney.

The mangos should be very ripe. Leave them in a paper bag at room temperature until very fragrant and squeezably soft. Note that if you have sensitive skin, wear rubber gloves when peeling the mangos. The oils in the mango skin can cause a poison ivy–like rash.

2 to 4 very ripe mangos
   (enough to make 1½
   cups strained purée)
3 to 4 tablespoons cold
   water, if needed
2 tablespoons vegetable oil
2 shallots, minced
1 clove garlic, minced
1 tablespoon minced fresh
   ginger
1 jalapeño chili, seeded and
   minced

¼ cup minced fresh cilantro
2 tablespoons fresh lime
   juice, or more to taste
1 to 3 teaspoons Thai chili
   paste or chili sauce
1 tablespoon light brown
   sugar, or more to taste
Coarse salt (kosher or sea)
   and freshly ground black
   pepper, to taste

1. Peel the mangos and cut the flesh off the seeds. Transfer the mango flesh to a food processor and process to

a smooth purée. Strain through a strainer into a large measuring cup. You should have 1½ cups. (If the mango is too thick to purée and strain, add a few tablespoons water.)

2. Heat the oil in a saucepan over medium heat. Add the shallots, garlic, ginger, and chili and cook until soft but not brown, 3 minutes. Add the mango purée and simmer for 3 minutes. Add the cilantro, lime juice, chili paste, and sugar and simmer for 2 minutes. Correct the seasoning, adding salt and pepper. For a sweeter chutney, add more sugar; for a tarter chutney, more lime juice. Transfer to jars, cover, cool to room temperature, and refrigerate. The chutney will keep for several weeks.

Makes 2 cups; enough to serve 6 to 8

CORIANDER-MINT CHUTNEY

TRY THIS!

Serve with any type of tandoori or Central or South Asian–style barbecue. Lamb is the most common meat in these parts, but don't pass it up as a sauce for grilled chicken, beef, or fish.

This bright green sauce turns up wherever sizzling skewers emerge from a tandoor, an Indian barbecue pit. It's the closest thing India has to a national barbecue sauce and tandoori chicken or lamb just wouldn't taste right without it. The mint cools and refreshes your mouth, while the cilantro and garlic tingle your taste buds. On top of that, the chutney takes all of five minutes to prepare, which makes it a big winner in my book.

1 bunch of fresh mint, rinsed, stemmed, and dried (about 1 cup packed)

½ bunch of fresh cilantro, rinsed, stemmed, and dried (about ½ cup packed)

2 cloves garlic, chopped

1 to 3 jalapeño chilies, seeded and chopped

1 tablespoon chopped onion

¼ cup fresh lemon juice, or more to taste

1 tablespoon vegetable oil

Scant 1 teaspoon coarse salt (kosher or sea), or more to taste

½ teaspoon sugar

Freshly ground black pepper, to taste

3 to 4 tablespoons cold water

Combine all the ingredients in a blender and purée to a paste, scraping down the sides of the blender a few times and adding water as needed to obtain a pourable sauce. Correct the seasoning, adding salt or lemon juice; the chutney should be flavorful and piquant. This chutney will keep for several days, covered, in a jar, in the refrigerator, but I find it tastes best served within a few hours of making.

Makes 1 cup; enough to serve 4

VARIATIONS

Yogurt Mint Chutney: Add ½ cup plain yogurt and 1 tablespoon minced fresh ginger to the blender with the other ingredients.

Afghan Coriander Chutney: Afghans make a similar chutney to serve with shish kebabs and grilled fish. Prepare as for Coriander-Mint Chutney, adding ½ cup walnut pieces. You'll probably need a little more water to obtain a pourable sauce. You may need more lemon juice for tartness. Some Afghan kebabi men use vinegar instead of lemon juice.

TOMATO CHUTNEY

TRY THIS!

Although this chutney comes from India, it's versatile enough to go with Western-style grilled chicken, pork, and lamb. I like to serve it in place of cocktail sauce on a platter of grilled shrimp.

If you're tired of ketchup and you can't look at another bottle of barbecue sauce, this tomato chutney from India is just the thing for reviving a jaded palate. The tomatoes are charred on the grill, which gives them a smoky flavor and concentrates their richness. The onions are soaked in cold water to rid them of their pungency while preserving their moist, crisp crunch. Put them together and you have the perfect accompaniment not just to Indian tandoori but to any Central Asian–style grilled poultry, seafood, and lamb.

1 medium red onion
Ice water
4 small ripe tomatoes
2 teaspoons vegetable oil
2 cloves garlic, minced
2 teaspoons minced fresh
  ginger
1½ teaspoons coarse salt
  (kosher or sea), or more
  to taste

½ teaspoon sugar
2 tablespoons fresh lemon
  juice, or to taste
Freshly ground black pepper,
  to taste
3 tablespoons minced fresh
  cilantro

1. Finely dice the onion and place it in a bowl with ice water to cover. Let soak for 1 hour, changing the water 2 or 3 times. Drain the onions in a colander and gently squeeze dry with your fingers.

2. Meanwhile, preheat the grill to high. For the best results make a wood fire.

3. Rub the tomatoes with oil and grill until charred on all sides, 3 to 4 minutes per side (9 to 12 minutes in all). Transfer to a plate to cool. Scrape off the burnt skins (you don't need to remove every last bit; a few bits of black add character). Finely chop the tomatoes.

4. Place the garlic, ginger, salt, and sugar in a bowl and mash to a paste with the back of a spoon. Place this mixture in a saucepan and stir in the tomatoes and lemon juice. Cook over medium heat until thick and fragrant, about 4 minutes. Add the cilantro and cook for 1 minute more. Remove the pan from the heat and stir in the onions. Correct the seasoning, adding salt or pepper. Cool completely, then transfer to tiny individual serving bowls. Or transfer to a large jar, cover, and refrigerate. The chutney will keep for up to 2 weeks.

Makes 1½ cups; enough to serve 4 to 6

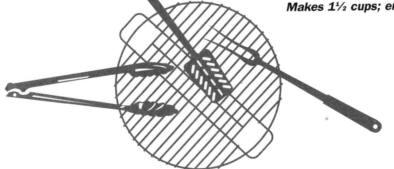

APRICOT BLATJANG

TRY THIS!

Serve *blatjang* as you would any chutney. It goes particularly well with chicken, pork, and lamb.

As a student of social history, I'm always fascinated by the cultural and geographic migrations of barbecue. Consider the chutneylike condiment served at South African barbecues, *blatjang*. The linguistic origin of the dish is obvious: *Blacan* is the Malay word for shrimp paste. Malay laborers brought it to South Africa at the turn of the century, when they came there to work in the gold and diamond mines. *Blacan* gave its name to *blatjang* and as time passed, the shrimp paste was supplanted by more European ingredients, like apricots, raisins, and onions. In the process, *blatjang* has become a sort of chutney that goes great with grilled chicken, pork, lamb, beef, and seafood. The garlic and ginger aren't sautéed in the traditional recipe, but I like the added layer of flavor that results.

2 tablespoons vegetable oil

3 shallots or 1 small onion, thinly sliced

2 cloves garlic, thinly sliced

1 tablespoon minced fresh ginger

1 to 2 jalapeños or other hot chilies, seeded and minced (for a hotter blatjang leave the seeds in)

2 cups (13 ounces) dried apricots, quartered

½ cup (4 ounces) dark raisins

5 tablespoons (packed) dark brown sugar, or more to taste

3 tablespoons chopped fresh cilantro

1½ teaspoons ground coriander

6 tablespoons cider vinegar

2 strips of lemon zest

2 tablespoons fresh lemon juice

1 cup cold water

½ cup chopped dry-roasted peanuts

Coarse salt (kosher or sea), to taste

Heat the oil in a heavy nonreactive saucepan over medium heat. Add the shallots, garlic, ginger, and chili and cook until lightly browned, 5 minutes. Add the remaining ingredients and bring to a boil. Reduce the heat and simmer, uncovered, until the apricots are soft and the mixture has thickened to the consistency of jam, about 15 minutes. If it starts to get too thick, add a little more water. Correct the seasoning, adding any of the ingredients to taste. Transfer to jars, cover, cool to room temperature, and refrigerate. The *blatjang* will keep for several weeks.

Makes about 3 cups; enough to serve 6 to 8

MAIL-ORDER SOURCES

GENERAL

Brugger Brothers
3868 NE 169th Street, Unit 401
North Miami Beach, FL 33160
(800) 949-2264
Telemanca peppercorns.

Dean & Deluca's
Catalog Department
560 Broadway
New York, NY 10012
(800) 221-7714
www.deandeluca.com
All manner of oils, vinegars, spices,
condiments, chilies, and hot sauces.

Foodalicious
2055 N.E. 151st Street
North Miami, FL 33162
(305) 945-0502
Oils, vinegars, chiles, spices, and Asian
ingredients.

Frieda's, Inc.
4465 Corporate Center Drive
Los Alamitos, CA 90720
(800) 241-1771; (714) 826-6100
www.friedas.com
Exotic produce, including habaneros
and other chilies, fresh sugarcane,
tamarind, and tomatillos. In addition to
mail order, they'll also tell you which
store in your area sells their products.

Melissa's Specialty Foods
P.O. Box 21127
Los Angeles, CA 90021
(800) 588-0151
www.melissas.com

All sorts of chili peppers; fresh and
dried Latin American produce.

The Spice House
1031 Old World Third Street
Milwaukee, WI 53203
(414) 272-0977
www.thespicehouse.com
Mail order is available; they carry
dried bell pepper flakes.

WILD MUSHROOMS, TRUFFLES, AND DRIED FRUITS

American Spoon Foods
P.O. Box 566
Petoskey, MI 49770
(800) 222-5886
www.spoon.com

Marché aux Delices
P.O. Box 1164
New York, NY 10028
(888) 547-5471
www.auxdelices.com

ASIAN INGREDIENTS

Anzen Japanese Foods and Imports
736 N.E. Martin Luther King Boulevard
Portland, OR 97232
(503) 233-5111

The Oriental Pantry at
Joyce Chen Unlimited
423 Great Road
Acton, MA 01720
(800) 828-0368
www.orientalpantry.com

ON-LINE PURVEYORS

www.ethnicgrocer.com
   Wide range of ingredients from around the world.
www.querico.com
   Latino ingredients.
www.Latingrocer.com
   Latino ingredients.
www.namaste.com
   Indian ingredients.
www.gongshee.com
   Chinese ingredients.

CARIBBEAN INGREDIENTS

Isla
P.O. Box 9112
San Juan, PR
(800) 575-4752

Jamaica Groceries & Spices
Colonial Shopping Centre
9587 S.W. 160th Street
Miami, FL 33157
(305) 252-1197

INDIAN INGREDIENTS

India Spice and Gift Shop
3295 Fairfield Avenue
Bridgeport, CT 06605
(203) 384-0666

Indian Emporium
68-48 New Hampshire Avenue
Tacoma Park, MD 20012
(301) 270-3322

Seema Enterprises
10635 Page Avenue
St. Louis, MO 63132
(314) 423-9990

MIDDLE & NEAR EASTERN, CENTRAL ASIAN, AND AFRICAN INGREDIENTS

Aphrodisia Products, Inc.
264 Bleecker Street
New York, NY 10014
(212) 989-6440

Haji Baba Middle Eastern Food & Restaurant
1513 E. Apache
Tempe, AZ 85281
(602) 894-1905

Neams Market
3217 P Street NW
Washington, D.C. 20007
(202) 338-4694

Oriental Pastry and Grocery
170-172 Atlantic Avenue
Brooklyn, NY 11201
(718) 875-7687

Pars Market
9016 W. Pico
Los Angeles, CA 90035
(310) 859-8125

Yekta Middle
Eastern Grocery
1488 Rockville
   Pike
Rockville, MD 20852
(301) 984-1190

MEXICAN, SOUTHWESTERN, AND SOUTH AMERICAN INGREDIENTS

Casa Lucas Market
2934 24th Street
San Francisco, CA 94110
(415) 826-4334
They carry Peruvian aji amarillo.

Catalina's Market
1070 Northwestern
Avenue
Santa Monica, CA 90029
(213) 461-2535
They carry Peruvian aji
amarillo.

The Chile Shop
109 E. Water Street
Santa Fe, NM 87501
(505) 983-6080
Fax: (505) 984-0737

Coyote Cafe General Store
132 W. Water Street
Santa Fe, NM 87501
(505) 982-2454
www.coyote-cafe.com

The El Paso Chile Company
909 Texas Avenue
El Paso, TX 79901
(800) 274-7468; (915) 544-3434
www.elpasochile.com
Fax: (915) 544-7552

Monterrey Foods Products
3939 Cesar Chavez
Los Angeles, CA 90063
(213) 263-2143

$50 minimum for mail orders on most products.

CHILI POWDERS AND HOT SAUCES

Mo Hotta, Mo Betta
P.O. Box 4136
San Luis Obispo, CA 93403
(800) 462-3220
www.mohotta.com

Peppers
2009 Highway One at
Salsbury Street
Dewey Beach, DE 19971
(800) 998-3473

DRY WORCESTERSHIRE SAUCE

Pendery's, Inc.
1221 Manufacturing Street
Dallas, TX 75027
(800) 533-1870
Call for a catalog.

INJECTORS

Chef William's Cajun Injector
P.O. Box 97
Clinton, LA 70722
(800) 221-8060
www.cajuninjector.com

WOODS AND CHIPS

Nature's Own/Peoples Woods
55 Mill Street
Cumberland, RI 02864
www.peopleswoods.com
Grapevine trimmings, dried herbs, and exotic woods, as well as premium charwood.

CONVERSION TABLE

LIQUID CONVERSIONS

US	IMPERIAL	METRIC
2 tbs	1 fl oz	30 ml
3 tbs	1½ fl oz	45 ml
¼ cup	2 fl oz	60 ml
⅓ cup	2½ fl oz	75 ml
⅓ cup + 1 tbs	3 fl oz	90 ml
⅓ cup + 2 tbs	3½ fl oz	100 ml
½ cup	4 fl oz	125 ml
⅔ cup	5 fl oz	150 ml
¾ cup	6 fl oz	175 ml
¾ cup + 2 tbs	7 fl oz	200 ml
1 cup	8 fl oz	250 ml
1 cup + 2 tbs	9 fl oz	275 ml
1¼ cups	10 fl oz	300 ml
1⅓ cups	11 fl oz	325 ml
1½ cups	12 fl oz	350 ml
1⅔ cups	13 fl oz	375 ml
1¾ cups	14 fl oz	400 ml
1¾ cups + 2 tbs	15 fl oz	450 ml
1 pint (2 cups)	16 fl oz	500 ml
2½ cups	1 pint	600 ml
3¾ cups	1½ pints	900 ml
4 cups	1¾ pints	1 liter

APPROXIMATE EQUIVALENTS

1 stick butter = 8 tbs = 4 oz = ½ cup
1 cup all-purpose presifted flour/
    dried bread crumbs = 5 oz
1 cup granulated sugar = 8 oz
1 cup (packed) brown sugar = 6 oz
1 cup confectioners' sugar = 4½ oz
1 cup honey/syrup = 11 oz
1 cup grated cheese = 4 oz
1 cup dried beans = 6 oz
1 large egg = 2 oz = about ½ cup
1 egg yolk = about 1 tbs
1 egg white = about 2 tbs

WEIGHT CONVERSIONS

US/UK	METRIC	US/UK	METRIC
½ oz	15 g	7oz	200 g
1 oz	30 g	8 oz	250 g
1½ oz	45 g	9 oz	275 g
2 oz	60 g	10 oz	300 g
2½ oz	75 g	11 oz	325 g
3 oz	90 g	12 oz	350 g
3½ oz	100 g	13 oz	375 g
4 oz	125 g	14 oz	400 g
5 oz	150 g	15 oz	450 g
6 oz	175 g	1 lb	500 g

OVEN TEMPERATURES

FAHRENHEIT	GAS MARK	CELSIUS
250	½	120
275	1	140
300	2	150
325	3	160
350	4	180
375	5	190
400	6	200
425	7	220
450	8	230
475	9	240
500	10	260

Note: Reduce the temperature by 20°C (68°F) for fan-assisted ovens

Please note that all the above conversions are approximate, but close enough to be useful when converting from one system to another.

INDEX